# Home Networking
# ANNOYANCES™

## How to Fix the Most ANNOYING Things
## About Your Home Network

Kathy Ivens

O'REILLY®

Beijing · Cambridge · Farnham · Köln · Paris · Sebastopol · Taipei · Tokyo

# Home Networking Annoyances™
### How to Fix the Most Annoying Things About Your Home Network

by Kathy Ivens

Published by O'Reilly Media, Inc., 1005 Gravenstein Highway North, Sebastopol, CA 95472.

O'Reilly books may be purchased for educational, business, or sales promotional use. Online editions are also available for most titles (*safari.oreilly.com*). For more information, contact our corporate/institutional sales department: 800-998-9938 or *corporate@oreilly.com*.

| **Print History:** | | **Editors:** | Brett Johnson |
| --- | --- | --- | --- |
| | | | Susan Silvius |
| January 2005: | First Edition. | **Production Editor:** | Emily Quill |
| | | **Art Director:** | Michele Wetherbee |
| | | **Cover Designer:** | Ellie Volckhausen |
| | | **Interior Designer:** | Patti Capaldi |

This book uses RepKover™, a durable and flexible lay-flat binding.

0-596-00808-2
[C]

# Contents

# Introduction

Installing a network is easier than most people think, but maintaining a network is almost as much work as raising children. It seems to go on forever.

Like all computer professionals, I'm constantly asked for help, advice, and opinions. Every event and occasion in my life seems to produce questions about computers, and for the past few years, the vast majority of questions were about home networks. Everybody's installing one; this is a hot topic!

These freebie consulting sessions have occurred at dinner parties, while standing in line at the bank, and even in an operating room where the anesthesiologist, poising the IV above my arm, asked me to solve her wireless network problem. After a satisfactory response, I was permitted to drift off.

Tons of requests for help arrive in my Inbox every day, and for some reason I saved the questions, along with my responses. When O'Reilly contacted me about doing this book, I knew the reason. Because my Inbox could be accurately described as a source of information for every annoyance a home network owner could encounter, it was fate that I should turn those messages into a book.

## IS HOME NETWORKING ANNOYANCES RIGHT FOR YOU?

This book is for people who installed a home network and now have to cope with maintaining it. Hardware, software, and users—*especially* users—provide daily challenges to smooth, error-free networking.

The person who installs a home network becomes the de facto network administrator. If you're the admin of your home network, this book is designed to help you prevent, solve, and understand the annoying problems that crop up.

## HOW TO USE THIS BOOK

This book isn't a novel, and it doesn't have a plot. That means you don't have to start at the beginning and read to the end to get the information you need. The chapters are arranged into semilogical categories, and the index will get you to the specific information you need.

## CONVENTIONS USED IN THIS BOOK

The following typographic conventions are used in this book.

*Italic*
Indicates new terms, URLs, filenames, file extensions, directories, and program names.

`Constant width`
Used to show the contents of files, commands and options, or the output from commands.

**`Constant width bold`**
Indicates commands or other text that should be typed literally by the user.

*`Constant width italic`*
Used for typed text that should be replaced with user-supplied values.

### Menus/navigation

This book uses arrow symbols to signify menu instructions. For example, "File → Print" is a more compact way of saying "Click File on the command bar at the top of the screen and choose Print from the drop-down menu." However, if an instruction directs you to click a tab, check an option, or click a button in a dialog box, I'll tell you.

### Pathnames

Pathnames show the location of a file or application in Windows Explorer. Folders are separated by a backward slash—for example, *C:\Windows\System32*.

## O'REILLY WOULD LIKE TO HEAR FROM YOU

Please address comments and questions concerning this book to the publisher:

O'Reilly Media, Inc.
1005 Gravenstein Highway North
Sebastopol, CA 95472
(800) 998-9938 (in the United States or Canada)
(707) 829-0515 (international or local)
(707) 829-0104 (fax)

We have a web page for this book, where we list errata, examples, and any additional information. You can access this page at:

*http://www.oreilly.com/catalog/homenetannoy*

To comment or ask technical questions about this book, send email to:

*bookquestions@oreilly.com*

For more information about our books, conferences, Resource Centers, and the O'Reilly Network, see our web site at:

*http://www.oreilly.com*

To suggest an annoyance or to comment on the Annoyances series, send email to:

*annoyances@oreilly.com*

## ABOUT THE AUTHOR

Kathy Ivens has spent more than 20 years as a computer consultant, and has been writing computer books for more than 10 years. She also writes about computers for a variety of magazines and newspapers, and is a senior contributing editor of *Windows IT Pro* magazine.

## ACKNOWLEDGMENTS

A hearty and heartfelt thanks to all the people who asked me for help with their home or small business networks. I owe a round of applause and an enthusiastic "Thank You" to Brett Johnson of O'Reilly Media for his help and patience.

# Hardware
# ANNOYANCES

Networking hardware is annoying on general principle. In fact, most people (including computer professionals) find installing routers, hubs, and network adapters boring. Worse, hardware troubleshooting is frequently quite difficult because the devices are stubbornly noncommunicative. Unlike software, hardware doesn't display error messages to help you determine what to do. I've spent many hours pointing a screwdriver at a computer in a threatening manner and muttering, "I hate hardware."

However, because a simple black box the size of a paperback novel can turn a bunch of individual computers into a network, there's no way to avoid messing around with hardware—this is where your network building starts. In this chapter, you'll learn about various types of network adapters and how to solve the most annoying problems associated with installing an Ethernet, phoneline, powerline, or wireless network.

# NETWORK ADAPTER ANNOYANCES

## A NIC IS A NETWORK CARD IS AN ADAPTER

**The Annoyance:** My computer-literate friends, and the articles I read about home networks, tell me I need to buy NICs or network cards. How do I know what I need?

**The Fix:** Those terms are nicknames for the same thing—a hardware device called a *network adapter*. The following are the most common adapters:

- PCI Cards fit in a PCI slot inside your computer (the slot is sometimes called a *bus*).
- USB adapters connect to a USB port on your computer.
- Embedded adapters are built into the computer by the manufacturer (which means you don't have to buy or install anything).
- PC Cards (sometimes called PCMCIA devices) slide into the PC-Card port of a laptop computer.

## FINDING AN EMBEDDED ADAPTER

**The Annoyance:** How am I supposed to know if my computer has an embedded adapter? I bought it a long time ago and I have no idea where I put the paperwork. A friend told me to see if the back of the computer has a device that looks like a phone jack, and if it does, I just have to plug in my Ethernet cable.

**The Fix:** Whoa, hold on. If it looks like a phone jack, it might be a phone jack. Many computers come with an internal modem built in, and that might be the device you see. Phone jacks and Ethernet jacks look the same, but they're certainly not the same, and they aren't interchangeable. However, you can find out what you have.

---

### WHAT THE HARDWARE DOES

The hardware handles communications among all the parts of your network. To understand how this happens, you need to know some of the terminology involved in the hardware setup of a network:

- ☒ *Topology* is the type of computer communication hardware your network uses: Ethernet, phone lines, electric lines, or wireless. All the hardware (network adapters, cable, hubs, etc.) must match the topology you've chosen. If you have mixed topology (e.g., a wireless network that feeds into an Ethernet router), you must have hardware that manages the transition, such as bridges and access points.

- ☒ *Medium* is the component that carries the data. The medium can be a wire, or radio frequencies.

- ☒ *Segment* is the total set of hardware (adapters, cable or wireless carriers, hubs, switches, routers, etc.) involved in creating an individual network.

- ☒ *Node* is the term for any device attached to the segment.

- ☒ *Frame* is the data message sent through the medium. Frames have rules of construction; a minimum and maximum size; and required information within the data, such as the addresses of the sending and receiving nodes.

---

An Ethernet jack (RJ45 jack) is slightly larger than a telephone jack (RJ11 jack). As a result, a phone cord won't fit snugly into an RJ45 jack. You won't hear that little click that indicates a connection, and if you gently pull on the telephone cord it'll fall out of the connector. Also, the connector at the end of an Ethernet cable won't fit into an RJ11 jack.

You can also ask the computer what it is by following these steps:

1. Right-click My Computer and choose Properties to display the System Properties dialog box.

2. In Windows XP and 2000, click the Hardware tab and then click the Device Manager button. In Windows 98SE and Me, simply click the Device Manager tab.

3. In the Device Manager dialog box, look for a listing named Network Adapters.

4. Click the plus sign to the left of the Network Adapters listing to display the name of the network adapter installed in your computer (see Figure 1-1).

5. If no adapter is installed, you won't see information about a specific network adapter.

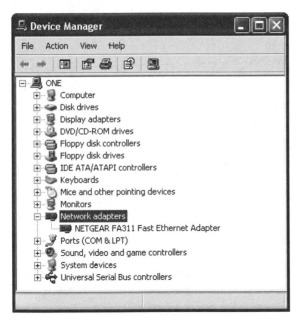

Figure 1-1. Aha! That connector at the back of the computer is really a network adapter.

The commonly used names for network adapters are *NIC* and *network card*. NIC stands for Network Interface Card, and the use of the word "card" in both nicknames dates back to the days when the only type of network adapter was a card you inserted in a slot inside your computer.

Today, in addition to a network adapter that's a card, you can buy a computer with the network adapter already built into the system board (called an *embedded adapter*), or buy a network adapter that connects to a USB port. Regardless of the way that you install a network adapter, most computer professionals use the term NIC. We're all too lazy and set in our ways to change our terminology.

Network adapters are designed for specific types of network topologies: Ethernet, wireless, powerline, or phoneline. You must install a network adapter that matches the network type you're installing.

## IT'S A PHONE, IT'S AN ADAPTER, IT'S...PHONELINE NETWORKING!

**The Annoyance:** The back of my computer has a metal strip with two jacks, and the documentation says the computer has a PNA network adapter. It doesn't say anything about a modem.

**The Fix:** PNA stands for Phoneline Networking Alliance. This group (*http://www.homepna.org/*) sets the standards for equipment that uses the telephone lines in your home to create a computer network. This is not Ethernet; it's phoneline networking. See the discussions (and annoyances) about phoneline networks later in this chapter.

# ENABLING USB PORTS

**The Annoyance:** I bought USB network adapters so that I didn't have to open my computers. One of the adapters didn't work. I switched it to another computer, and it worked fine. The computer that can't handle the USB adapter is several years old. Is the problem that the USB port is older?

**The Fix:** Age probably has nothing to do with it because most USB devices are compatible with older ports. I'm betting on a disabled USB port. When computer manufacturers first started including USB ports, there weren't many USB devices (and hardly anyone bought the few that were out there). Many of those manufacturers disabled the port, and had instructions in the documentation about enabling the port if and when you purchased a USB device. But who reads the documentation?

Restart your computer and type the appropriate keystrokes to enter the computer's setup program. The keystrokes vary depending on the manufacturer of your BIOS chip, but you should see a message that says "Press X to Enter Setup" (substitute the key mentioned in the message for X). The BIOS Setup program also varies among manufacturers, but it shouldn't be difficult to figure out which selection will let you see the state of the ports on your computer. Enable the USB port, save your changes, and let the computer continue to boot into Windows. Now you should be able to use your USB adapter.

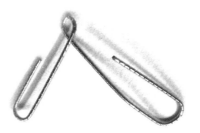

### About the BIOS

The BIOS (Basic Input Output System) is a chip that's in charge of the computer's basic hardware. It runs the startup POST (Power-On Self Test), part of which is visible in the form of text that appears on your monitor when your computer first starts. It checks memory, disks, ports, input devices, and other basic components. The last step of the POST is to find the Master Boot Record that Windows installed during setup, and turn the computer over to Windows.

# UNUSED EMBEDDED ADAPTERS

**The Annoyance:** My new computer came with an embedded Ethernet adapter, but I have a wireless network so I installed a wireless adapter. Now I have two icons for network connections in the Control Panel.

**The Fix:** The icon isn't bothering anyone or anything, so ignore it. If you're truly annoyed by two "live" adapters, and the computer is running Windows XP or 2000, you can disable the Ethernet adapter. Right-click the icon and choose Disable from the shortcut menu. The "disabled" status appears under the icon so that you won't accidentally try to configure it.

In Windows 98SE and Me, open the System applet in the Control Panel, click the Device Manager tab, and remove the adapter. However, if the device is Plug and Play (which means Windows notices its presence during startup), the device will constantly reinstall itself. So, as I said, ignore it.

# ETHERNET HARDWARE ANNOYANCES

## CABLING BETWEEN ADJACENT ROOMS

**The Annoyance:** We have two computers in our family room, connected to a router that sits between the two computers. My wife wants to add another computer to the network and put it in the den, which is next to the family room. What's the easiest way to do this?

**The Fix:** I'll tell you the easiest way, and then I'll tell you the best way. The easiest way is to string the cable along the baseboard, or below the quarter round, and take it through the opening (under the door if there's a door) and into the next room. This is the easy way because it requires no tools.

The best way is to drill holes and string cable through the holes. This method uses less cable, and in the end, the holes are less conspicuous (and less ugly) than the cable. Drill a hole in an inconspicuous place. I usually pick a corner of the room and drill the hole right above the baseboard. The hole only needs to be slightly larger than the connector at the end of the Ethernet cable, which is about half an inch. Do the same thing in both rooms (measure from a corner or the doorway, so the holes are directly opposite each other).

Cable is floppy, so when I'm cabling adjacent rooms I tape the cable to a thin dowel (I keep the chopsticks I get from the local Chinese restaurant takeout counter for this purpose). Duct tape is great for this type of work because it doesn't come loose if you scrape against the wall. Electrical tape works almost as well. Shine a flashlight through the hole from one room so that you can see the opening clearly, and push the cable through from the other side.

> **Warning. . .**
> Don't put tape on the Ethernet connector. You don't want to get sticky stuff on the business part of your cable.

## CABLING BETWEEN NONADJACENT ROOMS

**The Annoyance:** Our network currently consists of two computers in two adjacent bedrooms. I drilled a hole between those rooms to run cable between both computers and the router. Now we have to add another computer in a bedroom at the end of the hall (with a bathroom and a linen closet between the bedrooms that currently have computers and the bedroom that gets the new computer). The router that connects the computers is in the bedroom closest to the new computer. I think the straightest run, using the least amount of cable, is to drill holes through each room, bringing the cable along the top of the wall in the bathroom and linen closet. However, that's six holes, which seems like a lot of work.

**The Fix:** If the bathroom has tile walls, it's *really* a lot of work. Drilling through tile requires special tools, and also requires experience. I can tell you that even with the right tools, it's amazingly easy to crack the tile sufficiently to have it fall off the wall, followed by the fall of the surrounding tiles, and eventually the cost of a tile installer to repair all the damage.

It's best to go up or down, using the space above the ceiling or the space below the floor. If your computers are on the second floor, run cable across the attic or crawl space (depending on the way your house is built). If your computers are on the first floor, run your cable across the basement ceiling or through the crawl space beneath the first floor.

To cable from the attic or a crawl space above the rooms, drill a hole in the wall of the room that has the router, putting the hole as close to the ceiling as possible. Then drill through from the space above. Do the same thing in and above the room that holds the new computer.

When you're ready to run the cable, work downward, so you have the assistance of gravity. Go into the attic or crawl space and drop one end of the cable down the wall above the router. Then move to the hole you drilled above the new computer and drop the other end of the cable through the hole. Use an electrician's fish, or a bent piece of thick wire, to fish the cable through the hole you drilled in the wall of the bedroom.

To cable from the basement or a crawl space below the floor, drop the cable from the room with the router, and walk the other end of the cable to its position below the room with the new computer. Drop a piece of strong string with a weight attached to the end through the hole in the room. From below, tape the cable to the string, and pull up to bring the cable to the new computer (see Figure 1-2).

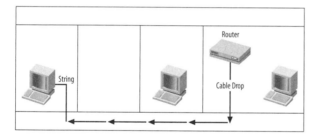

Figure 1-2. Gravity is a great assistant when you're running cable between floors.

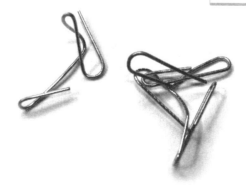

## ETHERNET CABLE: THE NAME GAME

Ethernet cable has more aliases than an international jewel thief. When you're looking for cable, or looking for advice, you might see any of the following terms:

- ☒ **Category 5 or Cat5 cable.** There are Ethernet cable categories from 1 to 6, each with different technical specifications. Category 5 is the common choice for computer networks.

- ☒ **Category 5e or Cat5e cable.** This is category 5 cable that can handle gigabyte speed.

- ☒ **Twisted pair cable.** The name describes the wires in Ethernet cable, which are twisted around each other to reduce crosstalk and other interference problems.

- ☒ **100BaseT cable or 10BaseT cable.** The numbers describe the speed of the transmission in megabits per second (mps). 100BaseT is called "fast Ethernet." The "T" is a code that identifies the wires inside the cable as copper. Fiber optic cable has an F in the name (e.g., 100BaseF). Base stands for baseband cable, which means that only Ethernet signals are carried on the cable. Broadband cable, on the other hand, can carry multiple types of signals simultaneously. Electric, telephone, and cable television lines are examples of broadband.

- ☒ **Gigabit cable.** This cable supports Ethernet connections measured in gigabits per second (gps). We're talking billions here, not millions. To use gigabit cable, your switch and network adapters must also support the gigabit standard.

**6** CHAPTER 1 HARDWARE ANNOYANCES

## CABLING BETWEEN FLOORS

**The Annoyance:** What's the trick for cabling Ethernet when you want to add a computer on a different floor?

**The Fix:** Take the cable through the wall, just like the people who wired your house for electricity did. Your walls have enough empty space for cable, even if there's insulation inside the walls. The empty space in the wall that you use for running cable is usually called a *chase* by people who install cable. After you run cable through the walls to get to the right floor, use the space across the beams to get to the right room. Drill your holes near the corner of the room. If radiators or heating pipes are accessible, use the opening around the pipes instead of drilling holes.

Work from the top down to let gravity work for you. Put a weight on the end of strong string or twine and drop it down to the lower floor. Then, tape the cable to the weight and haul it up.

If you have HVAC (Heating, Ventilation, Air Conditioning) ducts, use them. However, some local governments have strict building codes that might forbid using this easy method. I've also run into building codes that don't forbid the use of HVAC, but require you to use shielded cable.

> Ethernet cable is available with shielding. Look for (or ask for) Ethernet cable that's labeled STP, which means shielded twisted pair. (Unshielded cable is labeled UTP.) STP has a metal shield encasing the wires to reduce interference. Shielded cable is sometimes called *plenum* cable.

> **Warning. . .**
> Never go into the HVAC system by drilling a hole. Use existing entries and exits, which are the spaces behind the grates in each room.

## SIGNAL INTERFERENCE

**The Annoyance:** I want to run cable through the walls and the space between floors, but those spaces have electrical lines, speaker wires, and telephone wires. I'm afraid that either the Ethernet cable will interfere with existing wires, or the existing wires will interfere with computer data. Are there any guidelines?

**The Fix:** Worry about electric power lines interfering with computer data transmissions, and don't worry about anything else. The real worry is fluorescent lights, which will definitely interfere with data communication, so keep your Ethernet cable several feet away from the fluorescent light fixtures in the ceiling. To avoid interference with electric power lines, cross the Ethernet cable at a 90-degree angle. Don't run Ethernet cable parallel to electric lines.

## CABLING OUTSIDE THE WALLS— INSIDE THE ROOM

**The Annoyance:** We rent, and can't drill holes. Aside from being ugly, is there any reason we can't just run cable along the walls?

**The Fix:** You can certainly run cable through rooms instead of within walls, and it doesn't have to be ugly. Several companies make products that help you hide the cable. Look for a raceway (sometimes called an architectural raceway) that you can attach to the wall or baseboard (peel-off tape on the back of the raceway exposes the adhesive). The raceway is a vinyl, almost-flat tube with a front panel that flips up to insert the cable and then snaps shut securely. It comes in several neutral colors, or can be painted. You can find these inexpensive helpers at any hardware store or home center.

## MANAGING THE CABLE BETWEEN THE WALL AND THE COMPUTER

**The Annoyance:** We ran all our cable inside the walls and brought the cable to the computer. That last length of cable, running along the floor between the wall and the computer, is unsightly. Also, it's dangerous because every once in a while somebody trips over it.

**The Fix:** If you can't put the computer against the wall at the point where the cable comes out of the wall, you can cover the loose cable, which makes everything more attractive and less dangerous.

Floor cable covers are vinyl contraptions that are available in two forms:

- Cable covers fit over the cable. They're heavy so they don't move easily, and the sides are gently sloped so you don't trip over them.

- Cable tubes surround the cable on all sides. You can use double-sided tape to affix them to the floor surface.

> **Warning. . .**
> Don't run naked cable under a rug. The underside of the rug can rub against the cable and weaken or break the cable's insulation jacket. Instead, use a cable cover under the rug.

## WALL JACKS

**The Annoyance:** My computer at work is connected to a wall jack, so we don't have naked cable running out of the walls. Can I do this on my home network?

**The Fix:** Sure, just buy and install an RJ45 jack and a faceplate. The combined price is less than $10. Pull the cable through the hole in the wall, and remove about an inch of insulation from the cable with a wire stripper. (If the cable is a patch cable, cut off the connector.) Then insert the wires into the jack (the insertion points are clearly marked) and push against the socket to seal the connection (these work just like electrical boxes that snap the wires into place). Attach the jack to the wall, and then attach the faceplate over the jack (see Figure 1-3). Plug the cable from the computer into the faceplate to connect to the cable you ran through the wall.

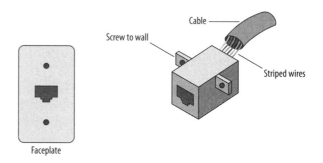

Figure 1-3. Make the final connection look professional with a jack and a faceplate.

> **t i p**
> You can also buy multiple-line jacks and faceplates to use in the room where your hub/switch/router connects multiple cable runs.

## ADDING A HUB TO THE SYSTEM

**The Annoyance:** We have two computers connected to a router on the first floor of our house. Now we need to add two computers on the second floor. The new computers are not only on a different floor, but also on the opposite side of the house from the router and existing computers.

**The Fix:** Instead of making all those cable runs, connect the two new computers to a hub or a switch (see the next annoyance) and then run a single length of cable through the walls from the hub/switch to the router. (If the new computers are not in the same room, see "Cabling Between Nonadjacent Rooms.")

## DECIDING BETWEEN A HUB AND A SWITCH

**The Annoyance:** We want to enlarge our network, but we'll end up with two "bunches" of computers. Two computers are already connected to the router. Three more computers, at the opposite end of the house, will be connected together with a hub, and the hub will be connected to the router. My geeky friends tell me to buy a switch (more expensive), not a hub, because switches send data faster.

**The Fix:** Your geeky friends are correct—switches speed up computer communications (see the sidebar "Hub, Switch, What's the Difference?" for the techie explanation). The real question is whether you'll notice the difference in a network that has five computers (or ten computers, for that matter). Personally, I don't think you will, so save some money and buy a hub.

---

### HUB, SWITCH, WHAT'S THE DIFFERENCE?

When data is exchanged among computers, the data packet holds the address of the receiving computer in addition to the actual data being exchanged.

A hub ignores the address contained in the packet and ships the data to every computer connected to the hub. The bandwidth speed of the hub (the number of bits per second the hub is capable of transmitting) is split among the number of occupied ports, as the data is sent to everyone at once. The computers read the address, and only the designated receiving computer accepts the data packet (the other computers just ignore it).

A switch, which is a more intelligent device because it keeps information about the computers in its memory, knows where the receiving computer is. The switch sends the data to that computer's port, dedicating all its bandwidth speed to that port.

We're talking about speeds that are measured in millions of bits per second, so when a hub divides that speed among several computers, the communication slows to hundreds of thousands of bits per second. Think you can tell the difference? If so, go with a switch.

This is a greatly oversimplified description of the way hubs and switches send data, but it should give you a picture of the processes. You should also realize that I'm describing a rather simple switch, and more complicated technology is available for the powerful switches used in large networks.

Incidentally, routers have built-in switches, not hubs.

## MIXING COMMUNICATION SPEEDS

**The Annoyance:** Our existing network has two computers attached to a router. We're adding two more computers, and we're going to install a hub to connect them to the router. The new computers have embedded Ethernet adapters that communicate at 100 mbs; the old computers have adapters that communicate at 10 mbs. It's really annoying to have to replace the old adapters.

**The Fix:** You don't have to replace the old adapters. Hubs and switches are built to recognize the speed at which any given computer operates and deliver that speed to that computer. This means you can mix speeds within your network. If you think you'll notice the speed difference (I'm betting you won't), replace the adapters.

## MAKING YOUR OWN CABLE

**The Annoyance:** The computers in our network are widely scattered, and the distance between the router and two of the computers is more than 100 feet. I can't find patch cable of the right length, and ordering special cable is expensive. Can I make my own Ethernet cable?

**The Fix:** Lots of people make their own Ethernet patch cables (you aren't really making cable, you're adding connectors to cable). You can take this step when you need very long cable lengths, when you're cabling many computers and want to save money, or if you're one of those folks who enjoy do-it-yourself projects. Here's what you'll need:

- Bulk Ethernet cable
- RJ45 connectors
- A wire stripper
- A cable crimper

Cut the cable to the length you need, plus about 3 feet for slack. Use the stripper to remove about a half-inch of insulation and expose the wires. Push each wire into the appropriate hole on the connector, using Table 1-1 as your guide.

To get the numbering right on the connector, point the connector away from yourself (the holes toward you), with the little plastic tab at the top. Wire #1 is on the left.

Set the crimper for RJ45 connectors, and place the crimper where the connector and the wires meet. Then press firmly. Do the same thing at the other end.

Table 1-1. Cat 5 wiring scheme.

| Wire number | Color | Used for |
|---|---|---|
| 1 | White and orange | Transmitting data |
| 2 | Orange | Transmitting data |
| 3 | White and green | Receiving data |
| 4 | Blue | Nothing |
| 5 | White and blue | Nothing |
| 6 | Green | Receiving data |
| 7 | White and brown | Nothing |
| 8 | Brown | Nothing |

You can buy bulk cable in lengths of 250 feet, 1,000 feet, or more (depending on the manufacturer). The cost is usually less than 10 cents a foot. RJ45 connectors cost about a half-dollar. A wire stripper costs a few dollars, and a crimper costs about $20 (and also crimps RJ11 connections if you want to run your own telephone cable).

## PATCH VERSUS CROSSOVER CABLE

**The Annoyance:** We're expanding our network by attaching several computers to a hub, and then connecting the hub to our router. The documentation for the hub says to use a crossover cable instead of a patch cable for the connection to the router. What is crossover cable?

**The Fix:** The term *patch cable* is used for straight-through cable. The wires go through the cable without changing their positions, so wire 1 at one connector is wire 1 at the connector at the other end. Patch (or straight-through) cable is the standard cable you use to attach components of your network together.

In *crossover cable*, the wires change position between connectors. Wires that start at one position end up at a different position, as follows:

- 1 crosses to 3
- 2 crosses to 6

(Only wires 1, 2, 3, and 6 are used for Ethernet communication.)

Crossover cable isn't used to connect computers to hubs/switches/routers. It's used only for special connections, such as attaching a DSL (Digital Subscriber Line) modem to the uplink port of a hub or switch, or to link two hubs through the uplink port. The documentation for the hardware device tells you whether a crossover cable is required.

Most of today's hubs and switches can automatically sense whether a crossover cable is connected to the uplink port, and will cross the wires electronically if a patch cable is found. Therefore, it's unusual to need crossover cable.

## CABLE DISTANCE LIMITS

**The Annoyance:** We're adding computers to our network, and I read that the total distance you can have on a network is limited to 300 feet. How do businesses manage large networks with such a limitation?

**The Fix:** Your number is right (well, it's close), but your definition is wrong. The maximum length limitation applies to a single cable run between a computer and a hub/switch. That maximum is 100 meters, which is 328 feet.

The reason for the maximum distance is the loss of signal over distance. Fiber optic cable doesn't lose signal as easily, and the length of a single fiber optic cable run can be about 10 times the length of standard Ethernet cable.

If you need a longer cable run (unlikely in most households), you can buy converters that let you connect a standard Ethernet cable to fiber optic cable, and then connect the fiber optic cable to standard Ethernet cable at the other end.

Another solution for a longer-than-permitted cable run is a repeater. This device looks like a hub and it takes care of signal loss by regenerating the signal, allowing you more than 100 meters for a cable run. Usually, you can double the distance with repeaters.

# PHONELINE HARDWARE ANNOYANCES

## SHARING A PHONE JACK

**The Annoyance:** I want to add a third computer to our two-computer phoneline network. The room where I need the computer has a phone jack, but the jack is being used by a telephone.

**The Fix:** You can share the phone jack between the telephone and the computer by inserting a modular duplex jack into the wall receptacle. This nifty device, which most people refer to as a *splitter*, has a regular RJ11 plug on one side. Plug that in the jack. The other side has two RJ11 female connectors. Use one connector for the telephone, and the other for a length of telephone cable that you run to the new computer. Splitters are available everywhere you can buy telephone equipment, including your local supermarket.

## SHARING A PHONELINE NETWORK ADAPTER

**The Annoyance:** One of the computers on our phoneline network is in a bedroom without a telephone. We now want to add a telephone in that room, but the PC is monopolizing the only jack.

**The Fix:** You have two methods for solving this problem:

- Use a modular duplex jack as described in the previous annoyance.
- Use the second connector on your phoneline network adapter.

### UNDERSTANDING PHONELINE BANDWIDTH

The telephone cable that runs through your walls has multiple wires, and not all of the wires use the same frequency. When cable can contain and manage multiple frequencies, we call it *broadband* cable. The technical term for the broadband capacity in telephone lines is Frequency Division Multiplexing (FDM). The Plain Old Telephone Service (POTS) frequency serves any device that requires a dial tone: telephones, fax machines, and modems. Because POTS devices share the same frequency, you can't use two POTS devices at the same time.

High-speed Internet access frequency is for special devices that provide high-speed Internet access, such as DSL and ISDN devices. This is why you can use DSL and a POTS device simultaneously.

The hardware in your phoneline network uses yet another frequency to communicate. Because POTS and high-speed Internet connection devices run on their own frequencies, you can have a phoneline network, POTS services, and a high-speed Internet connection all at the same time.

Your phoneline network adapter has two jacks: one has an icon or a label for the line (the wall jack), and the other has an icon or label for a telephone. Use the line jack to connect the computer to the wall jack, and use the telephone jack for your telephone.

## CHAINING COMPUTERS TOGETHER

**The Annoyance:** I want to add another computer to our phoneline network, in the same room as an existing computer. The room has only one phone jack, and I'm already using a splitter to share the jack with the telephone.

**The Fix:** You can attach the new computer to the existing computer, whether it's in the same room or another room. Run telephone cable from the new computer's network adapter to the second jack in the first computer's network adapter. This is called a *daisy chain*.

Incidentally, the fact that you can daisy-chain phoneline adapters proves the point made in the sidebar "Line Jacks, Telephone Jacks—Don't Worry About the Labels."

In fact, if you don't mind stringing telephone cable around the house, you can daisy-chain your entire network to one wall jack. Connect the first computer to the wall jack, and then connect the next computer to the empty jack in the first computer's network adapter. Connect the next computer to the empty jack in the second computer's network adapter, and on and on. This frees up all the other wall jacks in your house for telephones, modems, and fax machines.

**tip**

A phoneline daisy chain can accommodate up to 25 computers, but no two computers on the chain can be more than 1,000 feet apart. However, I can't imagine you'd run into that problem in a home network.

## USING JACKS FROM DIFFERENT PHONE LINES

**The Annoyance:** One of the computers we want to put on our phoneline network is in a room with a jack. However, we wired that jack for a different telephone number. Can we still use it?

**The Fix:** Sorry, all the computers on the network must operate on the same telephone line. Oh, wait—I'm supposed to provide a "fix." OK then. Use the "other" wires in the jack with the different phone number. Open the jack and find the wire pair combination that matches the first phone line (you just have to match the colors). Put them into a jack (you can buy one anywhere), and connect the computer to that jack. Use your favorite Internet search engine to find one of the many web sites that illustrate do-it-yourself wiring.

## TELEPHONE CABLE PROBLEMS

**The Annoyance:** My phoneline network stopped exchanging data. At the same time, the telephones had a lot of static. Why would static on the phone line cause a problem with my phoneline network? I thought they didn't use the same part of the telephone lines.

**The Fix:** The squirrels that chewed away the insulation on the telephone cable aren't fussy, and when they gnaw they don't go after only the wires producing a dial tone. If you don't have squirrels, substitute the same lack of discrimination for corrosive liquids that eat away the cable in underground conduits. When telephone cable has a problem, all the wires and all the frequencies on the cable share the problem. Call your telephone company for assistance.

## CREATE A MINI PHONELINE NETWORK

**The Annoyance:** We have an Ethernet network on the first floor of our house, and we want to add two computers on the second floor. I can't face the task of moving all that cable through the walls and rooms. Someone told me that if the rooms on the second floor have telephone jacks, I could create a phoneline network and connect it to the Ethernet network. This seems too good to be true.

**The Fix:** Most things that seem too good to be true are false (ever fall for any of the stuff offered in pop-up ads?). Happily, this case is different; it's true, and it's a great solution to your problem. In addition to the network adapters for the upstairs computers, you'll have to buy a phoneline bridge. A bridge is a network device that bridges two network topologies—in this case, your Ethernet and phoneline networks. All manufacturers of network devices sell bridges, and you can expect to spend about $50.

Set up your phoneline network on the second floor by plugging both computers' network adapters into the telephone jacks. Then, on the first floor, connect the bridge to both networks. The back of the bridge has ports for each connection you need (see Figure 1-4).

Figure 1-4. Connect cables to ports to merge your phoneline network with your Ethernet network.

Connect the bridge's phoneline port to a wall jack with telephone line. Connect the bridge's LAN port to your Ethernet hub/switch/router with Ethernet cable. Read the documentation for the bridge and the Ethernet device to see whether you have to use special ports (such as an uplink port). Most phoneline bridges have an uplink port in addition to a LAN port.

**tip**

You can also use a phoneline bridge to connect your phoneline network to a wireless network by connecting the bridge to a wireless access point.

## PHONELINE PORTS ARE LABELED HPNA

**The Annoyance:** I can't figure out which port to use to connect to the phone jack. None of my phoneline devices has a port labeled Phoneline, Phonejack, or Jack.

**The Fix:** Look for a port labeled HPNA, which is the official term for a phoneline port that uses the specifications set forth by the Home Phoneline Networking Alliance. This group sets standards for phoneline networking. You can learn more about the alliance by going to its web site, *http://www.homepna.org*.

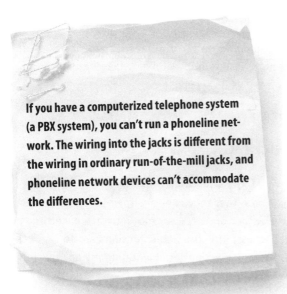

If you have a computerized telephone system (a PBX system), you can't run a phoneline network. The wiring into the jacks is different from the wiring in ordinary run-of-the-mill jacks, and phoneline network devices can't accommodate the differences.

## EVEN UNUSED PHONE LINES CAN RUN A PHONELINE NETWORK

The rule for phoneline networks is that all the computers must be on the same phone line. If you have multiple phone numbers in your house, you have to be careful to connect all the computers to the same line.

However, the phone line you use doesn't need to be an active telephone line (a line that's been assigned a number and has a dial tone). You can use the spare telephone pair on any jack (the telephone cable has multiple pairs of lines, and a "pair" is a specific combination of colors).

As long as all the computers are connected to the same telephone pair, you can have a phoneline network. This works because the phoneline adapter doesn't use the part of the phone wire that the telephone uses. The part the adapter uses isn't connected to a dial tone.

# POWERLINE HARDWARE ANNOYANCES

## LOOK FOR THE HOMEPLUG LOGO

**The Annoyance:** I find that powerline devices have a wide range of prices, and they have different specifications on the box. Some say they operate at 12 or 14 megabits per second, others are slower (and cheaper). Is there a difference?

**The Fix:** Yes, and this is another one of those cases where you get what you pay for. The cheaper, slower devices aren't using today's standards for powerline network technologies. Look for the HomePlug logo on the box, which means the device is built to the specifications of the HomePlug Powerline Alliance (*http://www.homeplug.org*).

---

### UNDERSTANDING POWERLINE BANDWIDTH

**The electric wires running through your walls can do more than deliver power to electric appliances. A great many wires, operating at different frequencies, are enclosed in the electric cable. In fact, the range of frequencies is split into 84 separate carriers.**

**Multiple technologies exist for sending computer data along the carriers, but the most reliable is the technology endorsed by the HomePlug Powerline Alliance. This industry group has developed the specifications for accessing the bandwidth of power lines by using *orthogonal frequency-division multiplexing* (OFDM). You can learn more about the HomePlug Powerline Alliance, and the specifications for powerline networking, at *http://www.homeplug.org*.**

**OFDM sends packets of data along several of the carrier frequencies simultaneously, which provides more speed and reliability than previous powerline technologies. Today's powerline network devices operate at 14 mps. Specifications are being considered and tested for powerline communication speeds of 100 mbs.**

**If a power surge or any other problem disrupts one of the frequencies, the data switches to another carrier automatically. The carriers carry data, not power, so your electric bill is not affected by your use of powerline devices.**

## POWER STRIPS AND POWERLINE DEVICES

**The Annoyance:** Finding free outlets in a room with a computer and peripherals can be difficult. I have power strips plugged into outlets to handle the multiple devices. Can I plug the powerline adapter into a power strip?

**The Fix:** Maybe, maybe not. Sorry, but this question doesn't have a clear-cut answer. My experience differs from the recommendations of powerline device manufacturers. I've plugged powerline adapters into power strips without problems. The manufacturers' instructions all say that this action is not recommended, and they advise you to plug the adapter directly into the wall. They claim the circuitry in the strip (especially if it has surge protection) can interfere with network communication. Try it and see what happens.

## POWERLINE NETWORKING FROM THE DECK OR VERANDA

**The Annoyance:** My friends who have wireless networks brag that they can take their laptops outdoors in nice weather and stay on the network (giving them Internet access). If I string an extension cord to my deck (which has no power outlet), can I plug my adapter into it?

**The Fix:** Of course you can—an extension cord is a direct line to a wall outlet. And unlike your wireless-enabled friends, you won't have to reposition your chair several times to find the network signal.

## INSTALLATION SOFTWARE IS A MUST

**The Annoyance:** In addition to installing drivers for my powerline adapters, I have to install a whole software program. Why?

**The Fix:** Security. The software that comes with a powerline adapter includes the security program that makes sure your network communication can't be hacked by an outsider. The software enables the powerline device to apply security without requiring you to go through a complicated configuration process.

---

### DES SECURITY

Powerline network devices that adhere to the HomePlug standard use DES security to make sure nobody can grab your network communications. DES stands for Data Encryption Standard, and it's so strong that the United States Department of Defense uses it. With DES security, data that's moving between computers is encrypted.

DES provides a minimum of 72 quadrillion (that's 15 zeros after the 72) possible encryption keys that your powerline device can use. For each data packet that's exchanged across the network, the device chooses one key at random from this enormous number of possible keys. When the encrypted data is received, the receiving computer's powerline adapter takes care of finding the key and decrypting the data. Because of the strength of this type of security, it's almost impossible for anyone "eavesdropping" on the communication to read the data.

---

## WHAT'S THE SECURITY RISK FOR POWERLINE NETWORKS?

**The Annoyance:** I know that wireless networks have a reputation for being prone to security breaks, but my powerline network exists totally inside my house. None of the network data is floating around the air the way wireless transmissions can. Why do I have to worry about data communication security?

**The Fix:** You're right when you say the risk of data being grabbed as it travels between one computer and another on a powerline network isn't anywhere near as high as it is on a wireless network. However, your data isn't as enclosed in the safety of your electric wiring as you might think.

The gateway, or barrier, for your powerline network is the transformer that supplies electricity to your building. Anyone sharing that transformer is on "your side" of that gateway. That means anyone who plugs in a powerline computer on your side of the gateway gets to participate in your network (see "Change the Default Security Password"). For most single-family homes, this doesn't present the problem that occupants of multidwelling buildings face. However, even a single-family dwelling can share a transformer with the building next door. Install the security software that came with your powerline adapter to avoid any problems.

---

### Warning. . .

Any discussion of security for data moving between networked computers represents only a small part of the security problem. Beyond data packets, you have to worry about viruses, worms, and interlopers who get to your data over the Internet. Security is probably the biggest annoyance in computing! Chapter 7 has plenty of information about securing your computers and your network.

---

## SECURITY PASSWORDS MUST MATCH

**The Annoyance:** All three computers on our powerline network seem to be working properly. The link lights are on, the TCP/IP settings are right, and all three can get to the Internet. But one computer can't participate in the network. It can't access the other two computers, and the other two computers can't get to its files. This is really annoying. In fact, it's driving me crazy!

**The Fix:** I'll bet that the security password for the isolated computer doesn't match the passwords you installed on the other two computers. All the passwords must be the same. Anyone (well, in this case, anything) that doesn't know the password can't play!

## CHANGE THE DEFAULT SECURITY PASSWORD

**The Annoyance:** It takes time to go to every computer on my powerline network and change the password. The default password is already the same on every computer, and I don't have to worry about an unmatched password. Why can't I just leave well enough alone?

**The Fix:** Because leaving it alone isn't "well enough." The same default password comes with every adapter sold by the manufacturer of your adapters. Anyone with the same adapter can plug into the wires connected to your transformer and get to all the files on your network.

Generally, if you use computers, you just have to get into "paranoia" mode because security is such an issue in the computer world. Changing a bunch of passwords takes only a few minutes, and it secures your network communications, so just do it!

## MIXING POWERLINE WITH OTHER NETWORK TOPOLOGIES

**The Annoyance:** I loved being able to create a network on our second floor without stringing cable through the walls, but in our family room we have a router and two computers with Ethernet adapters. The computers are plugged into the router. I have empty Ethernet ports on the router, but no more Ethernet-enabled computers. How do I add the powerline network to the router?

**The Fix:** You need a powerline-to-Ethernet bridge. This nifty device, available for about $50 from all manufacturers of network devices, has two types of connections: powerline and Ethernet. Plug the powerline side of the bridge into an electrical outlet near the router (ta-da! the bridge joins the network), and run Ethernet cable between the Ethernet port and the router (ta-da! the network joins the router). Is this easy, or what?

# WIRELESS HARDWARE ANNOYANCES

## YOUR ELECTRIC GARAGE DOOR ISN'T A PROBLEM

**The Annoyance:** I want to expand my wired network with wireless technology, but I keep hearing about interference with the wireless signals. Is it true that opening an electric garage door can stop wireless communications, or that sending data from a wireless computer can open the garage door?

**The Fix:** I hear that question constantly, and I've never figured out how that warning became so ubiquitous. Even though wireless computers and remote-controlled garage doors operate with radio frequency (RF) technology, they're on frequencies far, far apart from each other. Most (probably all) garage doors, and the doohickeys you use to open them remotely, use the 433MHz frequency range. Wireless computers in home networks (802.11b and 802.11g) operate in the 2.4GHz range.

## AVOIDING STUFF THAT BLOCKS WIRELESS TRANSMISSIONS

**The Annoyance:** I like the idea of wireless connections. Can you give me a list of things to avoid so that the transmissions aren't blocked?

**The Fix:** Wireless users, and manufacturers of wireless equipment, have pretty much agreed on a list of things that are sure to cause problems. Here are the "top five":

- Metal. Don't put an antenna under a metal desk or next to a metal file cabinet. Metal in the walls and ceilings can also block transmissions.
- Water. Drain your moat if you want to use your computer outdoors. Move that large fish tank to a room that doesn't have a wireless device.
- Cordless telephones (when they're in use).
- Microwave ovens (when they're in use).
- Amateur radios (when they're in use).

Other transmission blockers exist, but those listed here are the "sure things."

## WORKING WITH OMNIDIRECTIONAL ANTENNAS

**The Annoyance:** Our wireless signals occasionally drop out, but even when the computers are communicating, the signal is weak and data transmissions are slow.

**The Fix:** A common reason for these problems is incorrect placement of the antennas. The antennas that come with most wireless devices are omnidirectional, which means they radiate signals in every direction—a 360-degree arc. However, most users put their wireless devices (computers, access points, routers) near a wall. If the wall has any material that can block transmissions (metal) or degrade the signal (brick, cement, thick glass), the signal in that portion of the 360-degree arc is compromised. The antenna doesn't strengthen the signal going toward the middle of the room enough to make up for the lost signal.

With omnidirectional antennas, the way to maintain signal strength and speed is to put all the wireless devices in the middle of the room. And I mean the middle of the *room*, not the middle of the floor. You can locate this by finding the midpoint of the horizontal plane and the midpoint of the vertical plane. If your room is 10 feet by 12 feet, with an 8-foot ceiling, the midpoint of the room is 5 feet in from one wall, 6 feet in from the other wall, and 4 feet above the ground.

It's difficult to put a computer in the middle of a room because it messes up the décor. However, you should make every effort to "middleize" (I think I invented a word) the router and any access points you might have added to your system. Hang the router from the center of the ceiling—duct tape is a great tool. Or investigate directional antennas.

## DO I NEED A DIRECTIONAL ANTENNA?

**The Annoyance:** Our wireless router is perched on a bookshelf in the corner of a room, and a geeky friend told me to use a directional antenna on it. How do I do this, and what difference will it make?

**The Fix:** You can buy a directional antenna from any manufacturer of network devices, and replace the existing antenna (they're removable on some devices). A directional antenna uses all its energy to transmit and receive signals from a single direction (forward—so position it according to the instructions), instead of spreading its signal in a 360-degree sweep. When an antenna is in a corner, or against a wall, it's usually more efficient to use a directional antenna.

## SIGNAL DISTANCE PROBLEMS

**The Annoyance:** Our wireless network works fine until one of the computers moves more than 40 or 50 feet away from the router. What's the maximum distance for wireless?

**The Fix:** The "rated" maximum distance for wireless network adapters is usually about 1,500 feet outdoors and 300 feet indoors. The word "rated" means "under perfect circumstances," and that's something to think about carefully.

For outdoor distance maximums, "perfect circumstances" means your entire network is outdoors—the router, any access points, and all the computers on the network. The indoor distance maximum depends on structural elements in the house. I've never seen a building that passes a "perfect circumstances" test. Almost anything in the walls, except for air, can block or degrade the wireless signal. Because no wall stays up with air as the only component, you lose some of the signal as soon as you ask it to pass through a wall. The nails in the studs, metal in plaster lath, air conditioning ducts, cast iron pipes, and even lead paint can interfere with the signal. In the end, don't count on getting more than about a 50-foot range, a little more if you're lucky.

## DON'T GET TOO CLOSE TO THE ROUTER

**The Annoyance:** One of the computers on our wireless network sits on the same table as the router, and yet it frequently can't communicate with the network or get to the Internet. What's going on?

**The Fix:** Too close for comfort—I'm not singing the song (though I am humming it as I type this), I'm telling you what's going on. Usually, the "don't get too close" problem isn't documented in the manual that comes with your network adapter. Search the support files at manufacturers' web sites, or call their support technicians and you'll be told that a computer directly below the antenna of an access point or router will have a weak or nonexistent signal.

## DISTANCE, BUT NO SPEED

**The Annoyance:** I can take my wireless laptop to the next floor, or even out on the front porch, without losing the signal. However, the transmission speed drops so much that it takes almost a full minute to open or copy a small file from another computer. What good is a wireless network if you're not totally portable?

**The Fix:** There's an inverse ratio between speed and distance in wireless transmissions; it's just one of those things (oh no, another old song). You can try to eliminate some of the things degrading the signal. For example, your front door might be metal, or have metal parts. Move away from it, perhaps close to a window.

## GIVE YOUR SIGNAL A BOOST

**The Annoyance:** I see that manufacturers offer new routers and other devices advertised as "boosters." Are they worth buying to improve signal speed and distance?

**The Fix:** Speed, yes; distance, no. The boosters do improve the speed of communications, but they don't help you achieve greater distances. Even with boosters, as you move away from the other wireless devices, you lose speed. However, a boosted signal means the speed loss isn't as dramatic until you move far, far away. Also investigate replacing the antenna with a more powerful model (almost all routers or access points permit you to replace the antenna).

## ROUTERS ARE ALSO ACCESS POINTS

**The Annoyance:** I'm planning to buy an access point so that I can get the additional security it provides for wireless networks. Can I put the access point near the wireless router, or will the signals interfere with each other?

**The Fix:** Your router already has a built-in access point, and it provides all the same security advantages that a standalone access point would give you. I just saved you some money!

# TROUBLESHOOTING AND TECH-SUPPORT ANNOYANCES

## LIGHTS FLASH DURING COMMUNICATION

**The Annoyance:** When I move a group of files between computers, sometimes I'm not sure the computers are actually communicating. Isn't there some way to tell?

**The Fix:** Follow the flashing lights. Most network hardware comes with LEDs that glow or flash, depending on what's going on. Usually a steady green light means that all connections are working properly, and a flashing green light indicates data exchanges between computers. If you look at your hub or switch and see two flashing green lights, those two computers are talking to each other.

If you use Windows 2000 or XP, you can put an icon for your network adapter on the taskbar. The icon looks like a monitor, and when the computer is communicating over the network, the monitor color changes from black to green. To add the icon to your taskbar, open the Network Connections applet in the Control Panel, right-click Local Area Connection, and choose Properties. On the General tab, check the "Show icon in notification area when connected" box.

---

### THE HARDWARE TROUBLESHOOTING DRILL

Computer professionals have a set of procedures they follow when faced with an apparent hardware failure. These procedures, designed to make hardware troubleshooting efficient in a large corporate computer environment, work just as well in a small home network.

Rule #1. **Start with the easiest thing to fix. If you're right, you've fixed the problem in a minute.**

Rule #2. **Change only one thing at a time. For example, if you think the problem is between a network adapter and a router, first plug the cable into a different port on the router. Then put that back and replace the cable, then move the cable from a working computer to the adapter on the nonworking computer, and so on.**

Rule #3. **Write down everything you do, even if it seems unimportant. For example, list each change you make ("switched cable between computer #1 and computer #2). That way you can easily retrace your steps if necessary.**

---

# INTERPRETING THE COLORS OF LIGHTS

**The Annoyance:** Three of the ports on my hub have a yellow light, but one port doesn't. The computers all seem to be communicating properly, and everyone is getting to the Internet through the router attached to the hub. Why is one yellow light missing? Is it a sign of impending doom?

**The Fix:** A yellow light, available on some hubs, switches, and routers, indicates that the port is operating at 100 mps. The port missing the yellow light is connected to a computer that has a 10mps network adapter. (The ports on your hub are *autosensing*, which means they automatically determine the speed of your network adapter and communicate with that adapter at that speed.) If you want to see a yellow light, replace the older adapter with a new 100mps device.

## USING A KNOWLEDGE BASE

**The Annoyance:** After I fill out the Search text box in a knowledge base web page, I get so many articles listed that it would take days to read all of them. Sometimes, the article titles seem to have no relationship to my problem.

**The Fix:** A knowledge base is a database, indexed by all the important words in each article (which means that words such as "the" and "and" aren't in the index). To use the knowledge base search engine efficiently, type a series of words that describe the problem. For example, enter flashing and green. Most of the time you can't tell how the search engine is programmed, and there's a real difference between assuming "or" and assuming "and."

- A search engine programmed to assume "or" will show you every article with the word *flashing* and every article with the word *green*.
- A search engine programmed to assume "and" will show you every article that has both words.

> When you work with a search engine, you can also use a plus sign (+) to indicate the word "and."

To ensure you get articles that include all your words, insert the word "and" in the text box that accepts your search terms—e.g., "flashing and green".

If you want to search for an exact phrase, such as "unable to connect," enclose the phrase in quotation marks. This tells the search engine to find those words in that order.

## RETURNING BROKEN EQUIPMENT

**The Annoyance:** My router stopped working shortly after I installed it. I changed the cables into both LAN ports, which didn't help. I changed the cable between the router and the DSL modem, which didn't help either. If I connect the DSL modem directly to one of the computers, that computer can get to the Internet. Obviously, it's the router. I called the manufacturer's support line to find out how to return the router, and they insisted on wasting my time running tests and turning the router on and off. Then, they told me to take the router back to the store where I bought it. The store says they're not an official repair site for this manufacturer, so they can't test or fix the router, and they won't take it back without charging me a restocking fee.

**The Fix:** The usual rule of thumb is that returns go to the seller, not the manufacturer (unless you bought the product directly from the manufacturer's online sales web site). When you bought the device, the sales receipt probably had the "rules for returns" (frequently in very small type).

A restocking charge is technically the cost of repacking the device correctly so that it can be put back into stock and sold to another user (scary, huh; you know the device is broken). Some stores put returned, restocked items on sale, and advertise the fact that the product was returned. Many retailers, both brick-and-mortar and online, don't have a restocking charge. Those are the retailers to use from now on.

> ## USER FORUMS FOR TIPS, TRICKS, AND WARNINGS
>
> The Internet is filled with web sites designed for user-to-user communication (usually called *user forums*). These sites are run as a courtesy to users, and are usually not sponsored by manufacturers. You can find user forums for your hardware manufacturer by going to your favorite search engine and entering the phrase "manufacturer and user and forum" (substitute the name of your manufacturer).
>
> Many of the participants who answer user questions or complaints aren't experts, so take advice with a grain of salt. However, you'll find that some user advice includes addresses for web sites that are extremely helpful, and that you may not have found on your own.
>
> You'll also find warnings about faults or annoyances in products, along with reports of what happened when the user who's writing the message called the manufacturer. You might find that magic phrase that gets you free help, or a way to return a product without aggravation or a restocking charge.

## RETURNING WORKING EQUIPMENT

**The Annoyance:** I want to buy a hardware print server, but some friends have told me I probably won't like it. Other friends use them and think they're great. Are there places to buy computer equipment that will take the stuff back if I just change my mind?

**The Fix:** Yes, a number of computer retailers are willing to take back equipment that's working, as long as you return it within a short time. A week is a short time, two months is not a short time. The only way to tell which retailers have this policy is to ask the question, or search their web sites for information about return policies. Look for a link to Customer Support, or Return Policy, to find the terms of sales and returns.

# Software
# ANNOYANCES

To get your network up and running, you have to go through a great many software configuration processes. The hardware devices you install to create a network have software components; the computer communication features must be enabled correctly; drives, folders, and peripherals (e.g., printers) must be configured so that network users can access them; and so on.

In this chapter I'll discuss some of the annoyances you might encounter as you go through these tedious, but necessary, software processes. I'll cover the technical specifications for setting up your network adapters, and the various ways you can set up users so that everybody has their own personalized computer environment. I'll also discuss security and controls for user access (who can do what on a computer).

# CONFIGURING NETWORK ADAPTERS

## GETTING THE FACTS FROM YOUR ISP

**The Annoyance:** The configuration of my network adapter seems to go on forever. There are all these tabs in the Properties dialog box, and each tab has many options. How am I supposed to know the correct selections?

**The Fix:** Your Internet Service Provider (ISP) has all the facts you need to get online. When you signed up for the service, you should have received instructions describing how to configure your network settings. Sometimes the information comes in the mail, sometimes you're directed to a web site. Most ISPs mail you a CD that contains a setup program that runs automatically, or text files that explain the tasks you must perform. (Many people find the setup program annoying—see the next annoyance.)

Once you have the information at hand, you can configure the adapters manually or with the help of a Windows wizard (I discuss these options later in this chapter).

### Adapter Settings

Your network adapter is the device that communicates with the other computers on the network. The data is exchanged over the medium you select for your network: Ethernet cables, phone lines, electric wires, or wireless RF signals. The settings you assign to the adapter provide the necessary information needed for network communications and Internet access.

## DO I NEED TO USE THE SOFTWARE FROM MY ISP?

**The Annoyance:** My ISP sent me a CD that sets up and configures all my Internet and network settings. A neighbor said that the CD from his ISP installed stuff he didn't need or want, changed his browser settings, and put toolbars on his screen. He told me not to use my ISP's CD. Can I set up my network and Internet connection without this CD?

**The Fix:** Yes, you can set up everything manually. Your neighbor is right, and I've seen a number of ISP software setup programs that went way over the top. Call your ISP or go to your ISP's web site and look in the Support section. You should see instructions for setting up your network adapters manually.

The only exception is for an ISP that requires the use of its own software, instead of letting you choose your own email software (such as Outlook Express, Eudora, or another email client application). For example, AOL and NetZero provide their own proprietary client software.

## WHAT INFORMATION DO I NEED FROM MY ISP?

**The Annoyance:** My ISP support information includes a ton of topics such as DNS settings, FTP settings, gateways, IP address choices, and lots more. Do I need all of this stuff to set up my network?

**The Fix:** You need most of it, but probably not all of it. The important stuff is the information about IP addresses and DNS settings. Those are the options you need to configure your adapter. The easiest way to see what information is required is to open the Properties dialog box for your Local Area Connection (which is also the Properties dialog box for your adapter). You'll find this under Start → Settings → Network and Dial-up Connections → Local Area Connection, or in the Network applet in the Control Panel (depending on your version of Windows). Select the listing for TCP/IP and click the Properties button to open the Internet Protocol (TCP/IP) Properties dialog box (see Figure 2-1).

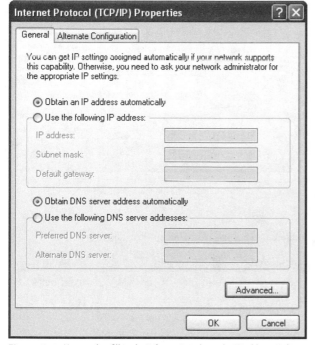

Figure 2-1. You need to fill in the information about the IP address and DNS.

Most ISPs provide the IP address automatically. However, if you've purchased specific IP addresses for your network, you must enter one of those addresses in the IP Address field for each adapter. The computer's IP address must be unique, so if you're creating a whole network of specific IP addresses, you have to buy enough IP addresses for your network.

Most ISPs also provide the DNS server's address automatically. However, if your ISP points your Internet connection to a specific DNS server, enter that server's IP address. Most of the time, you're given two DNS IP addresses; and the second one is a "fallback" server. Enter both IP addresses in the dialog box.

> **t i p**
>
> Most ISPs offer specific IP addresses for business DSL packages. This is always more expensive, but for businesses that want to run their web sites themselves (instead of using a web hosting service), an IP address is required.

## WHAT'S A GATEWAY?

**The Annoyance:** The instructions from my ISP include information on configuring the gateway. What the heck is a gateway and why do I need one?

**The Fix:** A *gateway* is a device that connects a network to the Internet. Your gateway is either a router or the computer that hosts Internet Connection Sharing.

# CONFIGURING ROUTERS

## ENTERING INFORMATION FROM YOUR ISP

**The Annoyance:** My ISP said to configure my network adapter to "Obtain an IP address automatically" and enter the IP address provided by my ISP for the DNS server. The instructions say to enter that data in either the Local Area Network Properties dialog box or the router's configuration pages. Which is the best choice?

**The Fix:** You don't really have a choice. If you installed a router, the ISP's instructions should have told you to enter the DNS server information in the router's configuration software. If you're using Internet Connection Sharing instead of a router to share your Internet connection, you have to enter the DNS server information in the Local Area Network Properties dialog box on the computer that's hosting the connection (the computer that has the modem).

## GETTING TO THE ROUTER

**The Annoyance:** An article on the manufacturer's web site suggested I make a change to the router's configuration to resolve a problem we're having. A consultant walked me through the original setup, and I can't find the documentation. How do I open the router's configuration pages?

**The Fix:** Assuming you didn't change the router's login name and password, you can get into the router's setup pages by opening your browser and entering the router's IP address in the Address Bar. The IP address is provided in the documentation, and all the major manufacturers offer a copy of the manual for download (usually a PDF file, so you'll need Acrobat Reader). However, to save you some time, the following list gives you the default IP addresses of the routers from some of the most popular vendors:

- Belkin: 192.168.2.1
- D-Link: 192.168.0.1
- Linksys: 192.168.1.1
- Netgear: 192.168.0.1

A login screen appears, looking something like Figure 2-2. Again, assuming the login name and password haven't been changed, and the default values are in place, enter the login data using the values in Table 2-1. These values are valid for the routers in the last year or so, but manufacturers can change the defaults as they upgrade their models, so check the documentation.

Figure 2-2. Log in to the router's configuration utility.

Table 2-1. Default login data for router configuration.

| Manufacturer | Login name | Password |
|---|---|---|
| Belkin | No Login Name field | Leave blank |
| D-Link | admin | Leave blank |
| Linksys | Leave blank | admin |
| Netgear | admin | password |

> **Warning...**
> Login names and passwords are case-sensitive.

# LOST ROUTER LOGIN NAME OR PASSWORD

**The Annoyance:** I did one of those stupid things you always read warnings about—I lost the piece of paper on which I'd written the login name and password I created for our router's configuration utility. I need to make an adjustment to a setting, but I can't get into the router's configuration pages.

**The Fix:** You must start all over by putting the router back to its factory settings. The factory settings include the original default login name and password. However, the factory settings don't account for all the configuration options you set.

Locate the reset button on the router. Press and hold the button for at least 30 seconds, though 60 seconds is preferable. Depending on the manufacturer, you might see a link light change color when the router's settings have been returned to the factory defaults. Now use the manufacturer's default login and password (listed in Table 2-1) to enter the configuration utility. Go through all the dialog boxes or wizards to reset your router for your network.

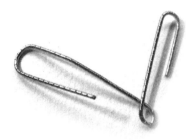

# WHY CHANGE THE LOGIN DATA FOR ROUTERS?

**The Annoyance:** I don't see any reason to change the default login and password for my router's configuration utility because it's just one more password to remember. My home network isn't in the middle of a public place, where strangers can get into the utility and mess up my network. What's the harm in leaving the default data alone?

**The Fix:** If your network is physically secure (the computers are not publicly accessible and you're not using wireless technology for your network), there are no negative side effects to leaving default values in place. However, you need to think carefully about the term "physically secure." I'll give you some things to think about based on the calls I've received from clients whose networks stopped performing properly because somebody messed around with settings.

Is there someone in your household who knows just enough about computers to be dangerous? These are people who can figure out how to get into dialog boxes and program settings, and are totally fearless about making changes because they think they know what they're doing. Of course, they usually don't know what they're doing—they know only enough to be dangerous. These folks aren't malicious, just well meaning and incompetent.

Is there someone in your household who lets outsiders who might fall into the "knows enough to be dangerous" category work on one of your network computers? For example, do your teenagers invite friends to share network games or work on homework assignments together?

Do you meet people who sound like geeks at social occasions, and ask them (or hire them) to help you tweak your settings? Approach the hiring of a computer consultant the same way you'd approach hiring an electrician or plumber—ask people for recommendations before you give anyone login names and passwords.

## YOU OWN YOUR LOGIN DATA

If you hire a consultant to install and configure your network or install and train you on a software application, make sure the consultant gives you all the login names and passwords he set up on your behalf, in writing. I've been in many businesses and homes in which my attempts to work on equipment and software were thwarted because the owner didn't know the login name and password of a software component, and they'd stopped using the consultant who installed and configured their systems.

Their consultants had told them it was too dangerous to turn that information over because the owner wasn't sufficiently knowledgeable to access administrative features. This is a form of job security that unethical and unprofessional consultants use. Don't accept it. Have the consultant come to your computers and access every password-protected feature. Change all the logins and passwords and then fire the consultant. If the consultant won't cooperate, contact a lawyer.

A lot of people spend a great deal of money with software companies to unlock their datafiles because they couldn't gain administrative access to their own software. You, not the consultant, own the password information, and you're entitled to it.

# WHAT'S DHCP AND WHERE CAN I GET SOME?

**The Annoyance:** I had intermittent problems with computers that suddenly couldn't be accessed across the network. I wrote to the router manufacturer's tech-support team, and they sent email advising me to change the duration of DHCP leases. What? Huh?

**The Fix:** DHCP (Dynamic Host Configuration Protocol) is a system in which a server, configured to be a DHCP server, assigns IP addresses to all the computers on the network the server serves. The DHCP server depends on your network setup:

- When a single computer connects to the Internet, a server at the ISP is the DHCP server.
- When a network is configured for Internet Connection Sharing, the host computer (the computer with the modem) is the DHCP server.
- When a network is configured to share an Internet connection via a router, the router is the DHCP server.

When you configure your network adapter to "Obtain an IP address automatically," the address is obtained from a DHCP server. DHCP "leases" an IP address to each computer for a given amount of time. If a computer is still connected to the network when the lease expires, it's automatically renewed. If you restart the computer, a new lease is issued during Windows startup.

If you want to know the current terms of your IP address lease, first open a command window. Do this by clicking Start → Run and typing Command in the Open field for Windows 98 and Me, or Cmd for Windows 2000 and XP. At the command prompt, enter ipconfig /all. The system returns the type of information seen in Figure 2-3.

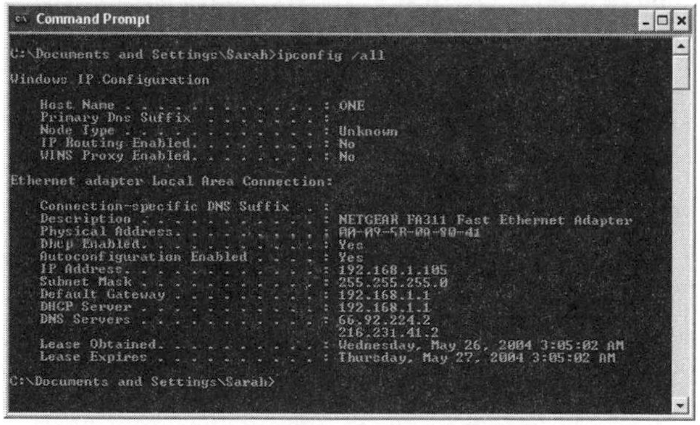

Figure 2-3. The DHCP server for this computer is giving out leases that last 24 hours.

Each DHCP server is equipped with a range of IP addresses that it can assign to the computers on the network. By default, most routers assign a lease for 24 hours, but you can change the duration by entering the router's configuration utility. The dialog box, the name of the option, and the choices you have depend on the manufacturer of your router, so you have to read the manual.

## MAC ADDRESS? I DON'T HAVE A MAC!

**The Annoyance:** According to a knowledge base article on my router manufacturer's web site, the problems I'm having might be related to a problem with MAC addresses. I'm supposed to delete the computers from my router and then boot them back into the network, but I don't have any MACs on my network.

**The Fix:** In this context, the term *MAC* has nothing to do with Macintosh computers. MAC stands for Media Access Control, which is a unique number for a computer. The number is related to a piece of hardware, which is the network adapter in a small network.

The DHCP server also tracks the IP address it assigns each computer and links that IP address to the computer's MAC and the computer's name. This feature lets you access network computers by name using My Network Places or Network Neighborhood. The network doesn't access the computer by name; it works with IP addresses. Your router's database links the names, MAC addresses, and current IP addresses. You can find that database, which is usually called the Client Table (or something similar), in your router's configuration utility. Look for a tab by that name, or go to the DHCP tab and look for a button or link with that name. Figure 2-4 shows a typical Client Table for a small network.

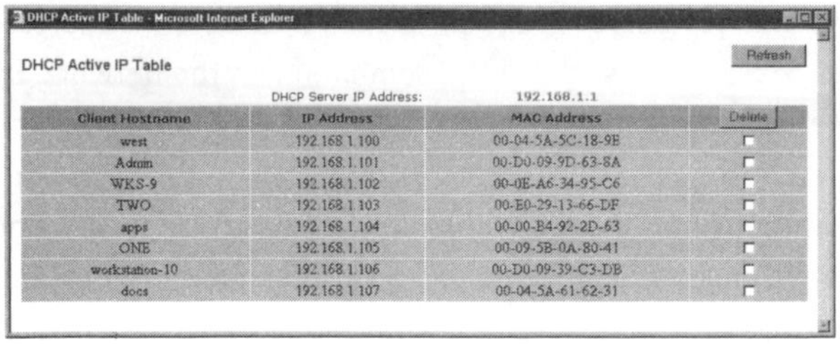

Figure 2-4. If you delete a computer, the router rediscovers it the next time it logs on to the network.

## HOW HARDWARE GETS AN ID BADGE

A number of computer hardware devices (for instance, hard drives and network adapters) come with an ID badge—a number created by the manufacturer that can be read by the operating system and software applications. The number's uniqueness in the world is derived with the use of a complicated algorithm involving the date of manufacture, a random number generated by a software program, and other factors. The process has been standardized and tested, and all manufacturers adhere to those standards. The algorithm is incredibly complicated, and is designed to make it statistically impossible for duplicates to occur anywhere in the world.

## OH NO, MY COMPUTER IS USING APIPA

**The Annoyance:** I couldn't get to the Internet from any of the computers on my network. I called a friend, who told me to check the IP addresses of my network computers by typing ipconfig at the command line. Then he told me my computers were using APIPA, which meant my router wasn't working. What in the world is APIPA, and how did it break my router?

**The Fix:** APIPA stands for Automatic Private IP Addressing, and it didn't break your router. It's a "last resort" feature computers use to communicate with each other when they don't get the IP addresses they expect from a DHCP server (in this case, your router). When communication between the DHCP server and a computer fails, the operating system automatically applies a unique private IP address to each computer. The APIPA addresses use the range 169.254.0.0 through 169.254.255.254. When you entered ipconfig at a command prompt, you could see that the IP address was within that range.

When computers use APIPA addresses, everything on the network slows down. Computers boot slowly because there's the delay of looking for the DHCP server, and then, when no DHCP server is found, the computer must peek down the pipes (the wires or wireless RF signal) to see what other computers are on the network and what their APIPA addresses are. Finally, the computer gives itself an APIPA address that isn't in use. The computer also sets the subnet mask to 255.255.0.0. The APIPA address is considered temporary until a DHCP server is located, and in fact, the computer continues to search for one.

If you're using APIPA addresses, it means your DHCP server (in this case, your router) isn't working. You need to check the connections and link lights on your router, and call the manufacturer's technical support line.

## SWITCHING LAPTOP IP ADDRESS SETTINGS BETWEEN WORK AND HOME

**The Annoyance:** I have a laptop computer that I bring home from the office. At work I have a fixed IP address, and at home I have a router so that my network adapter is set to obtain an IP address automatically. Obviously, these settings don't match, and at home I can't get on the Internet. The systems administrator at work told me I could go through a zillion steps to create an alternate hardware profile for the computer so that my network adapter settings match each network. Then he said it was too complicated to explain, and it was too much work to do it for me.

**The Fix:** Upgrade your laptop to Windows XP. If you don't, I vote with your administrator—a hardware profile is too complicated to explain, set up, and use, so fuggetaboutit.

Windows XP has a nifty feature for network adapters called "alternate configuration." It's available only if your main configuration is set to "Obtain an IP address automatically" (there's a DHCP server on the network), and the alternate configuration (the other network) doesn't have a DHCP server. You can set up the alternate configuration to use either an Automatic Private IP Address (APIPA) or a fixed IP address.

In your case, you must change your adapter so that its primary settings are for your home network (which obtains an IP address automatically), and then enter the fixed IP address for work on the Alternate Configuration tab. To do this (after you've upgraded to Windows XP, of course), open the Properties dialog for the Local Area Connection, select the TCP/IP component, and click the Properties button. Write down all the settings for the adapter, which are the settings for work. Be sure to click the Advanced button and take notes on all the settings on all the tabs.

Change the settings on the General tab to match the settings on your home network, then click the Alternate Configuration tab to enter the settings for work (see Figure 2-5).

Now, when you log on to your home network, your laptop receives an IP address automatically. When you log on to the network at work, the computer reads the adapter's settings. Because the primary settings are for obtaining an IP address automatically, the system looks for a DHCP server. You don't have a DHCP server at work, so when the computer can't find a DHCP server, it checks the Alternate Configuration tab and uses the settings it finds. Very cool!

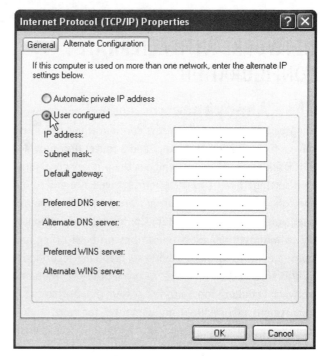

Figure 2-5. Enter the TCP/IP settings for the "other" network.

If the TCP/IP Properties dialog box doesn't have an Alternate Configuration tab, your primary settings are for a fixed IP address or for an APIPA address. The Alternate Configuration tab appears only when the primary settings are configured to "Obtain an IP address automatically."

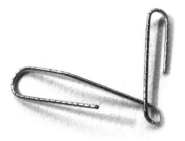

# CAN'T LOG ON TO DIFFERENT NETWORKS WITH ALTERNATE CONFIGURATION

**The Annoyance:** I configured my network adapter for alternate IP address configurations because I have a fixed IP address at work and a router that provides DHCP addresses at home (which is the primary configuration setting). I went to the Microsoft web site and found the following statement: "If you are a mobile computer user, you can use the Alternate Configuration functionality to maintain seamless operations on both office and home networks without having to manually reconfigure TCP/IP settings." After I set up my laptop for my home network I couldn't log on to the system at work, so the IT department reconfigured my computer for work. Now I can't access resources on my home network. This is what Microsoft calls "seamless"? I don't think so.

**The Fix:** I suspect that marketing departments tend to oversimplify stuff (is that a polite, politically correct statement, or what?). That assertion means "seamless TCP/IP settings," not "seamless logons." Take a look at the data on the Computer Name tab of the System Properties dialog box (right-click My Computer and choose Properties to get there).

Your computer identification setup probably looks a lot like mine, which you can see in Figure 2-6. My computer is set up to log on to my company domain, which has fixed IP addresses, while my home network has a router that supplies IP addresses. I don't have any trouble logging on to the company domain, because the computer fails to find a DHCP server and then uses the alternate configuration.

When I want to log on to my home network, I choose Local Computer in the logon dialog box (which has that

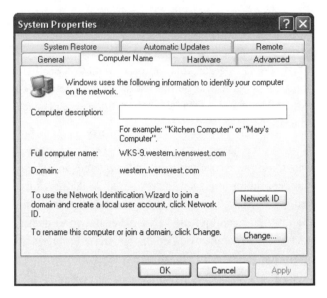

Figure 2-6. This computer is configured to log on to a domain, not a workgroup.

option because the computer is configured for a domain logon). I can get to resources on the other computers on the network by using the Run command (\\*Computer-Name*\*Sharename*). The other computers can't find this computer in Network Neighborhood or My Network Places. Because my laptop has no files or resources that the other computers on my home network need, I haven't bothered to figure out a way for the other computers to get to my laptop. Needless to say, this isn't efficient, so I looked for a better way. (See the next annoyance.)

## NETWORK SWITCHING PROGRAMS

**The Annoyance:** I move my laptop between my office, home network, four client sites, airport hot spots ...well, you get the idea. I spend half my work life trying to reconfigure my computer, and the other half dealing with error messages and trying to use a browser to connect to a network share.

**The Fix:** Sheesh! I only connect between my corporate and home networks and *that* drives me nuts. I can't imagine how you keep your sanity. I've discovered the solution—software designed to save computer settings and load them as needed. I'll mention two of these applications, NetSwitcher and Mobile Net Switch, because they've both received excellent reviews from respected sources.

NetSwitcher saves your network settings so that you can load them as needed. After you install the software, save your current configuration. Then select the command to define a different set of network settings, and enter the configuration for another network. Each set of configuration settings is called a *location*. When you boot the computer, select the location for the network you're joining. You can learn more about NetSwitcher at *http://www.netswitcher.com*.

Mobile Net Switch works similarly to NetSwitcher. However, for Windows 2000 or earlier, you must download and install some additional files (the Windows Management Instrumentation component, which is not installed in earlier Windows versions). You can learn more about Mobile Net Switch at *http://www.mobilenetswitch.com*.

# LAPTOP HAS MULTIPLE LOCAL NETWORK CONNECTIONS

**The Annoyance:** My laptop settings show two LAN connection items with identical properties. However, I own only one adapter. What's going on?

**The Fix:** You don't use the same slot every time you insert your PC Card (sometimes called PCMCIA) network adapter. Windows sees each slot as a unique device, and keeps information on devices even when they're removed from the computer.

At any given moment, one of those connections is showing an error—the one that Windows thinks should be in the slot you're not using at that moment (see Figure 2-7). If the adapter is for a wired network, the error says the cable is unplugged. For a wireless network, the error says no signal can be found.

Figure 2-7. Windows notices that one of the connections isn't available and displays an error.

You can ignore the error, and ignore the fact that your computer has two connections, without harm. If it really bothers you, decide once and for all which slot you want to use for your PC Card and remember to use that slot all the time. Then disable or remove the other LAN connection.

- To disable a connection, right-click its icon in the Network Connections window of the Control Panel, and choose Disable.

- To remove a connection, open the Device Manager and expand the listing for network adapters by clicking the plus sign to the left of the listing. Right-click the adapter currently showing the error and choose Uninstall.

To open the Device Manager, right-click My Computer and choose Properties to open the System Properties dialog box. In Windows XP and 2000 select the Hardware tab, and then click the Device Manager button. In Windows 98SE and Me, click the Device Manager tab.

> **Warning...**
> If you use the "other" PC Card slot in the future, your "disabled" connection will automatically be enabled, and the currently enabled connection will display an error. If you uninstalled the "other" connection, Windows will automatically go through an installation procedure.

# CONFIGURING AND MANAGING USERS

## ONLY ONE MY DOCUMENTS FOLDER IN WINDOWS 98SE/ME

**The Annoyance:** Several people share our Windows 98SE computer, and when anyone opens the My Documents folder, everybody's documents are in it. We've shared the My Documents folder so that we can get to our files when we work on another computer, but searching through everyone's documents to find your own stuff is annoying. How can I create a separate My Documents folder for each user of this computer?

**The Fix:** Apparently, the computer isn't set up for user profiles—a feature that automatically gives every user who logs on to the computer an individual copy of My Documents. You could enable user profiles (see the next annoyance), but the feature will work only for users you create after you enable the user profile feature; the system doesn't automatically reconfigure existing users. You can use any of the following workarounds:

- Move the My Documents folder (see the later annoyance "Move the My Documents Folder").

- Create subfolders for each user in the My Documents folder, and have everyone move his or her documents into the appropriate subfolders, and henceforth use that subfolder to save documents.

- Stop sharing the My Documents folder; instead, share each subfolder. Make sure the sharename includes the username to make it easy to identify the folder over the network.

- Delete the existing users, enable user profiles, and then add the users back to the system.

- Create individual folders for each user right on the root of the drive, and share those folders. This makes it easy for users to get to their documents from remote computers. However, this solution requires users to change their software configuration settings to make this new folder the default location for saving and retrieving files when they're working on this computer. Unfortunately, many software applications don't have a tool for changing the location of datafiles, and you can't ask people to use a whole bunch of mouse clicks to change folders every time they open or save a document. (Well, you can ask them, but they won't do it.)

## ENABLE USER PROFILES IN WINDOWS 98SE/ME

**The Annoyance:** I want to make sure users have their own profiles so that each user can have his own My Documents folder. I opened the Users applet in the Control Panel, but it doesn't have an option to enable user profiles. How do I do this?

**The Fix:** You apparently think user settings should be available in a dialog box named Users. With that kind of logic, you'll never get a job with Microsoft. To enable or disable profiles, open the Passwords applet in the Control Panel and click the User Profiles tab (see Figure 2-8).

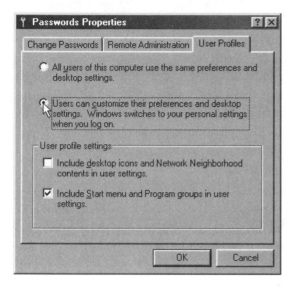

Figure 2-8. Open the Passwords applet in the Control Panel to enable User Profiles.

You'll probably notice immediately that neither of the two options at the top of the dialog box includes the term "user profile." The second option, which enables customized settings for each user, sets up user profiles (trust me).

> **Warning. . .**
> If you select the option to have all users share the same preferences and desktop settings, be aware that as each user logs on and makes configuration changes (such as adding or removing desktop icons), all the other users will have to live with those changes. The results can get ugly, as the "spare and lean desktop" folks do battle with the "shortcuts for everything" desktop decorators.

The bottom of the dialog box contains two options that cover the type of customized settings included in a user profile. Both options use the word "include," and the "included" components are those that currently exist. Before you enable user profiles, any customization of the desktop, software installation, and other configuration changes are saved as an "all users" profile. At the point that you enable user settings, those profile settings are automatically passed on to new user profiles.

By default, the first option (desktop icons and Network Neighborhood settings) is disabled. If you've customized the desktop and want to include these changes automatically for new user profiles, check the box. The second option, which includes the Start menu and Program groups in new profiles, is selected by default to make sure users can access the software installed on the Programs menu.

When you click OK, you must reboot the computer to put the new settings into effect. When Windows restarts, open the Users applet in the Control Panel and create users for this computer (see "Create Users the Right Way in Windows 98SE/Me").

## AUTOMATIC USER PROFILE FOLDERS CAN FOOL YOU

**The Annoyance:** I enabled user profiles on my Windows 98SE computer, and I know you're supposed to add each user to the computer with the Users applet in the Control Panel. But why bother? When a user logs on for the first time, the system displays the following message: "You have not logged on at this computer before. Would you like this computer to retain your individual settings for use when you log on here in the future?" If the user clicks Yes, she gets a user profile, without any effort on my part. If I open Windows Explorer and go to the Windows\Profiles folder, I see a subfolder for this newly logged-on user.

**The Fix:** Yep, sucks you right into believing you've created a user profile automatically, doesn't it? Expand the user's subfolder (see Figure 2-9). Notice anything missing? (Hint: My Documents.) This user, and the other users who log on to this computer in the same manner (without having a user profile created the right way) all share the same My Documents folder. Check the Properties for My Documents, and you see that the path for the folder is *C:\My Documents*. Do it the right way, as described in the next annoyance.

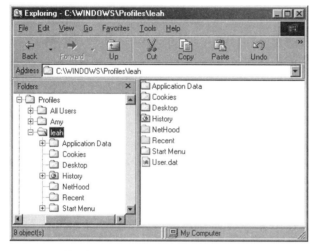

Figure 2-9. If you let Windows create a user profile automatically, it's not a real user profile.

# CREATE USERS THE RIGHT WAY IN WINDOWS 98SE/ME

**The Annoyance:** On my Windows 98SE computer, I set up user profiles in the Passwords applet in the Control Panel, but there's no option for creating users on that dialog box. How do I make sure everyone who logs on to the computer has a real profile, including a unique My Documents folder they can access locally or across the network?

**The Fix:** The Passwords applet in the Control Panel only contains the option to turn on user profiles. To create the actual user profiles, you must open the Users applet in the Control Panel. The first time you open it, the New User wizard launches automatically so that you can set up your own user profile. Thereafter, the User Settings dialog box lists your name as a user. You'll need to click Add User to start the wizard to set up another user.

Like all Windows wizards, you move through the windows by clicking Next, providing the appropriate information at each step. You must provide a username (the user's logon name) and a password. Then you can select the items you want to customize for this user profile. The components you select are configured for customization, which means the user's choices are saved as part of the profile. Click Finish to create the user.

# CHANGE USER PROFILE SETTINGS IN WINDOWS 98SE/ME

**The Annoyance:** I created two users (including myself) and realized I didn't set the customization parameters correctly. (I included everything, and nobody wants the original Downloaded web pages or Favorites list.) I'll know better for the next user, but do I have to remove and re-create the existing user profiles to change the settings?

**The Fix:** You can change the settings for any existing user in the Users applet in the Control Panel. Select the user's name and click the Change Settings button. In the Personalized Items Settings dialog box (see Figure 2-10), make the changes you need and click OK.

> **tip**
>
> If you remove settings you previously selected, choose the "Create new items to save disk space" option to clear out the stuff that had been previously put into the user's profile.

Figure 2-10. If you change your mind, change the settings to match your new choices.

# MOVE THE MY DOCUMENTS FOLDER

**The Annoyance:** I enabled user profiles, but an impatient user logged on before I had a chance to add her to the list of users. Now she has a profile, but it lacks a unique My Documents folder. Her My Documents folder is at *C:\My Documents*. I created a subfolder named My Documents in her user profile folders manually, but it's ignored when she saves documents.

**The Fix:** You can't create a My Documents subfolder in a user profile. OK, that's a lie; you can create one, but the system will ignore it. Instead, you have to move the existing My Documents folder for this user to her profile folder. Follow these steps:

1. Right-click the My Documents icon on the desktop and choose Properties. The Target text box displays *C:\My Documents* for the location of the folder (see Figure 2-11).

2. In the Target text box, enter `C:\Windows\Profiles\` `UserName\My Documents` (substitute the user's logon name for `UserName`).

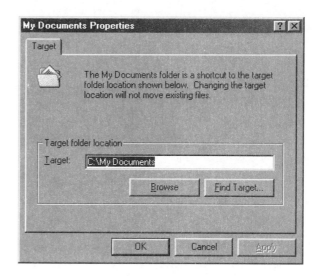

Figure 2-11. If a user's profile doesn't include the My Documents folder, that user must share a folder with other users.

3. Click OK.

4. If you previously created the folder manually, Windows accepts the change. If the folder doesn't exist, Windows displays a message to that effect and asks if you want to create it (see Figure 2-12). Click Yes.

From now on, the system will use the My Documents folder in the user's profile.

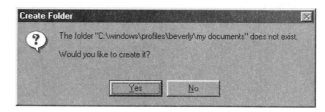

Figure 2-12. If the My Documents folder doesn't already exist, Windows creates it for you.

## DOCUMENTS DON'T TRAVEL WITH THE MY DOCUMENTS FOLDER

**The Annoyance:** After I moved the My Documents folder (on Drive C) to a user's profile, the system used it to save all of that user's documents. However, all the documents the user had created in the original My Documents folder disappeared. It's annoying that Windows removes documents when you move the My Documents folder.

**The Fix:** The documents weren't deleted, they just didn't travel with the folder. There's actual logic to this approach because a generic My Documents folder often has a slew of documents belonging to multiple users.

The documents still exist in the original My Documents folder, which is located at *C:\My Documents*. To move this user's documents into his new My Documents folder in his user profile, open Windows Explorer and select the My Documents folder in the left pane. The right pane displays the documents in the folder. You'll find all the documents this user saved before you moved his My Documents folder to his profile. Select all the documents that belong to the user, and then right-click and choose Cut from the shortcut menu.

>
> To select multiple documents, select the first document and hold the Ctrl key as you continue to select documents. To select all the documents, press Ctrl-A. To select contiguous documents, select the first document and hold the Shift key while you select the last document.

Expand the user's profile in the left pane by clicking the plus sign to get to *C:\Windows\Profiles\UserName\My Documents*. Right-click the icon for the user's My Documents folder and choose Paste from the shortcut menu. All the documents are now where they belong.

> t i p
> If the user had previously created a subfolder in the generic My Documents folder, don't cut and paste the subfolder. Instead, select the subfolder in the left pane and press Ctrl-A to select all the documents. Right-click any selected listing and choose Cut. Paste the documents into the My Documents folder in the user's profile.

## SEE A LIST OF USERNAMES WHEN YOU LOG ON TO WINDOWS 98SE/ME

**The Annoyance:** I like the way Windows XP displays all the usernames when you log on to the computer. It's a shame I can't do that with my Windows 98SE computers so that users who make typing errors when they log on don't create new users by mistake.

**The Fix:** You can have the same type of logon window on your 98SE computer—it's called Family Logon. To invoke it you need to replace your current network logon with Family Logon. Open the Network applet in the Control Panel and click the arrow to the right of the Primary Network Logon text box (see Figure 2-13). Select Family Logon and click OK.

Restart the computer, and Windows displays a list of users instead of the Logon dialog box you'd been working with (see Figure 2-14). Select your name, enter your password, and click OK.

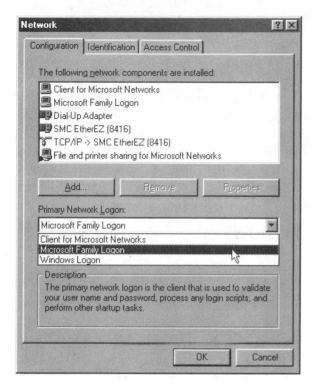

Figure 2-13. Change the dialog box Windows displays when you log on to the computer.

Figure 2-14. Select your name to log on.

If the selected user doesn't have a password, the Password field is grayed out.

# FAMILY LOGON ISN'T AVAILABLE

**The Annoyance:** My Window98SE computer doesn't offer the Family Logon option. That's really annoying because I think it's a good idea.

**The Fix:** Adding the Family Logon option to your 98SE computer is a piece of cake. You'll need your Windows CD to perform this task because the files for Family Logon have to be copied to your computer.

1. Open the Network applet in the Control Panel and click the Add button to open the Select Network Component Type dialog box.

2. Click the listing named Client, and click the Add button to open the Select Network Client dialog box.

3. In the left pane, select Microsoft. *Voilà*, the option you want is listed in the right pane (see Figure 2-15).

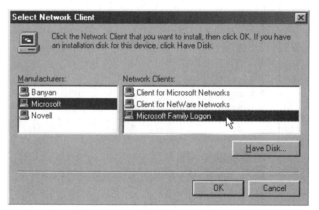

Figure 2-15. Microsoft Family Logon is available—just install it.

4. Select Microsoft Family Logon and click OK.

5. You're returned to the Network dialog box, where you can select Microsoft Family Logon from the drop-down list in the Primary Network Logon text box.

6. Click OK to close the dialog box, and Windows copies the files to your hard drive.

7. Restart the computer, and when Windows boots, the Family Logon dialog box appears.

## CAN'T ADD NAMES TO THE FAMILY LOGON USER LIST

**The Annoyance:** Two family members share our Windows 98SE computer, and today I had to use that computer because somebody was using mine. When the Family Logon dialog box appeared, my name wasn't on it. It's annoying that there's no way to add a username to the list.

**The Fix:** When you see the Family Logon dialog box, Windows hasn't yet finished booting, so the Windows features, including the Add User feature, aren't yet available. To add a name to the Family Logon dialog box list, you must add the user profile to the computer.

> If nobody in the Family Logon dialog box is available to log on and add your name to the Users list, click the Cancel button on the dialog box and do it yourself. Windows 98SE doesn't care who logs on, and lets anybody do anything (see "Earlier Versions of Windows Are Not Secure").

## EARLIER VERSIONS OF WINDOWS ARE NOT SECURE

**The Annoyance:** I installed the Family Logon feature so that only those users who exist on the computer (and appear on the Family Logon list) can get into the computer. However, there's a Cancel button on the Family Logon dialog box, and clicking it lets you into the computer, even if you're not an authorized user.

**The Fix:** If your computer runs Windows Me or any version of Windows that starts with a 9 (95/98/98SE), find a blackboard and write the following sentence 100 times until you've memorized and absorbed it: "My version of Windows is not secure, it can't be made secure, and anybody can get into the computer and reconfigure the settings, rip off the data, delete files, and generally do anything they want to do." If you want security and controls, update your computer to Windows XP.

## CAN'T BYPASS THE USER LIST IN WINDOWS XP

**The Annoyance:** I don't usually work on our Windows XP computer, but when I need to use it, my name isn't on the list. It's annoying that I can't bypass or add my name to the list so that I can use the computer.

**The Fix:** Security is annoying, but it's a great idea. Your Windows XP computer is imposing controls to keep out people who shouldn't be messing around on the computer. Have one of the authorized users add your name to the computer's User List. The user you ask must have Administrative status; a Limited User can't add names to the computer's user list.

## ELIMINATING PASSWORDS ISN'T A GOOD IDEA

**The Annoyance:** My Windows XP computer doesn't have any way to bypass the Logon window if your name isn't on the list. It's annoying that the instructions for using Windows don't point out that a good workaround is to skip entering passwords for the users you create. That way, anyone can select any name and use the computer. I've eliminated passwords and now we don't have a problem letting anyone use this computer.

**The Fix:** Sure, and "anyone" includes your kids' friends or any other person visiting your home who thinks it would be fun to log on to the computer with your name and look at your private documents, change your settings, and generally wreak havoc. Did you create automatic logons for web sites where you buy products and keep your credit information? Ouch! Want to rethink your solution?

## ONLY COMPUTER ADMINISTRATORS CAN CREATE USERS IN WINDOWS 2000/XP

**The Annoyance:** My daughter was using one of our Windows XP computers, and I asked her to add me to the user list for the computer. When she opened the User Accounts applet in the Control Panel, no option for creating accounts appeared. In fact, only her own account was listed, along with options for making changes to it.

**The Fix:** Your daughter doesn't have the permission required to create a new account. Only users who are configured as Computer Administrators can perform this task. Your daughter's account is configured as a Limited User. You'll have to have someone with administrative access create your user account.

## LOGON WINDOW DOESN'T INDICATE ACCOUNT TYPE

**The Annoyance:** When the Logon window appears, only the names are listed, without any indication of the user's account type. How do I know if I'm a Limited User or a Computer Administrator?

**The Fix:** I guess you're supposed to remember not only who you are (your logon name) and your password, but also what type of user you are. Unfortunately, the only way to find out is to try to perform some task that requires a Computer Administrator. Open the User Accounts applet in the Control Panel. If you see only your own account, you're a Limited User. If you see all the accounts, you're a Computer Administrator.

Any Computer Administrator can change the account type for another user.

## PASSWORD DISKS ARE LIFE SAVERS!

**The Annoyance:** One of our Windows XP users forgot his password and couldn't log on. Nobody could change his password because you have to know the original password to create a new password. In the end, I had to delete the user and re-create him. (Luckily, Windows XP copies the files in My Documents to another folder when you do this.) All the work involved with overcoming a forgotten password is very annoying.

**The Fix:** Setting up users on your network should include creating a password-reset disk. If you didn't perform that task as part of your user configuration for the computer, go back and create a password disk for each user now. A password disk lets you create a new password without entering the old password to complete the task.

> **Warning. . .**
> You can create password disks for other users only if your user account is configured for Computer Administrator. If your user account is configured for Limited User, you can create a password disk only for yourself.

To create a password disk, open the User Accounts applet in the Control Panel and select the user for whom you want to create the disk (start with yourself). In the User Accounts window, select "Prevent a forgotten password" in the Related Tasks section in the left pane. Put a floppy disk in the floppy disk drive and follow the prompts of the Forgotten Password Wizard. The only information you have to enter in the wizard's windows is the current password for this user.

> The wizard suggests you label the floppy disk "Password Reset" and put it in a safe place. I disagree because if anyone sees it, it could be difficult to fight the temptation to use it. Label the floppy disk with the user's name and some innocuous title, such as "Work Schedule." Or, just use the user's initials on the label.

To use the password disk, stare at the monitor for a few minutes as you try to remember your password. Scratch your head, bang the desk, or do whatever you usually do when you're having an annoying, frustrating memory lapse. Now go get your password reset disk from its safe hiding place.

Click your name (I'm assuming your memory lapse is limited to your password, and you still remember your name), and click the arrow (or press Enter) without typing in a password. Windows asks if you forgot your password, and offers a link to the password reset disk feature (see Figure 2-16). Put the password reset disk in the floppy drive and click the link.

Follow the wizard to create a new password and (if you want) a new password hint (see Figure 2-17). Windows changes your password and returns you to the Logon window. Enter your new password (you can't possibly have forgotten it this fast) and log on to the computer.

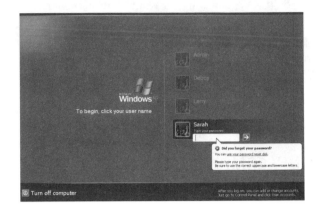

Figure 2-16. Windows offers to help you create a new password if you have a password reset disk.

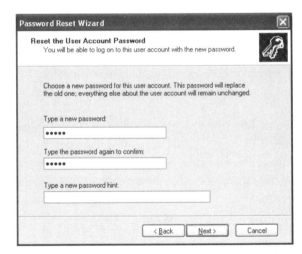

Figure 2-17. This is the only way to create a new password without having to enter the current password.

> Windows resets the password disk with your new password, so if you forget again, the password disk continues to work.

# CONFIGURING THE DESKTOP

## OTHER USERS CAN'T FIND SOFTWARE

**The Annoyance:** I installed a software program on our Windows XP computer, but the other users on the computer can't find it. I see it on the Programs menu when I log on, but other users can't see it when they log on.

**The Fix:** The software installed its menu item only into your user profile. Some software automatically installs itself for all users (a computer-wide installation), and some installs for the current user. What's annoying is that not all software offers the choice between computer installation or user installation during setup. More irritating is the fact that software that doesn't ask you to choose doesn't announce its installation plans. Once the software is installed, you can make it available to all users or some users.

In Windows Explorer or My Computer, expand *C:\Documents and Settings\YourName\Start Menu\Programs* (substitute your logon name for *YourName*). Shortcuts for

programs that appear on your All Programs menu are displayed in the right pane (see Figure 2-18).

Figure 2-18. The shortcuts for program menu items are stored in user profiles.

Right-click the shortcut for the program you want to provide for other users, and choose Copy. Then, expand the user profile for another user and paste the shortcut into that Programs subfolder. Do this for each user with whom you want to share the application.

> **Warning. . .**
> If your user account is configured as Limited User, you cannot access the user profile folders of other users.

## SOFTWARE NOT FOUND ERROR

**The Annoyance:** I selected a program and Windows displayed an error message telling me it couldn't find the software's file. I learned later that another user on the computer had uninstalled the software. It's annoying that Windows removes the program's icon only from the menu of the user who uninstalled it, and not from the other users' menus.

**The Fix:** You're right, it's very annoying. Windows should check to see whether the program's shortcut is on the menu of all the computer's users, and remove any shortcuts it finds. Unfortunately, Windows isn't smart enough to do that, so users have to remove the menu item manually. To do this, right-click the item on the menu and choose Delete, or you can go into each user's profile and remove the shortcut from the Programs submenu (see the previous annoyance).

## DISPLAY RESOLUTION IS GLOBAL IN WINDOWS XP/2000

**The Annoyance:** I like to work with high-resolution settings, but other users of my computer prefer the larger icons of a smaller resolution. On our Windows 98SE computer, Windows remembers the settings for each user, but on our Windows XP computer, anyone who changes his settings also changes everyone else's.

**The Fix:** Microsoft removed the ability to configure screen resolution settings starting with Windows 2000, and I don't know why. Surely there weren't complaints from users who said, "When I change my settings I want everybody else to live with my decision, so how dare you let them make their own choice?" You can't do anything about this, except change your settings whenever you log on, which takes only a few seconds. It's probably a good idea to change them back before you log off, unless you don't care about hearing the groans and complaints.

## LIMITED USERS CANNOT CHANGE POWER SETTINGS

**The Annoyance:** I don't like the default setting that Windows applies to turn off my monitor after a certain amount of time that I'm not using the mouse or keyboard. I opened the Power Options dialog box and changed the setting to Never, but when I clicked OK, I received an Access Denied message.

**The Fix:** For some reason that defies logic, Microsoft chose to forbid Limited Users to change power-saving options. What harm could come to the computer as a result of changing when (or whether) monitors and hard disks are powered down automatically for this user?

If you think that's annoying, check Microsoft's support web sites, where the suggested "fix" is to log on to the computer with an administrative account to make the change. Why is that a fix? The power options are part of the user settings, so they are unique to each user. Changing another person's power settings doesn't change the settings for a limited user. The only real fix is to have someone with administrative rights log on, change your account to an administrative account, make the power settings change, and then reset the account for limited permissions. Is this silly, or what?

## COPY DESKTOP THEMES IN WINDOWS XP

**The Annoyance:** I changed the look of my Windows XP computer by changing the desktop design and the way windows look when they're open (I didn't think the title bars and background colors were attractive). I named my new desktop design Debby. Windows doesn't seem to offer a quick list of the selections I made, so I can't tell other users how to duplicate them.

**The Fix:** Just give them a copy of Debby. Your desktop design is a theme file (named *Debby.Theme*), and you can give the file to any other Windows XP user. When you saved your theme file, Windows automatically located it in your My Documents file. Copy the file to the root directory, or to the desktop for easy access. If users on other Windows XP computers on the network want to use the file, copy it across the network. Heck, send it by email to everyone who has a Windows XP computer.

To load a theme file:

1. Right-click a blank spot on the desktop and choose Properties.

2. Click the arrow to the right of the Themes text box and choose Browse.

3. Navigate to the place where the theme file you want to load is located and select it. Click OK.

Copy your theme file to all the other Windows XP computers on your network. Load it the next time you log on to each of those computers to make your environment just as pleasing no matter which computer you work on.

## COPY DESKTOP DESIGNS IN EARLIER VERSIONS OF WINDOWS

**The Annoyance:** I customized my Windows 98SE desktop and saved it. I want to have the same desktop when I use the other Windows 98SE computer on our network. Also, my brother-in-law wants a copy for his Windows 98SE desktop. But unlike Windows XP, I can't create a theme file that I can copy to other computers.

**The Fix:** In earlier versions of Windows (98/98SE/Me/2000), you can provide your customized desktop settings to other users, but it's a bit more complicated than it is with XP. When you create a customized desktop and give it a name, the changes are written to the registry. You can export the registry key and then import it to another computer running the same version of Windows by following these steps:

1. Choose Start → Run, type regedit, and click OK.

2. Navigate to *HKEY_CURRENT_USER\Control Panel\Appearance* and select that key in the left pane.

3. In the right pane, you'll see the registry items for your current settings (see Figure 2-19). Choose Registry → Export Registry File and save the file using any filename you choose (Windows automatically adds the .*reg* extension).

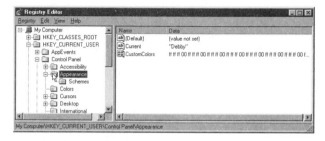

Figure 2-19. The details of your desktop are in the registry (and in incomprehensible binary data).

4. Copy the file to any other computer on the network that's running the same version of Windows. You can also email the file to anyone using the same version of Windows.

5. To import the registry file, double-click its listing. Windows asks if you're sure you want to merge the contents of the file to the local registry. Choose Yes to import the display settings for yourself (the current user).

If additional users on the computer want to use this desktop design, they must log on to the computer and import the file.

### Warning...

Playing in the registry can be *very* dangerous. If you're not comfortable with computers and don't have a thorough understanding of the way the registry works, ask somebody more experienced to help you. Before you import a registry file, export the current contents of the affected key as a backup in case something goes wrong and you have to return to the previous settings.

# INSTANT MESSENGER ANNOYANCES

## USE MESSENGER TO CHAT ACROSS THE NETWORK

**The Annoyance:** Our network is spread across three floors. Can we take advantage of the connections to send messages to each other?

**The Fix:** You have several ways of using the computers for communication, but if everyone is always connected to the Internet, the easiest solution is Messenger from Microsoft. The program comes with Windows XP, and you can download it from Microsoft for Windows 98 and later.

Microsoft has two Messenger software applications available for download. Windows Messenger runs on Windows 2000/XP, while MSN Messenger runs on earlier versions of Windows. You can chat with another user (see Figure 2-20), or even multiple other users, because you're not

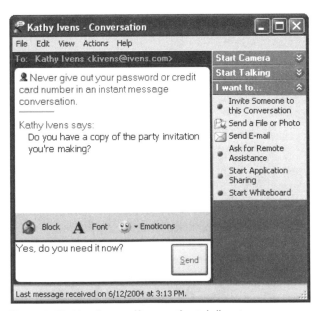

Figure 2-20. It's easier to use Messenger than to bellow at a user on another floor.

limited to just one other person in your conversation. Messenger also provides file transfer capabilities between users; two users can share a software window and discuss its contents in the chat window or by drawing directly on the window.

## SOME MESSENGER FEATURES ARE BLOCKED BY FIREWALLS

**The Annoyance:** When I try to take advantage of some of Messenger's features, I get an error message that I can't proceed because of a firewall.

**The Fix:** Some Messenger features use specific communications protocols that require support for Universal Plug and Play (UPnP). This isn't the same thing as the Plug and Play feature that automatically recognizes new hardware. UPnP is a technology that lets computers communicate through firewalls by helping the computers find each other (that's an extremely oversimplified explanation, so don't quote me). Most firewalls block UPnP by default, so you have to enable support for this technology manually. The method you use depends on the type of firewall you've employed (see the following annoyances for details).

## CONFIGURE WINDOWS XP SP2 FIREWALL FOR UPNP

**The Annoyance:** I'm using the built-in firewall for Windows XP Service Pack 2 (SP2), which is supposed to permit Messenger communications. However, I get error messages telling me the firewall has blocked communications when I try to use some of the Messenger features.

**The Fix:** The Windows XP SP2 firewall disables UPnP by default, but you can enable UPnP communications by changing the default configuration settings. Open the Windows Security Center applet in the Control Panel and click Windows Firewall. Next, click the Exceptions tab and check the "UPnP Framework" box (see Figure 2-21).

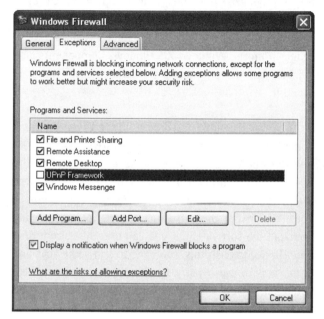

Figure 2-21. The Windows XP SP2 firewall can be configured to permit UPnP communications.

The firewall in Windows XP prior to SP2 cannot be configured at all and, in fact, doesn't support networking. You must disable it and replace it with a software or router firewall until you download and install SP2.

## CONFIGURE SOFTWARE FIREWALLS FOR UPNP

**The Annoyance:** We use a software firewall on our network computers, and we want to enable UPnP so that we can use all the features in Messenger. There doesn't seem to be a way to do this.

**The Fix:** Your software firewall might not support this configuration change. If you use ZoneAlarm from Zone Labs (*http://www.zonelabs.com*), the free version doesn't offer a way to enable UPnP communications. You can turn off the firewall for the Trusted Zone (the network) while keeping the firewall for Internet communications. However, that's risky because any computer on the network that has picked up a virus, worm, or other malicious program could deliver it to the other computers on the network. ZoneAlarm Pro (which isn't free) is configurable, as are all versions of BlackICE from Internet Security Systems (*http://www.iss.net/*). If you're using another software firewall, check the documentation or the support information on the company's web site.

## CONFIGURE ROUTER FIREWALLS FOR UPNP

**The Annoyance:** Our router provides our firewall, and it seems complicated to configure it without risking security. How do I find out whether I can open the firewall for certain types of communication, such as those required for Messenger?

**The Fix:** You can read the documentation (although the documentation for most network devices is annoyingly hard to understand) or visit the manufacturer's web site for support. However, to make it easier, Microsoft has put together step-by-step instructions for enabling UPnP in many of the popular routers. Visit *http://www.microsoft.com/windowsxp/windowsmessenger/equipment.asp* to see if your router is covered.

## STOP MESSENGER FROM OPENING AT STARTUP

**The Annoyance:** On a day-to-day basis, my use of Messenger varies between "hardly ever" and "never." It's annoying to wait for the software to load and sign in when I start my computer. It seems to take forever.

**The Fix:** Just stop Messenger from loading automatically. Open the software window and choose Tools → Options. On the Preferences tab, deselect the option to launch the software at startup (see Figure 2-22). When you want to use Messenger, just open it from the Programs menu.

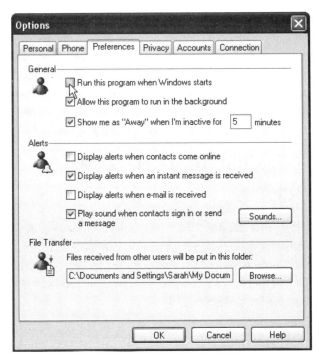

Figure 2-22. Deselect automatic startup to prevent Messenger from starting when you don't need it.

## REMOVE WINDOWS MESSENGER FROM WINDOWS XP

**The Annoyance:** I think our children spend too much time on the computer, although I encourage them to use the Internet for research and homework assignments. However, every time I walk past them, I see they're talking to friends and have at least six Windows Messenger chat windows open. I uninstalled Windows Messenger from the Windows XP Windows Components dialog box, but the program is still available and the kids found it.

**The Fix:** The uninstall process in the Windows Components section of Add/Remove Software in Windows XP uninstalls only the Windows Messenger shortcut on the All Programs Menu (and any shortcuts to Windows Messenger that are on the desktop). As you found out, it doesn't uninstall the software. In fact, you can't really uninstall the software, but you can prevent it from running. To accomplish this, you have to add some keys and data items to the registry. Registry changes can be very dangerous if you don't know what you're doing, so you might want to get help from a computer expert. Take the following steps to make the registry change:

1. Choose Start → Run, enter regedit, and click OK to open the registry editor.

2. Navigate to *HKEY_LOCAL_MACHINE\Software\Policies\Microsoft*.

3. Choose Edit → New → Key, and enter Messenger as the name of the new registry key.

4. Select the new key, *HKEY_LOCAL_MACHINE\Software\Policies\Microsoft\Messenger*, choose Edit → New → Key, and name the new key Client.

5. Select the new key, *HKEY_LOCAL_MACHINE\Software\Policies\Microsoft\Messenger\Client*, and choose Edit → New → DWORD Value. Name the new value PreventRun.

6. Double-click the new PreventRun value, and change the default value from 0 to 1.

7. Close the registry editor and restart the computer.

Now, when anyone tries to open Windows Messenger from any source—the Programs menu, a desktop shortcut, or the software's executable file—nothing happens. I mean nothing, not even an error message. This will drive your kids crazy unless you tell them you uninstalled the program.

If your computer is running a version of Windows earlier than Windows XP and you downloaded Messenger, you can uninstall it from Add/Remove Programs.

# USE BUILT-IN MESSAGING UTILITIES

**The Annoyance:** Our network uses a telephone modem for Internet access, so we don't have an always-on connection. Because Windows Messenger uses the Internet, we can't send messages unless every computer happens to be connected to the Internet.

**The Fix:** Well, you could walk up and down the stairs and tell everybody to connect to the Internet, or yell loudly "get on the Internet," and then use Messenger. Hmmm, I guess that defeats the whole purpose, huh? OK, I have a better idea: use Windows built-in message utilities.

For sending messages among computers, the net send command is available in Windows XP and Windows 2000. Earlier versions of Windows can send and receive messages with a program named WinPopup.

I've seen help files and articles that say net send and WinPopup don't talk to each other. Don't believe it!

### Using net send

In Windows 2000/XP, net send is available from the command line. The syntax is net send target "message", where target is a username or a computer name and "message" is the text of the message, enclosed in quotation marks.

For example, to send a message to a computer named Admin on my network, I enter the text in Figure 2-23. When I press Enter, the system tells me the message was sent successfully (unless the target computer wasn't running, in which case I'd see an error message that the system couldn't find the computer).

Figure 2-23. Send a note (or a demand) to a network user from the command line.

I could have substituted a username for the computer name, and the system would have routed the message to the computer where the user was logged on. But in this case, I chose the computer because it's next to the kitchen (where the sodas are), and I didn't care who was using the computer.

> **Warning. . .**
> If the name of the computer or user has a space, you must enclose the entire name in quotation marks.

You can also send a message to all the computers on the workgroup by using the syntax net send /domain:Work-groupName "message". Substitute the name of your workgroup for WorkgroupName.

If the target computer is running Windows 2000/XP, the message appears in a message dialog box (see Figure 2-24). Clicking OK simply makes the text box go away; there's no utility for responding to the message in the dialog box. To respond, you must open a command prompt and enter the appropriate syntax for net send. If the target computer is running an earlier version of Windows, the message appears in the WinPopup software window (as discussed next).

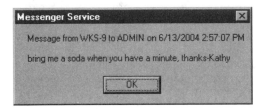

Figure 2-24. Read the message, then click OK to close it.

## Using WinPopup

For Windows versions earlier than Windows Server 2003, you have to use WinPopup to send messages. WinPopup is a program, and it has to be running to send or receive messages. Because it doesn't appear on a menu anywhere, there's a trick to getting it to run.

The best way to make WinPopup available is to create a desktop shortcut to the program. Of course, to create a shortcut, you first have to locate the program. In this case, open Windows Explorer and make sure it's not in full-screen mode (so that you have access to the desktop). Navigate to the Windows folder and look for the file named *WinPopup.exe*. Right-drag the winpopup.exe icon to the desktop. When you release the right mouse button, choose Create Shortcut(s) Here.

Because WinPopup has to be running for you to receive or send a message, you should start the software whenever you boot the computer. In fact, it's a good idea to make WinPopup start automatically, which you can do by putting a shortcut to the software in the Startup subfolder of your Programs menu. Use the following steps to accomplish this.

Open Windows Explorer and navigate to the Startup subfolder of the Programs folder in your profile (see Figure 2-25). To move the desktop shortcut to the Startup subfolder, drag it into the right pane. To copy the desktop shortcut to your Startup subfolder, right-drag it to the right pane and choose Copy Here from the menu that appears when you release the right mouse button.

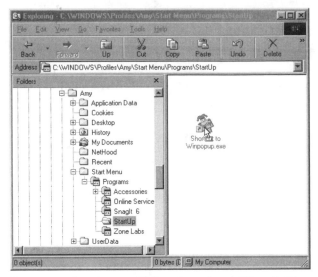

Figure 2-25. Put a shortcut to WinPopup in your Startup folder so that the program starts when you boot your computer.

When you're through using the WinPopup window, minimize rather than close it. Remember, it has to be running for you to send or receive messages. If you accidentally close it, Windows displays a message warning you of the consequences. Click Cancel on the error message, and then use the Minimize button (the minus sign) on the window instead of the Close button (the X).

If someone sends you a message, it appears within the WinPopup window (see Figure 2-26). The program keeps all the messages it collected since it started running, which is handy if you have a short memory. You can move through the messages using the arrows on the toolbar.

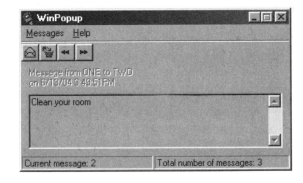

Figure 2-26. The message is displayed in the software window.

By default, WinPopup beeps when a message is received, but you can choose Messages → Options to tell the software to open the window instead of just beeping when a message arrives. If you change the option, also select the "Always on Top" option to be sure you'll see arriving messages come in if you have software windows open.

To send messages, click the Send icon on the toolbar (or press Ctrl-S, or choose Message → Send). Select User or Computer, or Workgroup, and fill in the appropriate name. Then enter the message text and click OK (see Figure 2-27).

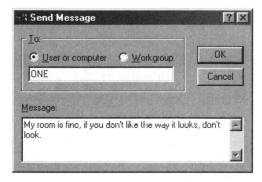

Figure 2-27. Direct your message to a computer name, a username, or the entire workgroup.

## CAN'T FIND WINPOPUP.EXE?

**The Annoyance:** I want to run WinPopup on our Windows 98SE computers, but the *winpopup.exe* file isn't in my Windows folder.

**The Fix:** Apparently, when the operating system was installed, the person performing the installation customized the process and neglected to keep WinPopup in the list of files to install. To install it:

1. Open the Control Panel and double-click the Add/Remove Programs icon.

2. Look in the Windows Setup tab of the Add/Remove Programs dialog box. WinPopup is listed under the category System Tools.

3. Put the Windows CD in the CD-ROM drive.

4. Select WinPopup, and then click OK twice.

# SOFTWARE SUPPORT ANNOYANCES

## GETTING SUPPORT FOR WINDOWS PROBLEMS

**The Annoyance:** Some of the network software configuration settings I applied in Windows don't seem to be working correctly (or at all). How do I figure this stuff out? I can't believe I have to hire a consultant to set up a small home network.

**The Fix:** Users who aren't computer experts can set up most home networks quickly and easily (although the combination of devices and settings sometimes does require expert help). For Windows support, you should start with Microsoft.

Check the web site for your version of Windows. If you start at *http://www.microsoft.com*, the left side of the web page has a section named Product Families. Click the listing for Windows to go to the Windows web page. Windows XP is listed on the left side, and if you hover your mouse pointer over the listing, you can select your version of Windows XP (Home Edition or Pro). If you want to look at support pages for earlier versions of Windows, hover your mouse pointer over Other Versions, and click the appropriate listing (see Figure 2-28).

Figure 2-28. Select your version of Windows to visit its web pages.

The web page for your version of Windows has tons of support in the form of Frequently Asked Questions, "How-To" articles, and sections on specific processes such as networking. Navigate through the pages to find the answer to your question. If your network problems prevent you from getting to the Internet in the first place, consult your computer's documentation to find a technical support number.

## USING THE MICROSOFT KNOWLEDGE BASE

**The Annoyance:** I'm not always sure what category to access on Microsoft's web site. I need a way to find the answer when I've encountered an error message, or have some specific question to ask.

**The Fix:** Try the Microsoft Knowledge Base, which is a terrific search engine to help your problem solving. To get there, start at the Microsoft home page; on the left side, under the heading Resources, hover your mouse pointer over the listing for Support, then select Knowledge Base.

When the Knowledge Base web site opens, fill in the fields to match your needs (the fields have drop-down lists for your selections) and click Go (see Figure 2-29).

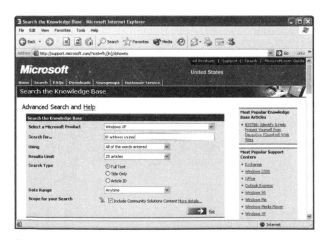

Figure 2-29. Fill out the fields to search for a solution in the Knowledge Base.

In a few seconds, a list of articles appears. Each listing has the article's title and the first sentence of the article. Select one that seems appropriate. If it doesn't provide the information you need, click the Back button to return to the list.

> **tip**
>
> Add the Knowledge Base web page to your browser's Favorites list so that you can access it quickly whenever you need an answer in the future.

> **tip**
>
> You can also call Microsoft's support line (the numbers are in the Support section of Microsoft's web site). However, unless the problem you're having is a bug that's Microsoft's fault, you'll probably be charged for the call. The Knowledge Base articles indicate whether a problem is a bug, and usually tell you that a fix is in the works or suggest you download an update.

## GETTING SUPPORT FROM THIRD-PARTY SOURCES

**The Annoyance:** I find the Microsoft web site annoying. It's vast, full of marketing hype, and takes forever to navigate. Isn't there a better, faster way to get a solution to a problem?

**The Fix:** Sure, the Internet is filled with experts anxious to provide advice and solutions, and a few of them actually know what they're talking about. The best way to approach your search is to ask somebody with expertise where to find the most reliable information. Or, until you know who to trust, visit the web sites of some of the computer publications (both print and online) that have been around for a long time.

# Network Access
# ANNOYANCES

One of the nifty advantages to a home network is that you can sit in front of one computer and access files on any other computer on the network. For example, perhaps Mom usually works at the computer in the den, and saves her files on that computer. Suppose one of the kids is using the den computer when Mom wants to work on a document. Before the network arrived, Mom would have to ask (or order) Junior to move so that she could work. With a network-enabled house, Mom can use any free computer, and just reach across the network to work on her files. I'm sure this contributes to a more harmonious family atmosphere. Of course, if you have more users than you have computers, you can still expect to have some discordant moments in your household.

In this chapter I'll provide some tips, tricks, and workarounds for the annoyances you might run into as you access all the computers on your network. I'll cover the problems you encounter in network windows (Network Neighborhood and My Network Places), methods for connecting to other computers quickly, and ways to solve connection problems when you can't find computers on your network.

# FINDING COMPUTERS ON YOUR NETWORK

## WINDOWS HAS A WINDOW FOR YOUR NETWORK

**The Annoyance:** There's no easy, intuitive way to see all the remote computers on my network. Why doesn't the Programs menu list commands such as "Go to Computer Named Charlie?"

**The Fix:** Imagine working in a large company with 100,000 computers on the network. If the Programs menu listed all the computers on the network, you could have Charlie 1 all the way up to Charlie 145. Which computer belongs to which Charlie? Not very practical. Instead, Windows provides special windows that make it easy to see all the computers on your network. The name of the window depends on your version of Windows:

- For Windows Me/2000/XP, the window is named My Network Places.
- For Windows 98SE (and earlier versions of Windows), the window is named Network Neighborhood.

Except in Windows XP (see the next annoyance), an icon for the network window exists on your desktop. Double-click the desktop icon to display an icon with the name of your workgroup. Double-click the workgroup icon to display icons for the computers on your network. Figure 3-1 shows a Network Neighborhood window in Windows 98SE.

The computer you're using is always referred to as the *local computer*. All the other computers on the network are called *remote computers*.

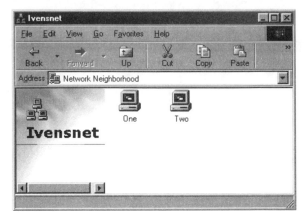

Figure 3-1. The Network Neighborhood window displays the name of the workgroup, as well as icons for the computers in the workgroup.

---

## UNDERSTANDING SHARE AND UNC

Any discussion about accessing computer resources across a network is certain to include the following references:

- ☒ *Share* is the term applied to a resource on a computer (drive, folder, or printer) that has been configured for access by other computers.

- ☒ *UNC* (Universal Naming Convention) is the "path" to a network resource. It is always notated in the following format: \\*ComputerName\ShareName*. The ComputerName is the name of the remote computer that has the resource; the ShareName is the name applied to the shared resource.

## HUNT FOR MY NETWORK PLACES IN WINDOWS XP

**The Annoyance:** I give up. Where is the listing for My Network Places in Windows XP? I can't find an icon on my desktop, and I can't find a listing on the Start menu.

**The Fix:** Don't you want to ask the programmers who designed Windows XP why they did this? I do, although I suspect I'd find their explanation as annoying as the feature design. The My Network Places window does exist—honest. You just have to go on a scavenger hunt every time you want to open it. (For a workaround that offers a quick solution, see the next annoyance.)

The road to your My Network Places window starts in your My Computer window. Begin your journey by selecting Start → My Computer. When the My Computer window opens, look for the link to My Network Places on the left side of the window. Click the link to open the My Network Places window, and then click the "View workgroup computers" link to see the computers in your network (see Figure 3-2).

Figure 3-2. The My Network Places window includes links to other folders and features in addition to icons for each computer on the network.

## CREATE A LINK FOR MY NETWORK PLACES

**The Annoyance:** There must be a way to open My Network Places in Windows XP without an interminable number of mouse clicks. This important window should have its own link in the Start menu.

**The Fix:** You're right, and you can create the link yourself. This task involves multiple mouse clicks, but it's a one-time thing, so it's worth it. To create a link for My Network Places, you have to change the configuration of the Start menu. To accomplish this, follow these steps:

1. Right-click a blank spot on the task bar and choose Properties.
2. In the Task Bar and Start Menu Properties dialog box, click the Start Menu tab.
3. Click the Customize button to the right of the Start Menu option to display the Customize Start Menu dialog box.
4. Click the Advanced tab.
5. Scroll through the listings in the Start Menu Items section and check the My Network Places box.
6. Click OK twice to close all the dialog boxes.

Now, when you click the Start button, you'll see a listing for My Network Places on the Start menu. One click now opens the window.

## CREATE A DESKTOP SHORTCUT FOR MY NETWORK PLACES

**The Annoyance:** I don't want to click the Start menu and then click a link to My Network Places. I want a shortcut, such as the one on my Windows 98SE desktop.

**The Fix:** That's the attitude of a truly efficient Windows user—good for you. Right-click the My Network Places listing on the Start menu and select Show On Desktop from the drop-down menu. While you're there, do the same thing for the My Computer listing on the Start menu.

---

### RECONFIGURE THE LOOK OF WINDOWS XP

If you moved to Windows XP from an earlier version of Windows, you might miss certain features, such as the desktop icons for My Computer and My Network Places. In addition, you might miss the "look and feel" of earlier Windows versions, especially the layout of the Start menu. If you feel this way, you can reconfigure Windows XP so that it looks almost exactly like earlier versions. Right-click a blank spot on the task bar and choose Properties. Click the Start Menu tab and select the Classic Start Menu option. The Start menu changes to resemble the older Start menu, and the desktop icons that appeared on older Windows desktops are placed on your desktop.

Think carefully before you make this change because you'll give up some of the nifty features built into Windows XP's graphical design. For example, I love the fact that the Start menu lists recently used software and offers one-click access to the windows I use most frequently (My Computer, My Network Places, Control Panel, etc.). Give yourself a chance to get used to the new graphical interface. I'll bet your annoyance eventually changes to appreciation.

---

## ADD THE NETWORK WINDOW TO THE QUICK LAUNCH TOOLBAR

**The Annoyance:** I always have application windows open, so to get to a desktop shortcut I have to click the Show Desktop icon on my Quick Launch toolbar, and then double-click the Network Neighborhood icon. Why isn't there an option for a Quick Launch toolbar shortcut to the network window? I love the fact that the icons on my Quick Launch toolbar require only a single click of the mouse.

**The Fix:** You'd think that Microsoft would offer the ability to create Quick Launch toolbar icons for all the major system windows, since the toolbar is so quick and efficient. You have several methods for accomplishing this task:

- In Windows XP, right-drag the My Network Places link on the Start menu to the Quick Launch toolbar area on your task bar. When you release the right mouse button, select Create Shortcut(s) Here.

- In all Windows versions, right-drag the My Network Places (or Network Neighborhood) desktop icon to the Quick Launch toolbar. When you release the right mouse button, select Move Here (or Copy Here if you want to keep the desktop icon) or Create Shortcut(s) Here (depending on your version of Windows).

## USE WINDOWS EXPLORER TO FIND COMPUTERS

**The Annoyance:** I'm trying to avoid "icon clutter," and I don't access the network window very often. Also, I don't like clicking my way through links and icons to get to a window displaying the contents of a network computer. I do keep a shortcut to Windows Explorer on my Quick Launch toolbar, but I'd like to configure it to display the network computers.

**The Fix:** You don't have to reconfigure Windows Explorer to display the network computers; that capability is built in. In the left pane, scroll down below the listings for the local computer to find Network Neighborhood or My Network Places (see Figure 3-3). Expand the listing by clicking the plus signs. Select the listing for the remote computer you want to access to display its shared resources in the right pane.

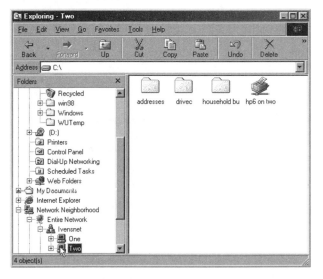

Figure 3-3. The remote computers and your local computer are available at the same time in Windows Explorer.

In Windows 2000 and XP, you can click the Folders icon on the My Computer toolbar to change the display of My Computer to a double-pane layout that looks just like Windows Explorer.

## TRICKS FOR QUICKER ACCESS TO REMOTE COMPUTERS

**The Annoyance:** I find it annoying to click my way through a series of windows, and I don't like using the mouse anyway. How can I access a remote computer without going through a lot of steps?

**The Fix:** As a touch typist, I try to avoid the mouse as much as possible. I find it faster and easier to use my keyboard. You can use either of the following shortcuts to access a remote computer:

- Click Start → Run and enter \\*ComputerName* (substitute the name of the remote computer for *ComputerName*).

- Open your browser and enter \\*ComputerName* in the Address Bar (substitute the name of the remote computer for *ComputerName*).

You'll see the shared resources of the remote computer displayed in the open window (see Figure 3-4). OK, I admit this doesn't eliminate the need to reach for the mouse altogether, but you certainly use fewer mouse clicks.

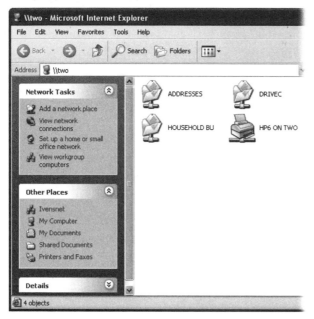

Figure 3-4. Go directly to a remote computer from the Run command or from your browser.

# TROUBLESHOOTING NETWORK CONNECTIVITY

## NEW COMPUTERS DON'T COME TO THE NEIGHBORHOOD

**The Annoyance:** I added a new computer to my network, but it didn't appear in My Network Places or Network Neighborhood on any of the other computers. I know the cabling and the network settings are correct, but I have to reboot all the computers on the network to see a new computer, which is really annoying.

**The Fix:** You don't have to reboot all the computers to see a newly added computer on your network. Just wait

12 minutes. Honest. Could I make that up? Go have a cup of coffee, empty the dishwasher, or change all the burned-out light bulbs in the house. Then open the network folder again, or press F5 to refresh the display if you didn't close the folder. You should now see the new computer.

Why does this happen? The icons in the network windows are controlled by a Windows service called the *Computer Browser Service.* The service browses the network, peers down the pipes (including the virtual pipes for wireless connections), and checks to see who's on board. The service runs every 12 minutes.

### The Computer Browser Service

All the computers on a network elect one of their own as a *browser master* using a complicated scheme that involves a private conversation among the computers. The conversation is held secretly, so you aren't aware of it and can't control or interfere with it. The browser master runs the browser service every 12 minutes, and populates the network folders of all computers on the network with icons representing the computers and shared resources it finds.

## TURNED OFF COMPUTERS STILL IN THE NEIGHBORHOOD

**The Annoyance:** After I shut down one of the computers, its icon continues to appear in the network window, even though nobody on the network can access it. It's annoying that Windows doesn't seem to know the computer isn't turned on.

**The Fix:** Although the icon eventually goes away, it remains in the network folders for quite a bit of time. Of course, because it's not available, selecting it produces an error message similar to the one in Figure 3-5. Before you see the error message, you have to stare at an hourglass for a while, which is a fairly good indication that something is wrong.

Figure 3-5. Windows eventually lets you know it couldn't connect to the computer.

The reason for the delay in removing a shut-down computer from the network window is once again something you can blame on the browser service. The next time the browser service runs after the shutdown, it notices the computer is missing. (Remember that it can take up to 12 minutes for the service to run.) However, if the computer is missing, its icon isn't removed from the other computers' network folders. The browser service assumes the computer is merely AWOL and won't declare it "gone" until it's been missing from the roll call three times (that's another 36 minutes!). The browser service gives the computer the benefit of the doubt before assuming it's not available, in case the inter-computer communication had a glitch of some kind.

If the computer you shut down was the browser master, the other computers notice the removal and eventually hold a new election (they must wait for the next scheduled browser service to run, so it can take up to 12 minutes). If you have a two-computer network, the remaining computer elects itself, of course.

# WORKGROUP NAME MUST BE IDENTICAL ON ALL COMPUTERS

**The Annoyance:** One of the four computers on our network never appears in My Network Places or Network Neighborhood on the other computers. When I open My Network Places on the missing computer (named PinkBedRm), the only computer that appears is PinkBedRm. The hardware is working, so why won't this computer join the network?

**The Fix:** Those symptoms indicate that PinkBedRm is configured for a workgroup that has a different name. Usually, this occurs because you made a typing error when you set up the computer, or you forgot to change the name from the default workgroup name Windows provided.

If PinkBedRm is running Windows XP or 2000, right-click the My Computer icon and choose Properties. Click the Network Identification tab and make sure the workgroup name matches that of the other computers. For Windows 98SE and Me, open the Network applet in the Control Panel, click the Identification tab, and (if necessary) change the workgroup name.

## ERROR MESSAGE ISN'T SPECIFIC

**The Annoyance:** When a computer isn't available, the error messages I see aren't specific, so I don't know what the problem is. I've seen error messages that tell me to try typing the computer name again (I never typed it in the first place—I clicked an icon), or that the path is unavailable, or to contact my administrator, etc.

**The Fix:** Alas, there's no way around this problem. Windows can't peek through the monitor to see if the computer is turned off or if the network cable is unplugged. A computer can become unavailable to the network for other reasons as well (see the following annoyances). All Windows can do is attempt to communicate with the computer and, if no response is received, determine that the computer is inaccessible.

# INSTALL FILE AND PRINTER SHARING SERVICES

**The Annoyance:** I set up a computer for our network, and I'm sure all the connections are right. The TCP/IP settings are right, too. But the new computer never shows up in My Network Places. How do I find out what's wrong?

**The Fix:** If you've performed all the appropriate troubleshooting steps for the network hardware (see Chapter 1), check the settings for your network connection. It could be that you forgot to install File and Printer Sharing services, which is one of the most common causes of this problem.

Right-click your network connection and choose Properties. On the General tab, make sure "File and Printer Sharing for Microsoft Networks" appears as an installed network component. If not, you need to install the service.

> **tip**
>
> To quickly learn whether the File and Printer Sharing service is missing, right-click a folder or printer. If the Sharing command is missing from the drop-down menu, the service isn't installed.

### Install File and Printer Sharing in Windows 9X and Windows Me

To install File and Printer Sharing in Windows 9X and Windows Me, open the Network applet in the Control Panel (see Figure 3-6).

Click the "File and Print Sharing" button. In the dialog box, select the option to share files, printers, or both (see Figure 3-7). Click OK, at which point the system asks you to insert the original Windows CD so that it can copy the files. After the files are copied, the system displays a message telling you that the new settings won't take effect

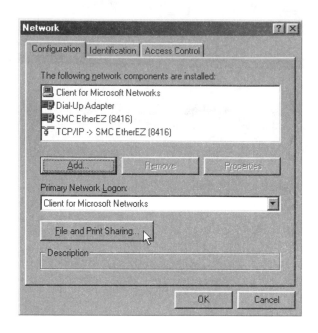

Figure 3-6. You must install File and Printer sharing to join the network.

until you restart the computer. Click Yes to restart your computer now, or click No if you want to restart the computer at a more convenient time.

Figure 3-7. You can choose the computer resources you want to share.

### Install File and Printer Sharing in Windows 2000 and Windows XP

1. In Windows XP, open the Network Connections applet in the Control Panel. In Windows 2000, open the Network and Dialup Connections applet in the Control Panel.

2. Right-click the icon for the Local Area Connection and choose Properties.

3. If File and Printer Sharing for Microsoft Windows isn't listed on the General tab, click the Install button (see Figure 3-8).

4. In the Select Network Component Type dialog box, select Service and click the Add button.

5. Choose File and Printer Sharing for Microsoft Networks, and click OK.

6. Click Close.

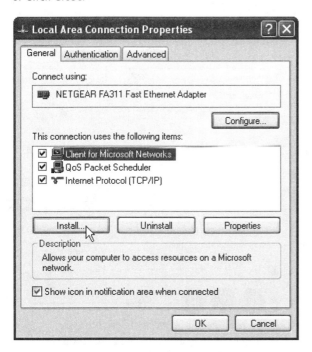

Figure 3-8. If the File and Printer Sharing service isn't listed, you have to install it.

**Unlike earlier versions of Windows, Windows 2000 and Windows XP don't require reboots every time you change configuration options (another good reason to upgrade your Windows 9X and Windows Me computers).**

# NETBIOS OVER TCP/IP MUST BE ENABLED

**The Annoyance:** After setting up our two-computer network, I opened My Network Places and selected the link named View Workgroup Computers. Then I double-clicked the icon named FAMILY (the name of our workgroup) and saw the following error message: "FAMILY is not accessible. You may not have permission to use this network resource." I logged on to the computer with a username that has administrative permissions, so what permissions am I missing?

**The Fix:** I'll bet this problem has nothing to do with permissions and is another one of those annoying error messages in which Windows takes a wild stab at the cause of the failure. The common reason for this message is that you have a small (but ruinous) configuration error in your network adapter's setup. Also, your network settings probably don't include NetBIOS over TCP/IP.

To check on the state of NetBIOS over TCP/IP, open the Properties dialog box for your Local Area Connection as follows:

- In Windows 9X and Me, open the Network applet in the Control Panel.

- In Windows 2000, open the Dialup Connections applet in the Control Panel, then right-click the listing for Local Area Network and choose Properties.

- In Windows XP, open the Network Connections applet in the Control Panel, then right-click the listing for Local Area Network and choose Properties.

Select the TCP/IP component and click the Properties button to open the TCP/IP Properties dialog box. Then proceed as follows:

- In Windows 9X and Me, click the NetBIOS tab. Most of the time, the "I want to enable NetBIOS over TCP/IP" box is already checked and inaccessible (grayed out). If not, check the box and then click OK twice to close all the dialog boxes. The system asks for your original Windows CD so that it can copy files. You must restart the computer to apply the new settings.

- In Windows 2000 and XP, click the Advanced button on the TCP/IP Properties dialog box, and click the WINS tab. In the NetBIOS Setting section, select the Default option (see Figure 3-9). Click OK three times to close all the dialog boxes.

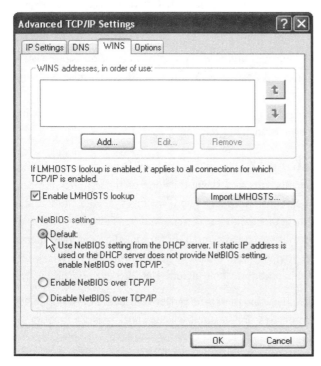

Figure 3-9. Select the Default option for NetBIOS to make sure NetBIOS is linked to TCP/IP when needed.

## OPEN NETWORK PROPERTIES QUICKLY

**The Annoyance:** When I have to view or change settings on my network adapter, I get really annoyed because I have to go through five steps to see the Properties dialog box for my Local Area Connection.

**The Fix:** Isn't that a pain? You can eliminate the first four steps by putting an icon for your Local Area Connection on the task bar. Open the Properties dialog box for the Local Area Connection (sorry about all those steps, but this is the last time you'll have to go through them). At the

bottom of the General tab, check the "Show icon in notification area when connected" box (see Figure 3-10).

Figure 3-10. Put an icon for your network connection on your task bar for quick access to configuration options.

> **tip**
>
> The notification area is the rightmost section of the task bar, near the time display. Older versions of Windows call this section of the task bar the TaskTray.

The task bar icon has several nifty features. Let your mouse pointer hover over it to see the speed at which your connection is transmitting data, or the signal strength if you're using a wireless adapter. You'll also see the number of data packets that have been sent and received since you booted the computer. (OK, I admit I can't think of a single reason you'd care about the number of data packets, but it's there. Hmmm, now that I think about it, there's probably some overhead on the system's resources to keep count of the data packets. OK, now *I'm* annoyed.)

If your cable connection becomes unplugged, either at the computer or at the hub/switch/router (depending on where your network comes together), a red X appears over the icon. The same red X appears if your wireless adapter loses its ability to send or receive transmissions. A tool tip over the icon tells you about the loss of connectivity, so you don't have to remember what that red X means.

When you click the icon (a single click—you don't have to double-click), you'll see a Status report for your connection (see Figure 3-11). The most important item on the Status dialog box is the Properties button. Click the button to open the Properties dialog box with one click!

Figure 3-11. One-click access to the Properties dialog box makes it easy to view or change configuration options for your Local Area Connection.

**t i p**

Windows 2000 also offers the option to put an icon for the Local Area Connection on the task bar with all the same cool features. Earlier versions of Windows don't support this feature.

# PING NETWORK COMPUTERS

**The Annoyance:** I'm getting an error message that tells me a computer is unavailable when I try to open it in My Network Places. It's annoying to go through all the hardware troubleshooting, followed by all the software configuration troubleshooting. Is there a way to narrow down the source of the problem?

**The Fix:** Sort of (don't you love answers like that?). You can test whether the computer is properly connected, whether its TCP/IP configuration is working, and whether the system can link the IP address to the computer's name (a process called *name resolution*).

If you know those features are working properly, you don't have to check the hardware and the TCP/IP settings. However, this knowledge doesn't eliminate the need to check all the other settings and configuration options involved in networking.

To carry out the investigation, use the Ping utility built into Windows. To run the Ping command, open a command prompt window and enter `ping ComputerName`, where `ComputerName` is the name of the computer you're trying to contact. (You can use the target computer's IP address instead if you don't know the name offhand.) If the system returns information about the target computer (see Figure 3-12), you know the computer's hardware and TCP/IP settings are working properly. But that's all you know.

Figure 3-12. The response means the computer named Two is turned on and connected to the network properly.

Because the Ping command only checks for limited information, a successful response doesn't mean the computer is set up to participate in the network. For example, Ping is successful when you use it on computers that don't have File and Printer Sharing services enabled. Without those services, the computer can't participate in the network, and you can't access it using the features and tools built into Windows networking.

> **Warning...**
> A computer running a firewall can respond to the Ping command only if it is configured to let local network traffic through. See Chapter 7 to learn about using firewalls properly.

## PING FAILURES

**The Annoyance:** I ran the Ping command for a computer named Tom, and the system returned the message "Unknown host tom." What specific problem do I fix?

**The Fix:** Sorry, but again I have to be wishy-washy because the failure to find the computer named Tom indicates any of several possible problems.

I'll assume there's actually a computer named Tom on your network. If not, I can give you a very specific answer, which is that your network has no computer named Tom. That was easy!

However, I suspect that's not the case, so I'll enumerate the possibilities. Any one (or more) of the following problems could exist when the Ping command returns the message "unknown host":

- The computer is shut down. You know what to do.
- The computer is running, but is not physically connected to the network. A cable is unplugged (or bad), or a wireless adapter isn't working, or the hub/switch/

router that connects your network isn't working. See the guidelines for troubleshooting physical network connections in Chapter 1.

- The computer is running and is properly connected, but Ping (which is a TCP/IP tool) can't resolve the computer name to its IP address. Try pinging the IP address instead of the computer name (see the next annoyance).

In addition to these possibilities, the "unknown host" message could mean the computer you're pinging *from* has a problem. Try pinging Tom from another computer on the network. If your computer and Tom are the only computers on the network, try pinging your computer from Tom. If the problem seems to point to your computer, make sure your computer is properly connected to the network by checking all the hardware. If you're sharing an Internet connection, see if you can get on the Internet. If not, you're the problem, not Tom.

## PING AN IP ADDRESS

**The Annoyance:** Using the Ping command on a computer's name to test connectivity failed. Somebody told me the problem could be that Ping can't put the computer name together with its IP address. How do I do this, and what does it prove?

**The Fix:** You can use Ping to determine whether a specific IP address is currently connected to your network. If you get a successful reply, it confirms that the computer assigned that IP address is physically connected to the network.

To ping a computer's IP address, enter the command ping X, where X is the computer's IP address (see Figure 3-13). If this command is successful but pinging the computer's name is unsuccessful, you have a problem with name resolution. Resolving it depends on the way your network resolves names. (See the sidebar "Resolve Names to IP Addresses" for more information.)

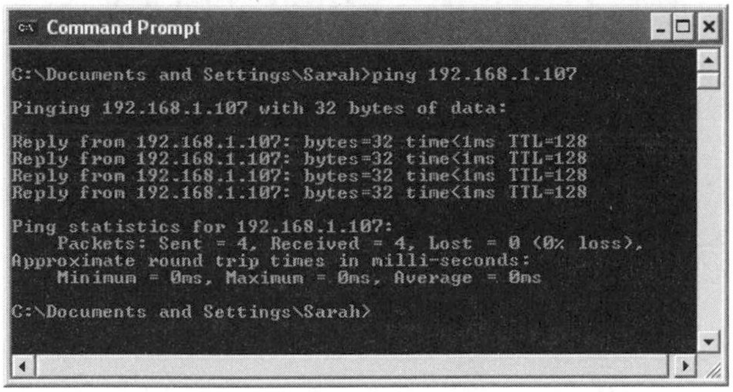

Figure 3-13. You can use the Ping command to contact a remote computer by its IP address.

# FIND A COMPUTER'S IP ADDRESS

**The Annoyance:** I looked at the TCP/IP Properties for my adapter, but it doesn't seem to have an IP address. I selected the "Obtain an IP address automatically" option, but no numbers appear.

**The Fix:** That means your computer lacks a permanent IP address. Instead, its address is dynamically assigned when your computer boots into Windows. Actually, it's being leased for a finite period from your router, *LMHOSTS* file, or ISP, depending on your network configuration (see Chapter 2 for more information).

## RESOLVE NAMES TO IP ADDRESSES

Any network using TCP/IP needs a name resolution function so that people can use easy-to-remember computer names instead of complicated, hard-to-remember IP addresses when they need to communicate with remote computers. Several methods are available for matching computer names on the network to their IP addresses. The most common methods follow:

*DNS* (Domain Name System) is the method most often used for name resolution, although you're almost certainly not using it as the internal name resolution method for your home network. The Internet (the largest TCP/IP network in the world) uses DNS, as do most businesses that run networks. With DNS, certain servers are assigned the task of maintaining the corresponding IP address for every computer name on the network. DNS name resolution on the Internet resolves domain names (e.g., *microsoft.com* or *ivens.com*) to the IP addresses of the servers that host those domains. DNS name resolution on business networks resolves a computer name (e.g., one selected by a user working in My Network Neighborhood) to the IP address of the target computer.

*WINS* (Windows Internet Naming Service) is another server-based name resolution method commonly used in corporate

networks. The server holds the WINS database, which maps every computer's name to its IP address. It also ensures that each computer on the network has a unique name. WINS doesn't handle growth well, so it's not as efficient as DNS. Most corporate networks are switching from WINS to DNS.

*DHCP* (Dynamic Host Configuration Protocol) assigns temporary IP addresses to computers from a central location. In a corporate network, this could be a DHCP server. On a home network sharing a broadband connection, the router is the DHCP server. The DHCP server has a range of IP addresses available for the network computers, and it leases an IP address to each computer for a given length of time. If you have a router on your network, you can see the terms of your computer's IP address lease, along with other information about the network, by entering `ipconfig /all` at a command prompt.

*LMHOSTS* is the name of a file stored on a network computer, which translates IP addresses to "NetBIOS over TCP/IP" names. Although the file is plain text, its format follows very strict rules. The *LMHOSTS* file method of resolution appears in home networks that use Internet Connection Sharing for telephone modems.

To determine a computer's current IP address, open a command prompt window and type `ipconfig`. The system returns the IP address (as seen in Figure 3-14).

Figure 3-14. Use the command ipconfig to ascertain the current IP address of a computer.

# MY NETWORK PLACES NEEDS HOUSEKEEPING

## CLEAN OUT THE CLUTTER

**The Annoyance:** When I open My Network Places, the window is filled with icons for the folders I've accessed. In fact, it's so full of icons that it's hard to find the folder I need. I access only a few of these folders on a regular basis. Can I delete the rest of them or will doing that make it impossible for me to get to the deleted folders later?

**The Fix:** By default, Windows XP and 2000 display an icon for any shared drive or folder you access. The icons are shortcuts to folders, and it's always safe to delete a shortcut because you're not deleting the original object (the drive or folder).

If you want to access a shared resource after you have deleted its shortcut, you'll have to navigate through the network window, starting with View Workgroup Computers or Entire Network. Of course, Windows will once again add a shortcut to My Network Places.

# LOCAL FOLDERS SHOW UP IN MY NETWORK PLACES

**The Annoyance:** The shortcuts that appear in My Network Places for folders I've accessed aren't all from remote computers. Why do folders from my own computer appear in the window? It just makes the window more crowded.

**The Fix:** Any time you access a local folder that's been shared, its shortcut appears in My Network Places. This window can't tell the difference between local and remote shared folders—a share is a share is a share.

This is another one of those things that makes me want to travel to Redmond and ask programmers, "What were you thinking?!" The only reason why I can imagine this "feature" was built into Windows XP and 2000 is that during the development of the operating systems, Microsoft had a contest. It must have awarded a prize to the programmer who wrote code to make My Network Places teem with objects faster than any other programmer could.

But back to your problem. Go ahead and delete the objects from the local computer—it's unlikely you'll ever use them. Why would you open files from one of these shortcuts rather than from within the appropriate software application or My Computer?

If you want to delete only the local shortcuts and keep the shortcuts to remote shares, select View → Details, and then click the Computer column heading to sort the list by computer (see Figure 3-15). Click the first listing for the local computer and hold the Shift key while you click the last listing for the local computer to select the entire list. Then press the Delete key.

Figure 3-15. Sort the My Network Places window by computer to make it easy to remove shortcuts to local folders.

# GET RID OF THE ALPHABET BREAKS IN MY NETWORK PLACES

**The Annoyance:** I sorted the icons in My Network Places by computer to get rid of all the shortcuts to local shared folders. When I changed the view so that it sorted by name, the window displayed letters of the alphabet between each alphabetic group. These breaks appear no matter which view I choose. This forces me to use the vertical scrollbar, which is really annoying.

**The Fix:** I don't know why Windows XP does this, but whenever you change the way the window is sorted, the alphabet breaks appear when you return to sorting by name (see Figure 3-16).

What Windows has done is automatically enable the option that arranges the display by group. You can turn off this option by choosing View → Arrange Icons By → Show in Groups, and removing the check mark.

# STOP SHORTCUTS FROM APPEARING IN MY NETWORK PLACES

**The Annoyance:** I'm tired of deleting all those shortcuts in My Network Places and watching them reappear. There should be a way to tell Windows to stop tracking my moves.

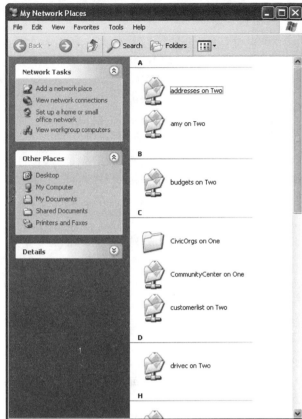

Figure 3-16. Breaking up the display like this creates more work for a user who wants to open a shortcut with a name near the end of the alphabet.

**The Fix:** It does feel like Windows is tailing you, doesn't it? There *is* a way to stop this behavior, but the solution differs among Windows versions:

- In Windows 2000 and XP Professional, you can change the behavior by enabling a Group Policy.
- Windows XP Home Edition doesn't offer the Group Policy, so you must make a change to the registry. The same registry change works for Windows 2000 and XP Professional, but it's usually preferable to use Group Policies than to mess with the registry.

## Using a Group Policy

To change the computer's policy to prevent Windows from adding shortcuts to My Network Places for shares you access, follow these steps:

1. Choose Start → Run to open the Run command.

2. Type mmc and click OK to open the Microsoft Management Console (MMC).

3. Choose File → Add/Remove Snap-in (Windows XP) or Console → Add/Remove Snap-in (Windows 2000).

4. In the Add/Remove Snap-in window, click the Add button to open the Add Standalone Snap-in window.

5. Select Group Policy from the list of available snap-ins, and click the Add button.

6. Accept the default (Local Computer) Group Policy Object and click Finish.

7. Click Close, and then click OK to return to the MMC window.

8. In the left pane, expand the User Configuration entry to *User Configuration\Administrative Templates\Desktop* (see Figure 3-17).

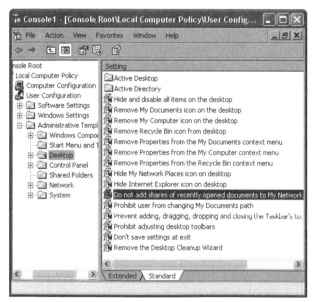

Figure 3-17. Expand the policy options to get to the local user's desktop policies.

9. In the right pane, double-click the "Do not add shares of recently opened documents to My Network Places" listing.

10. Select the Enabled option and click OK (see Figure 3-18).

11. Close the MMC.

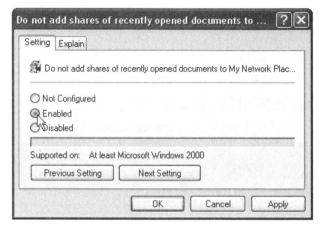

Figure 3-18. Enable the policy if you want to stop adding shortcuts to My Network Places.

### t i p

When you close the MMC, the system asks if you want to save the console settings. This has nothing to do with saving the policy change you just made; that's already saved. Most people say No. If you say Yes, you're saving this particular window and its configuration in case you ever want to return to it. Windows saves the console using a name you invent in the Administrative Tools folder of the Control Panel.

### Warning. . .

Working in the registry can be very dangerous because a wrong keystroke in certain places can prevent your computer from running properly, or at all. If you're not comfortable with this procedure, find a more experienced friend or relative.

### Changing the registry

Follow these steps to change the registry to stop Windows from adding shortcuts to My Network Places for every shared drive or folder you visit:

1. Choose Start → Run to open the Run command box.

2. Enter `regedit`, and click OK to open the Registry Editor.

3. In the left pane, select *HKEY_CURRENT_USER*, and click the plus signs to expand the left pane to the subkey *HKEY_CURRENT_USER\Software\Microsoft\Windows\CurrentVersion\Policies\Explorer*.

4. Choose Edit → New → DWORD value, to place a new registry item in the right pane. The placeholder text for the new item's name is highlighted, so the text is replaced as soon as you begin to type.

5. Enter `NoRecentDocsNetHood` as the name of the item and press Enter.

6. Double-click the new item to open it (see Figure 3-19).

7. Change the data value to 1.

8. Close the Registry Editor.

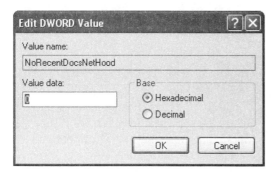

Figure 3-19. The default value is 0, which means the setting for this registry item is "disabled."

## SHARES YOU NEVER ACCESSED APPEAR IN MY NETWORK PLACES

**The Annoyance:** The My Network Places window on my Windows XP computer is getting incredibly crowded with shortcuts. What's weird is that some of the shortcuts are for folders I've never accessed. How did they get there? This is both annoying and confusing.

**The Fix:** This "feature," exclusive to Windows XP, can be very annoying. Don't worry, you're not imagining things, you weren't working at your computer during a sleepwalking episode, and your memory isn't going (well, maybe it is, but not in regard to this particular annoyance). Your confusion is perfectly normal and valid.

In a workgroup, Windows XP periodically peeks at all the computers on the network to see if any computers have new shared resources. If a user on any network computer creates a folder and shares it, or shares an existing folder, Windows XP gets so excited about discovering this new resource that it wants to share the discovery with the rest of the world (all the Windows XP computers on the network, anyway). Therefore, a shortcut to the newly created share appears in every Windows XP computer on the network. Think of it as Windows bragging to you, "Hey, look what I found!" The fact that you might not need or care about this shared folder enough to crowd your network window never occurs to Windows.

You can just delete these icons as they appear, or you can stop Windows from performing its scavenger hunt and bringing back the items (see the next annoyance).

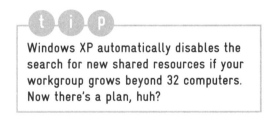

> Windows XP also hunts for newly shared printers, and when it finds one it places an icon for that printer in the Printers and Faxes folder of every Windows XP computer on the network. It doesn't matter whether you installed the printer or not—its shortcut is in the folder.

## DISABLE THE SEARCH FOR NEW SHARED RESOURCES

**The Annoyance:** Our network has five computers, and more users than computers. Users frequently create and share folders so that they can get to their files no matter which computer they work on. The My Network Places window on every Windows XP computer adds shortcuts faster than we can use the Delete key. How do we just say "STOP!"?

**The Fix:** You've probably already discovered that yelling "CUT IT OUT" at the monitor doesn't work. Luckily, it's quite easy to put a stop to this behavior. You need to change an option in the Folder Options dialog box, which you can reach from any system window (My Computer, My Network Places, and so on).

Select Tools → Folder Options to open the Folder Options dialog box. Click the View tab, *uncheck* the "Automatically search for network folders and printers" box, and then click OK (see Figure 3-20).

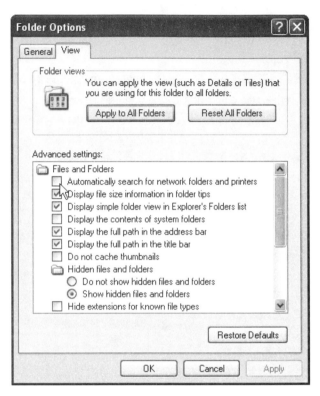

Figure 3-20. Stop Windows XP from searching for new shared resources.

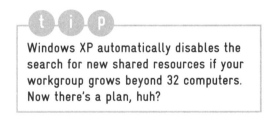

> Windows XP automatically disables the search for new shared resources if your workgroup grows beyond 32 computers. Now there's a plan, huh?

# A NETWORK SHORTCUT STOPS WORKING

**The Annoyance:** After working properly for a long time, one of my network shortcuts has stopped working. I see an hourglass for a long time, then a message appears telling me the folder is inaccessible. It worked yesterday. In fact, it worked an hour ago.

**The Fix:** The resource to which the shortcut is linked has changed. Perhaps the folder has been deleted, renamed, or moved, or the sharename was changed, or someone selected the option "Not Shared" for the resource.

What's annoying is that Windows doesn't check the links to make sure the shortcuts are accurate and remove shortcuts that no longer work. An operating system that can find newly created shares and put shortcuts for those shares into your My Network Neighborhood window is certainly capable of checking the status of shortcuts you actually visit. Apparently, nobody thought of writing the code for this step.

# CREATE YOUR OWN SHORTCUTS FOR MY NETWORK PLACES

**The Annoyance:** We changed the configuration of the Windows 2000 and Windows XP computers on our network so that they would stop filling up My Network Places with shortcuts. Now, some users would like shortcuts to the shares they access all the time. Is there a way to do this?

**The Fix:** Yes, you can create your own shortcuts in the My Network Places window. Windows provides a wizard to walk you through the process, which you can start by selecting Add Network Place in the My Network Places window.

The Add Network Place Wizard serves two purposes: setting up a file storage location on the Internet and creating a shortcut to a shared resource. For this fix, you're interested in the latter. Note that the Windows 2000 and XP versions of the wizard differ slightly.

### Adding a Network Place in Windows XP

In Windows XP, the first wizard window is introductory only, so click Next to get started. In the next window, you can choose between creating an account with MSN Communities or choosing a network location. Select the option to choose a network location and click Next.

Click the Browse button to open the Browse For Folder dialog box (see Figure 3-21), and select the appropriate computer and share. When you click OK, the wizard automatically enters the UNC for that share in the Internet or Network Address field. (Optionally, you can type the UNC for the shared resource into the Internet or Network Address field.)

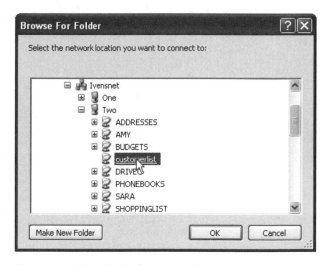

Figure 3-21. Select the share for your new shortcut.

Click Next and name the shortcut. The wizard enters the sharename as a suggestion (usually a good choice), but you can enter any name you wish. Click Next to see the final wizard window, and click Finish to complete the task. By default, the wizard selects the option to open the shared resource after you click Finish. If you don't have any particular reason to travel to that folder, deselect the option before you click Finish.

### Adding a Network Place in Windows 2000

The Windows 2000 wizard is quite straightforward. The first wizard window asks you which network resource you want to use for your shortcut (see Figure 3-22). You can manually enter the UNC, or click Browse to select the appropriate share in the Browse For Folder dialog box. Click Next again, accept or change the name the wizard suggests for this shortcut, then click Finish. Windows automatically opens a window that displays the contents of the shared resource.

Figure 3-22. The Add Network Place Wizard in Windows 2000 goes right to work with no introduction or welcoming messages.

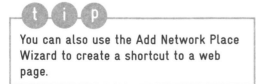

You can also use the Add Network Place Wizard to create a shortcut to a web page.

# NETWORK SHORTCUTS FOR OLDER VERSIONS OF WINDOWS

**The Annoyance:** Our network users like the self-created network shortcuts, but this feature isn't available on computers running Windows 98SE or Windows Me. This is really annoying.

**The Fix:** You can create your own folder for network shortcuts, which is more efficient and easier to use than the My Network Places folder in Windows XP and 2000. This task has two simple components:

- Create a desktop folder to hold your network shortcuts.
- Move shortcuts to network shares into the desktop folder.

The desktop shortcut is easier to access than the My Network Places window, which is why you might want to think about applying this solution to Windows XP and 2000 computers.

To create a folder on your desktop, right-click a blank spot on the desktop and choose New → Folder. Name the folder Network Shortcuts. Position the folder along an edge of the desktop so that it's visible when an application window opens (assuming the application window isn't maximized). Now that the folder exists, you can begin to fill it with network shortcuts using the following steps:

1. Open Network Neighborhood and reduce its size so that you can see the desktop folder you created.

2. Open the remote computer that has the share you want to save as a shortcut.

3. Right-drag the icon or listing for the target share to the Network Shortcuts folder icon. You don't have to open the folder—dropping the item on the folder's icon pastes the item inside it.

4. When you release the right mouse button, select Create Shortcut(s) Here.

# MAPPED DRIVES

## CREATE A MAPPED DRIVE QUICKLY

**The Annoyance:** I usually think about mapping a drive when I'm ready to access a shared resource in My Network Places or Network Neighborhood. The Windows Help files tell me to use the Map Network Drive command on the Tools menu. That in turn asks me to enter the path to the share I want to map, or makes me open another window and select the shared resource. There must be an easier way.

**The Fix:** Actually, mapping a drive to a share in front of your face is the fastest way to accomplish this task. In the window that displays all the shares of a computer, right-click the icon for the shared resource and select Map Network Drive. This action opens the Map Network Drive dialog box seen in Figure 3-23. Windows has already selected the next available drive letter and inserted the UNC to the shared resource. Specify whether you want to reconnect to this mapped drive every time you start the computer, and click Finish. The drive appears in My Computer.

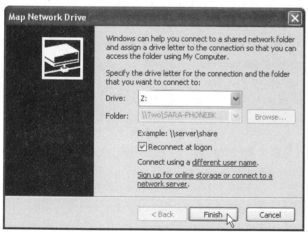

Figure 3-23. Mapping a drive can be a one-step process.

## CHOOSE A DRIVE LETTER FOR A MAPPED DRIVE

**The Annoyance:** I don't always use the same computer—I usually have to find one my kids aren't using. I mapped drives to my favorite resources on each computer, but I find the inconsistency of the drive letters annoying. Each computer seems to pick a different letter for the "next available drive letter."

**The Fix:** You don't have to accept the next available drive letter; just pick any letter that the computer you're working on isn't using already. To do this, click the arrow to the right of the Drive text box on the Map Network Drive dialog box and select another letter.

Usually, drive letters A through D are taken by physical drives in the computer. If you have multiple hard drives or have partitioned a hard drive, A through E might be taken. A second CD-ROM drive might also eat up another drive letter.

All versions of Windows except XP suggest the first empty letter for your mapped drive. As you map more drives, the system keeps offering the next available drive letter, working its way through the alphabet. Windows XP starts at Z and works backward.

If you want consistency in your mapped drives, pick a letter from the middle of the alphabet. For example, use M for your first mapped drive on every computer, N for the next mapped drive, and so on.

## AUTOMATICALLY RECONNECT A MAPPED DRIVE

**The Annoyance:** The Map Network Drive dialog box has an option labeled Reconnect at Logon. I don't know what effect this would have on restarting my computer, so I never know whether to select the option. It's annoying that the Map Network Drive dialog box offers no help.

**The Fix:** Although it *is* annoying that the Map Network Drive dialog box lacks both a help button and a "What's This?" feature, the explanation is rather simple.

Reconnecting at logon means the drive mapping is permanent and will be available every time you log on to this computer. Deselecting the Reconnect at Logon option creates a temporary drive mapping that expires when you log off the computer (whether by using the Log Off option, restarting the computer, or shutting down the computer). The next time you log on, the mapped drive doesn't exist.

Windows remembers the state of the Reconnect at Logon option. The next time you map a drive, the option is selected or not, depending on how you left it the last time you mapped a drive.

Except for Windows 98SE (see the next annoyance), selecting the Reconnect at Logon option means more than maintaining the mapped drive permanently. It also affects the logon process. Every time you log on, Windows verifies the mapped drive, which means it peers down the network cable (or virtual cable in a wireless network) to make sure the shared resource mapped to the drive is up and running. This verification slows the logon process a bit, but I doubt you'll notice the difference. If the share isn't available, the mapped drive still appears in My Computer, but is marked as inaccessible until its linked share is available again. (See the "Failed Automatic Reconnections" annoyances later in this section.)

## WINDOWS 98SE AUTOMATIC RECONNECTION OPTIONS

**The Annoyance:** On my Windows 98SE computer, I can configure the way mapped drives are reconnected in the Network dialog box. But why does my selection have no effect on whether the Reconnect at Logon option appears when I map a drive?

**The Fix:** This can be confusing, so let me try to explain what's going on. In Windows 98SE, open the Network Properties dialog box, select the Client for Microsoft Networks component, and choose Properties. The bottom half of the Client for Microsoft Networks Properties dialog box offers two options for managing your mapped drives (see Figure 3-24):

- The "Quick logon" option means Windows doesn't confirm the availability of the shares linked to your mapped drives during logon (saving the time the process takes). The first time you access the mapped drive, Windows checks its availability. If the share is available, you're connected. If the share isn't available, an error message appears.

- The "Logon and restore network connections" option means Windows 98SE behaves the same way as later versions of Windows (described in the previous annoyance).

Because these options manage the logon process, the selection you make is unrelated to the Reconnect at Logon option (making the mapping permanent) when you're creating a mapped drive.

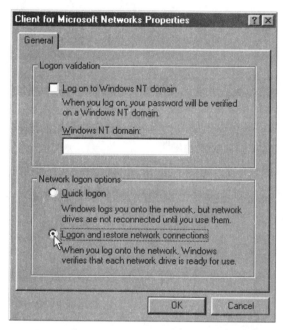

Figure 3-24. Choose the way mapped drives are managed when you log on.

# FAILED AUTOMATIC RECONNECTIONS IN WINDOWS XP

**The Annoyance:** When I log on to my computer, Windows XP displays a balloon over the notification area of the task bar telling me that a mapped drive failed to reconnect to its share on a remote computer. It also says to click the balloon to see which mapped drives are connected and which are not. But before I can click the balloon, it disappears. How can I tell which mapped drives are connected?

**The Fix:** The balloon quickly disappears to make room for another Windows XP balloon that says "Stay Current With Automatic Updates" (a balloon that doesn't disappear quickly). The original balloon is unimportant because clicking it merely opens My Computer, which you can do for yourself. My Computer displays mapped drives that aren't currently connected to the shares they represent with a red X on the icon (see the bottom icon in Figure 3-25).

Figure 3-25. A mapped drive that failed to connect with its remote share displays a red X on its icon.

When the computer that holds the share linked to the mapped drive becomes available, double-click the mapped drive icon to open the share and reestablish the connection. The red X goes away.

---

### AUTOMATIC RECONNECTION TO MAPPED DRIVES FREQUENTLY FAILS

It's not unusual for the reconnection to a mapped drive to fail when you log on to a computer. Let's say you have two computers on your network, both of which have mapped network drives configured for reconnection at logon. What happens when you start both computers? The computer that runs the logon procedure first loses, and the computer that logs on second wins. When you're logging on to the first computer, the second computer isn't yet up and running. Therefore, the share on the second computer is not yet available, so the mapping function fails.

---

## FAILED AUTOMATIC RECONNECTIONS IN WINDOWS 2000

**The Annoyance:** When I log on to my Windows 2000 computer and a mapped drive isn't reconnected, how am I supposed to know? I don't see any error message during logon or after logon is completed.

**The Fix:** For some reason, Windows 2000 refuses to share information about its failures. You can learn which mapped drives were successfully reconnected and which were not by opening My Computer. A mapped drive with a red X on its icon is not available.

When the computer that holds the share linked to the mapped drive becomes available, double-click the mapped drive icon to open the share and reestablish the connection. The red X goes away.

## FAILED AUTOMATIC RECONNECTIONS IN WINDOWS 98SE

**The Annoyance:** When I log on to my Windows 98SE computer, I sometimes see a message telling me a mapped drive isn't connected. It also asks whether I want to reconnect the next time I log on. What should I say?

**The Fix:** Say Yes. If you say No, the mapped drive is deleted from your system forever (well, until you go through the steps required to map the drive again). Windows 98SE offers you this option in case the mapped drive is linked to a share that you've removed. Of course, if you have removed the shared resource, you should say No to save yourself the trouble of removing (disconnecting) the mapped drive from your system.

Windows 98SE provides the most logical, most helpful, and least annoying method of dealing with failed reconnections of mapped drives. Why did Microsoft abandon this method with later versions of Windows?

## DISCONNECT MEANS DELETE THE MAPPED DRIVE LETTER

**The Annoyance:** I have a mapped drive to a remote computer out for repair. I decided to disconnect the mapped drive while the remote computer was unavailable (a week or more) because I didn't want to worry about reconnection error messages whenever I logged on. I figured I'd just be able to reconnect when the remote computer came back on the network. Imagine my surprise when I selected the Disconnect command and the mapped drive disappeared.

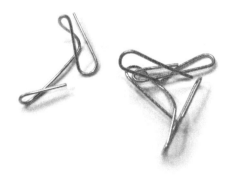

**The Fix:** This is another one of those annoying situations in which we learn the hard way that Microsoft invents its own meanings for words. Microsoft should have named the command "Delete Mapped Drive" because, as your experience indicates, people who don't work in Redmond don't generally think of "disconnect" as a synonym for "delete."

Of course, you're deleting the mapping rather than the shared resource, so you can continue to access the share from My Network Places, Network Neighborhood, Windows Explorer, or My Computer.

## CAN'T MAP A NETWORK SHORTCUT

**The Annoyance:** I decided to map a drive to one of the network shortcuts I use frequently, but the command Map Network Drive isn't available when I right-click the icon. What happened?

**The Fix:** You can't map a drive from a shortcut. Although this seems annoying, the reason for the restriction is actually quite logical—you have no guarantee that the shortcut is linked to a real live shared resource. As I pointed out in a previous annoyance, Windows doesn't monitor the health of network shortcuts. They can remain in the network window long after the original shared resource has been removed or renamed (which is the real annoyance).

## MAP SHARED PARENT FOLDERS

**The Annoyance:** I use one computer on the network more often than the others. I keep my private files in a subfolder named Larry, which is under a shared folder named OfficeFiles. To maintain my privacy I don't share the subfolder, but when I'm working on another computer I need to get to the files. I tried to map a drive to the subfolder (a temporary mapping), but the mapped drive command isn't available when I right-click the icon.

**The Fix:** When you use the Windows graphical interface, you can't map a drive to a folder that hasn't been explicitly shared. You have to map the shared parent folder, and then move to the subfolder. But wait, don't give up yet. You can map subfolders if you perform the task from the command line (see "Map Subfolders of Shared Folders").

> A good method for keeping the contents of a folder private is to configure the folder as a hidden share. Only those users who know of its existence can get to it (so don't tell anyone). Read Chapter 4 to learn about this nifty trick.

## PREVENT THE SHARE FROM OPENING WHEN YOU MAP A DRIVE

**The Annoyance:** When I create a mapped drive, a window opens and displays the contents of the shared folder I just mapped. This is really annoying.

**The Fix:** I hate that! To prevent this time-wasting exercise, hold the Shift key while you click Finish.

## USE THE COMMAND LINE TO MAP A DRIVE

**The Annoyance:** I want to map several folders on multiple remote computers, but winding my way through the maze of windows is annoying. It would be nice to be able to do this quickly. I'll bet there's a command I could use.

**The Fix:** Good guess—there is. And good thinking, too. As a rule of thumb, almost any task you ever have to perform on a computer can be accomplished more quickly at the command line. Well, that's *my* rule of thumb, because I'm a command-line junkie.

The magic is in the net use command. At the command line, enter net use *driveletter:* \\*ComputerName*\ *ShareName*.

- Substitute the drive letter you want to use for *driveletter*, followed by a colon and a space.
- Substitute the name of the target computer for *ComputerName*.
- Substitute the sharename of the shared resource for *Sharename*—use the sharename, not the folder name.

For example, let's assume the following:

- A computer named Bedroom1 has a folder named Family Budgets.
- The Family Budgets folder is shared as FamBudget.
- G is the next available drive letter on the local computer.

Enter net use g: \\bedroom1\fambudget. The system displays the message "The command completed successfully." Drive G now appears in My Computer and Windows Explorer.

## MAP SUBFOLDERS OF SHARED FOLDERS

**The Annoyance:** Sometimes I want to map a subfolder of a shared folder or a folder of a shared drive. I can access the folder in My Network Places by opening the share and then opening the folder. But when I open the share and right-click the subfolder, the command for creating a mapped drive doesn't exist.

**The Fix:** You can map a drive to an unshared folder only under the following circumstances:

- The parent folder of the folder you want to map is shared.
- You perform the drive mapping at the command line with the net use command.

The command is net use *driveletter:* \\*ComputerName*\ *ShareName*\*FolderName*. If any of the names contain spaces, enter quotation marks before the double slash and at the end of the command. For example, on my corporate network I have a computer named Workstation-10. The computer contains a folder named Client Kit for QB2004, which has the sharename ClientKit2004. A subfolder named Importing Report Templates exists, but it isn't shared. When I'm working on the files in that subfolder, I map a drive on the computer I'm currently using. As you can see in Figure 3-26, as long as I use the right format and remember the quotation marks, it's easy to create the mapped drive.

Figure 3-26. Use the command line to map a drive for an unshared subfolder of a shared folder.

> **tip**
>
> The format required for a command is called its *syntax*.

## DETERMINE THE AVAILABLE DRIVE LETTERS

**The Annoyance:** When I work in My Network Neighborhood, the system tells me the next available drive letter, but not all the other available choices. If I want to use a drive letter of my own choosing, I have to use the drop-down list of mapped drives to see what's free. It's annoying to have to go through the steps to map a drive using the graphical windows just so that I can see what drive letters are available.

**The Fix:** You can find out which drive letters are currently being used for mapped drives right from the command line. Enter `net use` to see a list of current mapped drives (see Figure 3-27).

Figure 3-27. Enter "net use" without any parameters to see the current mapped drives.

You can also see the drive letters currently in use for mapped drives in Windows Explorer or My Computer.

## LET THE COMPUTER PICK THE DRIVE LETTER FOR A MAPPED DRIVE

**The Annoyance:** When I use Windows' graphical interface to map a drive, the computer automatically picks the next available drive letter. If I'm mapping drives from the command line, I have to keep entering `net use` to remind myself of the next available drive letter.

**The Fix:** No, you don't, because you can let the computer automatically select the next drive letter. To accomplish this, use an asterisk (*) in the command instead of specifying a drive letter. Don't put a colon after the asterisk. As you can see in Figure 3-28, the system picks the next available drive letter and tells you what it is. Is this cool, or what?

Figure 3-28. Let the computer find the next available drive letter when you're mapping a drive.

## PERMANENT VERSUS TEMPORARY MAPPED DRIVES

**The Annoyance:** I mapped a drive at the command line yesterday, but when I logged on today, I couldn't find it. Are mapped drives not reconnected at logon when you create them at the command line?

**The Fix:** Mapping a drive at the command line works exactly like mapping a drive in Windows. In this case, you've run into the situation where the computer remembers the current state of the Reconnect at Logon feature discussed earlier in the chapter (see "Automatically Reconnect a Mapped Drive").

When you're working in the Windows interface, you can see whether the Reconnect at Logon option (which makes the mapped drive permanent if you choose it) is the current selection by noting whether the box is checked. At the command line, you can determine the same thing from the system's response when you enter `net use`. After you type the command, one of the following lines of text appears:

- New connections will be remembered (the current state is that mapped drives are permanent).
- New connections will not be remembered (the current state is that mapped drives are temporary).

The command line works in the same manner as the graphical window, and lets you decide whether you want to reconnect to the mapped drive you're creating. Of course, you don't have a checkbox when you use the command line; instead, you have the persistent parameter, which lets you specify Yes or No.

To make the mapping permanent, enter net use *driveletter:* \\\\*ComputerName*\\*ShareName* /persistent: yes. Enter /persistent:no to make the mapping temporary.

## MANIPULATE FILES BETWEEN LOCAL AND MAPPED DRIVES

**The Annoyance:** It's a real pain to move or copy files between computers. I have to navigate my way through the network windows to get to the right folder, and then open the local folders sending or receiving the files. Once both windows are open, I can copy files between them. Isn't there an easier way?

**The Fix:** If you map drives to the folders on the remote computer, everything you need is available in Windows Explorer. The mapped drive is listed in the left pane of the Explorer window along with all the folders on your local hard drive.

> **t i p**
>
> In Windows XP and 2000, you can open My Computer and click the Folders icon on the toolbar to create two panes, which makes My Computer look and act like Windows Explorer.

## OTHER USERS DON'T HAVE THE MAPPED DRIVES

**The Annoyance:** For two of the computers on our network, I created mappings to folders on a third computer. Those folders contain files that everyone uses. However, when anyone other than me logs on to those two computers, the mapped drives aren't there. What happened?

**The Fix:** Mapped drives, along with many other configuration settings, are user settings, not computer settings. This is why the reconnection option is worded "Reconnect at Logon" instead of "Reconnect at Startup." Your computer joins the network when it finishes booting, but your username doesn't log on until you complete the logon routine. Each user has to create his own mapped drives.

# 4

# File-Sharing
# ANNOYANCES

One of the most common activities of network users is accessing files across the network. Sometimes you need to move or
copy files from one computer to another, and sometimes you
need to use files on another computer when you're working in
a software application. In this chapter, I'll discuss some of the
annoying "features" in the networkwide file-sharing paradigm,
and offer some workarounds that can help you create the
perfect scenario for sharing files. I'll explain how to use files
from any computer on the network when you're working in
a software program, how to share datafiles among multiple
users working on different computers, and how to set up your
My Documents folder so that you can access its contents from
any computer.

# ACCESSING FILES ON REMOTE COMPUTERS

## SHARE WINDOWS XP MY DOCUMENTS FOLDERS ON THE NETWORK

**The Annoyance:** I usually work on a particular Windows XP computer, but sometimes one of my kids is at that computer and I have to do my work from another one. I can't figure out how to get to my documents on the Windows XP computer. I know my My Documents folder isn't marked "private" because my kids can access it when they are logged on to the computer. Why can't I get to the folder from another computer on the network?

**The Fix:** The fact that you didn't configure your My Documents folder as private means its contents are accessible to other users, but only on the computer on which the folder resides. To access the folder over the network, you must specifically enable the option to share the folder on the network.

1. Right-click the folder icon and choose Properties.
2. Click the Sharing tab and check the "Share this folder on the network" box (see Figure 4-1).

## SHARE WINDOWS 98SE/ME MY DOCUMENTS FOLDERS ON THE NETWORK

**The Annoyance:** I want to share my Windows 98SE My Documents folder on the network so that when I'm working at a different computer I can access my own files. When I right-click the folder's icon on my desktop, the shortcut menu doesn't have a Sharing command. It's annoying that Windows won't permit sharing of My Documents.

Figure 4-1. You must specifically enable the option to share your documents folder on the network if you want to use the contents from another computer.

**The Fix:** The My Documents icon on your desktop isn't a folder—it's a shortcut to a folder, and you can't share a shortcut. The actual My Documents folder, which you *can* share, exists within your user profile at c:\ *Windows\username* (substitute your logon name for *username*).

Luckily, you don't have to go to all the trouble of opening Windows Explorer and navigating to the real folder because you can ask the shortcut to take you there. Right-click the desktop icon and choose Properties from the shortcut menu to open the shortcut's Properties dialog box (see Figure 4-2).

Click the Find Target button and *voilà*, you're transported to your user profile. Right-click the My Documents folder and you'll see the Sharing command.

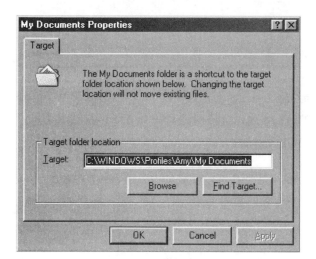

Figure 4-2. A shortcut's properties include the path to the target, and a button that lets you travel that path in a split second.

# MANIPULATING FILES ON THE NETWORK

## DRAG FILES BETWEEN COMPUTERS

**The Annoyance:** I needed to copy a bunch of files from a shared folder on a remote computer to the computer I was working on. I got really annoyed by all the folder-opening and right-clicking involved in copying and pasting from one computer to the other. Is there a faster way?

**The Fix:** It's a drag—I mean the solution, not my sympathetic response to your annoyance. Open both folders and drag between them. You can also use Windows Explorer to drag files between the right pane of the shared folder to the left pane of the local folder (or the other way around).

## WINDOWS EXPLORER DISPLAY IS ANNOYING

**The Annoyance:** It's annoying that the Windows Explorer program listing moved to the Accessories menu, causing an extra step to open it. But that pales compared to the real annoyance—the display it presents in the left pane. It takes several mouse clicks to get to Drive C and expand it. This is where Windows Explorer used to open, and where I almost always want to start.

**The Fix:** Microsoft introduced the changes to Windows Explorer in Windows 2000, and kept them in Windows XP. I hate it, too. You can force Windows Explorer to open with Drive C selected and expanded. To do so, you have to change the properties of the shortcut to the program. The listing on the Accessories menu is a shortcut (all menu listings are shortcuts), so you could do it right on the submenu, but you might as well create a more convenient shortcut to the program and change that.

To create the more convenient shortcut, right-drag the listing on the Accessories submenu to your desktop (or to your Quick Launch toolbar). When you release the right mouse button, choose Copy Here. Now you've eliminated one annoyance—you no longer have to move to the Accessories submenu to open the program.

Right-click the icon for the shortcut you just created and choose Properties. In the Target text box, add the following parameter to the existing path: `/e,c:\`. Be sure to leave a space between the end of the current path and the new parameter (see Figure 4-3).

Figure 4-3. Change the command for opening Windows Explorer to alter the way that it displays the left pane.

## MOVING VERSUS COPYING

**The Annoyance:** When I'm working on a computer that isn't my "home base," I like to move the files I want to work on to the current computer, and then move them back when I'm done. When I drag the files back, Windows always asks me if I want to replace the files that currently exist. Dragging files moves them, it doesn't copy them, so why are the original files still there?

**The Fix:** Dragging files between folders on the same computer moves those files. However, when you cross disks, dragging files results in a copy action, not a move. Dragging files between computers is, of course, a drag across different disks. The Cut and Paste functions are the simplest way to accomplish what you want.

## USE THE SEND TO COMMAND TO COPY FILES AND FOLDERS

**The Annoyance:** I think the Send To command on the right-click menu is nifty; I use it all the time to copy files to floppy disks. However, it's annoying that the Send To command doesn't include remote computers for fast transfers of files across the network.

**The Fix:** The Send To command is niftier than you think. You can use it to copy files or folders to any shared folder on the network—you just need to know how. You merely add the target to the Send To command, which is quite easy to do. In Windows 2000 and XP, you can create discrete Send To targets for each user. In Windows 98SE and Me, you can only create global Send To targets for all users.

### Add Send To targets in Windows XP/2000

To add a target to the Send To menu in Windows 2000 and XP, expand Windows Explorer or My Computer to display your profile in the left pane. One of the folders in your profile is named SendTo, and selecting it displays the current targets of the Send To command in the right pane (see Figure 4-4).

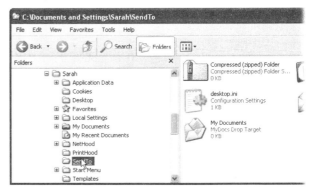

Figure 4-4. The submenu of the Send To command is a list of items in a folder.

1. Choose File → New → Shortcut to open the Create Shortcut Wizard. Either use the Location text box to enter the path to the remote folder or click the Browse button to navigate to the remote folder.

2. To enter text in the Location text box, use one of the following methods:

    • If the remote folder is a mapped drive, enter the drive letter followed by a colon (e.g., M:).

    • If the remote folder is not a mapped drive, enter its path in the format \\*ComputerName*\*ShareName* (the path is technically called the UNC, for Universal Naming Convention).

You can learn about mapped drives in Chapter 3.

If you don't know the path, or don't want to bother typing it, click the Browse button to open the Browse for Folder dialog box. Expand My Network Places and expand the remote computer to display its shares (see Figure 4-5).

Figure 4-5. Expand any computer on the network to display and select a folder.

3. Select the share you want to use as the target of your Send To command, and click OK to enter the UNC in the Location text box.

4. Click Next and enter the name for this shortcut (which will be the text on the Send To submenu).

5. Click Finish. The new shortcut shows up on the Send To command's submenu (see Figure 4-6).

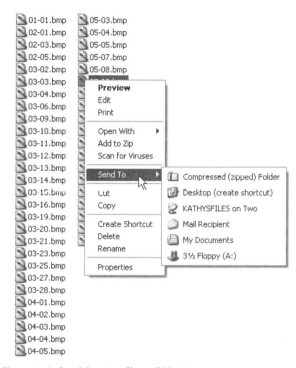

Figure 4-6. One click copies a file to a folder on a remote computer.

Warning. . .
When you expand My Network Places, you'll see shortcuts to network places you've previously visited. You can select one of those items instead of expanding the remote computer's object, but you face the risk of a nonexistent share. Windows doesn't track the listings for network places you've previously visited to make sure they still exist. When you expand the listing for a remote computer, the shares listed for that computer are currently valid.

If the target folder you want to use isn't shared, but is a subfolder of a shared folder, expand the shared folder to select it.

### Add Send To targets in Windows 98SE/Me

To add another target to the Send To command in Windows 98 and Me:

1. Open Windows Explorer and expand the Windows folder.

2. Select the Send To subfolder and choose File → New → Shortcut to open the Create Shortcut Wizard.

3. Enter the UNC to the remote shared folder, or enter the drive letter if the share is mapped to a drive. For reasons known only to the folks who designed it, the Browse button in the Windows 98SE and Me Create Shortcut Wizard locates only files, not folders, so it's useless for this task. After you enter the UNC or mapped drive letter, click Next.

4. Enter the name for the shortcut and click Finish. All users of the computer see this target on their Send To submenu.

## MY SEND TO FOLDER IS MISSING

**The Annoyance:** When I expand the folder for my username under Documents and Settings, I don't see a Send To folder.

**The Fix:** You've been victimized by one of the most annoying features in Windows. The Send To folder is a hidden folder, and by default, Windows doesn't display hidden folders. To correct this annoying "feature," open Windows Explorer or My Network Places. Choose Tools → Folder Options, click the View tab, and choose the "Show hidden files and folders" option (see Figure 4-7).

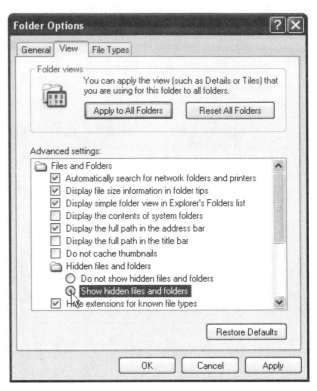

Figure 4-7. Change the default display settings so you can see the files and folders that Windows hides.

## THE WEIRDNESS OF THE RECYCLE BIN

**The Annoyance:** When I work at a computer other than my own, I occasionally need to access the Recycle Bin of my regular computer. I shared the drive, so it's easy to see the Recycle Bin. However, if I want to restore a file I just realized I shouldn't have deleted, I can't find it.

**The Fix:** You're not looking at the Recycle Bin of the remote computer. Instead, you're looking at the local Recycle Bin. Even though you're looking at a Recycle Bin that appears under the shared drive of a remote computer in Windows Explorer or My Computer (see Figure 4-8), you're not really looking at the remote computer's Recycle Bin. If you don't believe me (and I wouldn't blame you because there's not much logic to what I'm saying), double-click the desktop icon for your local Recycle Bin. Compare the contents to the one under the shared drive of the remote computer—they're identical.

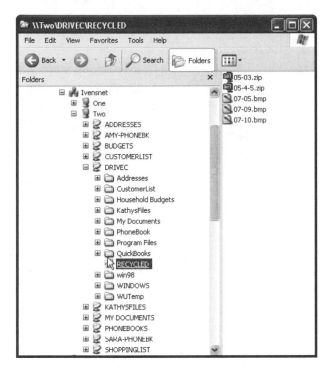

Figure 4-8. Don't believe your eyes.

# USE REMOTE FILES IN SOFTWARE

**The Annoyance:** When I open a software application and want to work on the files I created and stashed on a different computer, it's annoying to have to copy the files to the computer I'm currently using and then copy them back when I'm finished.

**The Fix:** You don't have to copy the files you want to use in a software application because you can open them right from the software window:

1. In the software window, choose File → Open.

2. Select My Network Places and navigate to the file you need.

## SOME DEFAULT VIEWING OPTIONS ARE DANGEROUS

The Windows "feature" of not displaying hidden files and folders is annoying, but it doesn't begin to match the stupidity and annoyance level of another Windows "feature"—the default setting that suppresses the display of filename extensions. Open Windows Explorer or My Network Places. Choose Tools → Folder Options, click the View tab, and *uncheck* the "Hide extensions for known file types" box.

This setting probably launches more viruses than we'll ever know. Viruses usually travel in executable files, so when you receive an email attachment named *filename.txt*, you'll think it's a safe file. However, because you can't see file extensions, you can't tell that the real name is *filename.txt.exe*. The executable extension is at least a clue that the file could be dangerous, but with the default view settings set to hide extensions, you'll never see it. Even if you keep your antivirus software up to date, you can get a new virus before a detection method is available from your antivirus software vendor, so your antivirus software doesn't automatically take care of the file.

# CAN'T SAVE FILES ON THE REMOTE COMPUTER?

**The Annoyance:** While using a software application, I opened a file from my own My Documents folder on a remote computer and made changes. When I tried to save the file, I received an error message.

**The Fix:** You didn't change the default permission settings when you shared the folder. When you share a folder, all versions of Windows except Windows 2000 set a folder's permissions to Read Only by default. Change the setting as follows:

- In Windows XP, right-click the folder and choose Properties, click the Sharing tab, and check the "Allow network users to change my files" box (see Figure 4-9).

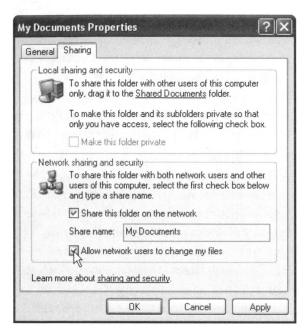

Figure 4-9. By default, Windows XP doesn't let a remote user save files in a shared folder.

- In Windows 98SE and Me, right-click the folder and choose Properties, click the Sharing tab, and select the Full option (see Figure 4-10).

In Windows 98SE and Me, if you're sharing your own My Documents folder, you can password-protect it. If you don't give the password to anyone, you'll have a private, remote folder.

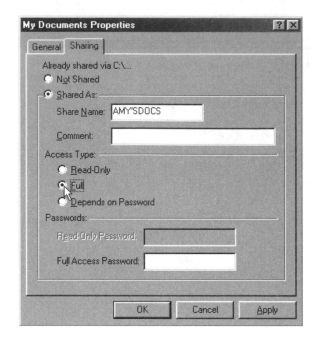

Figure 4-10. Change the Access Type to Full to be able to save files in a shared folder in Windows 98SE and Me.

# FILE CONTENTS CHANGE MYSTERIOUSLY

**The Annoyance:** Sometimes I add or change contents of a file, and when I open the file later, the contents don't match what I entered. Then I find out that while I was working on the file, somebody else was working on the same file from a different computer. This is truly annoying.

**The Fix:** It sure is annoying, and unless the software is designed to manage simultaneous users, there's nothing you can do about it. Two annoying things are going on:

- "The last save wins" rule is in effect.
- Each user's copy of the file is static except for the changes that user is making. As each user makes changes and saves them, the other user's file doesn't update with the changes being saved to the disk.

When you save and close the file and then reopen it, everything might look fine—the last save wins! However, if you're the user who saved the file earlier than the last save, you're probably rather surprised by the contents.

> **Warning. . .**
> Two software applications that can't manage simultaneous users, and therefore cause this problem, are WordPad and Notepad.

# USE SOFTWARE THAT PERMITS SIMULTANEOUS USERS OF THE SAME FILE

**The Annoyance:** Sometimes I open a file in a software application and I'm told that someone else is using the file. The message that appears explains the Notify option, but what's the Read Only button for?

**The Fix:** You'll see this message if you use software designed to manage multiple users opening the same file (e.g., Microsoft Word). And you're right, the message only explains what happens if you click the Notify button (see Figure 4-11).

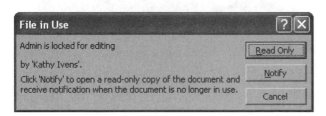

Figure 4-11. The message explains the Notify button, and assumes you understand the Read Only option.

The Read Only button lets you open the file as read-only, which means you can't save the file under its original filename (you can't click the Save button on the toolbar or select File → Save). When you want to save your work, you must choose File → Save As and save the file under a different name.

> **t i p**
> When you save the file with a different name, pick a name that connects the file to the original, such as *Filename-2* (substitute the real filename for *Filename*).

If you click the Notify button, the file opens with the contents it had the last time it was saved by the user currently working on the file. You can begin working on the file, but if you want to save your work before you're notified that the other user has closed the file, you must use a different filename (you're working in read-only mode and creating a separate file, which won't merge its contents with the original file).

Windows tracks the other open copy of the file, and when it's closed, you're notified that the file is available for editing (see Figure 4-12), which means you can save it using the original filename. The file, of course, now contains any new or changed material inserted by the user who was working on it.

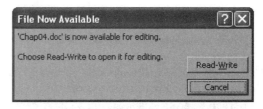

Figure 4-12. Choose Read-Write so you can save the file with its original filename.

> **Warning. . .**
> The next time the "other" user opens the file, your changes are there, which might be a surprise, and a surprising annoyance. You should tell the other user what you did, or make changes in a way that's suitable for collaboration (see "Collaborating on Files").

## COLLABORATING ON FILES

**The Annoyance:** We have several files on our network that multiple users work on. We keep shopping lists, calendars, and other family notes in those files. Everyone puts text in front of or behind their changes, such as "Mom, I changed the previous sentence from xxx to yyy." This makes it more difficult to read the files, and it's a rather complex task to create a final file.

**The Fix:** Most software designed for Windows offers a way to track each person's contribution to a document, and to accept or reject changes easily (to create a finished document). When the tracking feature is enabled, as each person opens the document and types, that person's characters appear in a different color. When text is deleted, it remains on the screen with a special character to indicate that the document was changed by that deletion. You can accept or reject each person's work, one change at a time, or all at once. See the Help files for your software to learn how to use this nifty feature.

> **Warning. . .**
> After you've accepted or rejected all the changes and saved the document, turn off the collaboration features. Be sure to turn off the ability to see changes in the screen or print document, then test it by opening the document again and turning on the feature that shows changes (not the one that tracks changes). If you see any original text that was changed or deleted, delete it without the tracking feature to make sure it's permanently deleted. Otherwise, if you send the document to anyone, they'll be able to turn on the feature that shows the changes and see all the contributions, notes, and comments. This could be embarrassing to you and extremely interesting to the recipient. I've received documents from major corporations (including Microsoft) in which I was able to see notes, comments, and rejected text, at least some of which I'm sure they didn't want me to see.

## CREATE A FILE SERVER

**The Annoyance:** We keep a number of files on our network for everyone in the family to access. As the number of files grows, we constantly lose track of where they are. At work, we have a file server that holds all the files that multiple employees need to use, but at home we have a peer-to-peer network with no file server.

**The Fix:** You can add the services of a file server to your network simply by assigning one computer to that role:

1. Choose a computer with plenty of disk space, and make sure it's a computer that's either on all the time or easy to get to if you need to turn it on (a computer you keep in a locked room on the third floor isn't a good choice). Create a user for that computer named Family, and share the My Documents folder for Family with full access (which lets other users change files).

2. Make sure the folder is shared on the network.

> **Warning. . .**
> Don't name a user Everybody, because Windows XP and 2000 have an Everybody user built into the system for permissions purposes.

## MAP LOCAL FOLDERS TO DRIVE LETTERS

**The Annoyance:** Some of the files I create need to go into a folder other than My Documents. Most of the software I use opens the My Documents folder by default when I want to save or open a file. It's annoying to go through all the mouse clicks needed to change the folder. Is there a faster way?

**The Fix:** When you're working in software, it's much easier to change the drive letter in the Save or Open dialog box than to click your way through the computer's hierarchy. If you have a specific folder on your drive that holds certain files, you can map a drive letter to that folder on the local computer. If you're working remotely, share the folder and map a drive on the remote computer. If you use this folder often, save your sanity by using the same drive letter for the local and remote mappings.

Mapping a local folder is different from mapping a remote folder (read Chapter 3 for detailed instructions on mapping drives to remote folders). There's no way to do this in the graphical Windows interface; you must use the command line. The format (the technical term is *syntax*) of the command is:

```
subst driveletter: path
```

If you have a folder named Project-1 on Drive C of your computer, and you want to substitute the drive letter P, enter the following command: `subst p: c:\project-1`. You can use a longer path if the folder to which you want to assign a drive letter is a subfolder, or even a subfolder of a subfolder. For example: `subst p: c:\project-1\budget\2005`.

> **Note. . .**
> **If any folders in the path have a space in the name, enclose the entire path in quotation marks. For example:**
>    `subst p: "c:\my projects\budget"`

Alternatively, you could keep these files in your Favorites list and fetch them from the Favorites folder available in the Open dialog box.

## SAVING DATABASE DATAFILES

**The Annoyance:** We have a database program to track our family budget and spending. Two of the computers on the network have a copy of the program. If each user saves the data to his or her own computer, we don't have a complete record on either computer. This can't be the way it's supposed to work.

**The Fix:** It certainly isn't the way it's supposed to work. Most database software for small businesses or home users is designed to hold all the data, from all computers, in one location. These database applications don't have "merge" features that let you save multiple copies in different locations, then later merge the data. Larger, more robust databases usually have a merge feature that puts all the information into one file and checks for duplicate information.

The way to resolve this problem depends on the database application's design. If the program you're using is designed for multiuser access (e.g., QuickBooks), you must decide which computer holds the datafile, and then configure the software on all computers to use that datafile.

If the program isn't designed for multiuser access (e.g., Quicken), you have two choices:

- Designate one computer as the database computer and stop using the other computer.
- Designate one computer as the database computer, and then configure the other computer to use the file on the first computer (use a mapped drive). Make sure only one computer at a time accesses the database file.

## DATABASE FILE LOCKING

**The Annoyance:** We use a multiuser database program to track our finances. Sometimes a user enters data and sees a message such as "access denied" or "file is locked." We purchased this database because it can handle multiple users, so what's the deal?

**The Fix:** The database file-lock feature is kicking in. The solution is to wait a few seconds, then enter the data again. All databases have "file-lock" features to prevent users from entering different data in the same place simultaneously. Depending on the way the database is designed (programmed), the locking feature can kick in at any level of the hierarchy. The general hierarchy of a database (presented in an oversimplified manner) is as follows.

File

The database datafile.

Record

A particular record, such as a bank account or vendor name.

Field

A particular field, such as the check number or the invoice number for a vendor's bill.

The general rule of thumb is that the more robust (and expensive) a database, the lower the level of the lock. The only databases that lock the entire file are those that don't permit simultaneous access by multiple users.

If your database locks at the record level, when any user is accessing a record, other users are locked out until the first user moves on to a different record. For example, if you're using a vendor record to enter a bill, write a check, or change the vendor's address, no other user can create a transaction involving that record.

If your database locks at the field level, when one user is entering a check for a particular vendor using the vendor's invoice number, the other users are locked out of the field until the first user has moved on. For example, if you and someone else are both entering checks in the Check Number field, the first person to save the data (usually by pressing the Tab key or clicking the next field) wins. The second user is locked out for the few seconds it takes for the first user to move on before the Check Number field becomes available again.

## TEMPORARY FILE LOCKING OF DATABASE DATAFILES

**The Annoyance:** We have a financial database program designed for multiple simultaneous users. Every once in a while, no remote users can get into the file, and the error message says the file is not available for multiple users. This problem is sporadic, and it always goes away eventually, but it's annoying to have an error that seems to occur randomly.

**The Fix:** Most databases designed for multiple simultaneous users lock out remote users when certain activities are taking place, such as backups, major configuration changes, software updates, and other processes that involve the entire file. When the task ends, the database is once again available.

> **Warning. . .**
> Some database programs (QuickBooks, for example) require the user who performs the file-locking task to manually put the file back into multiuser mode. If your database doesn't automatically return the file to remote users, train everyone in the household to go back to multiuser mode manually after performing a file-locking task.

## BACK UP DATABASE FILES TO REMOTE COMPUTERS

**The Annoyance:** We run our family financial software on a Windows 98SE computer. We don't want to reinstall the software on our new Windows XP computer, but we'd like to take advantage of the ability to burn CDs on the new computer. Is there a way to back up the datafile across the network?

**The Fix:** I know this is possible in Quicken, Money, and QuickBooks (and surely in other financial software as well). Here are some guidelines:

- Make sure you share the folder that will hold the backup; configure the share for network users and allow them to change the files.

- Quicken and QuickBooks will both work with a network path, but your life will be easier if you map a drive to the remote shared folder before you make your backup.

- Money will not work with a network path, so you have no choice but to map a drive to the remote shared folder before backing up the drive.

Chapter 3 has detailed instructions on mapping drives to shared folders.

## USING SOFTWARE ON A REMOTE COMPUTER

**The Annoyance:** I have a software application installed on a computer, and I usually use a different computer to do my work (so that all my files are on that computer). Can I run the software remotely, from my usual computer, by double-clicking the software's program file?

**The Fix:** Almost certainly not. Software installations are rather complicated, and in addition to the executable file that launches the software, there are probably close to 100 related files scattered around the hard drive of the computer that holds the software. In addition, there are registry entries that control and manage the software on the registry of the computer that holds the software.

Even all the old DOS software I still use on my Windows machine won't run from a remote computer. DOS software doesn't have an installation routine and doesn't write to the registry, but it is hardcoded to use the local drive and doesn't understand network paths—if it's not launched from its own drive (usually C), it won't run.

However, you do have some ways to accomplish this, all of which are much more complicated and expensive than getting up and moving to the computer that holds the software. You can subscribe to an Internet software sharing service, such as WebEx (*http://www.webex.com/*). Search the Internet (and magazine stories with reviews of services) for Internet support and training services. You can also buy remote computing software, which lets you enter a remote computer on the network and take over its screen, keyboard, and mouse controls and open software.

# NETWORK ENTERTAINMENT CENTERS

## CONNECT YOUR NETWORK TO GAMING DEVICES

**The Annoyance:** We have an Xbox that everyone enjoys. Is there a way to connect the device to our network?

**The Fix:** If you have gamers in the house, look for game adapters that let you attach PlayStation 2, Xbox, or GameCube devices to the network. Most network equipment manufacturers offer these adapters, and many of them support wireless communication.

Installation might seem a bit complicated, but that's because you can't configure the game adapter unless it's connected to a computer via Ethernet cable. After you've configured the adapter, you can remove it from the computer and attach it to the game console. Complete directions come with the device.

## MUSIC EVERYONE?

**The Annoyance:** Everyone in our household has a music collection on his or her computer. Sometimes you can hear different music from every computer, which is incredibly annoying. On the other hand, sometimes someone is playing something everyone likes, but with computers on different floors, it's hard for everyone to enjoy it. We need some suggestions for fixing our music problems.

**The Fix:** For the first annoyance (the cacophony of multiple tunes echoing through the house), buy headsets. Every sound controller I've ever seen has a headset jack. For the second annoyance, the solution is a network music device. These nifty gadgets are available from almost any manufacturer of network hardware.

I've tested two different types of network music boxes: one that lets any network user send a tune to the family stereo system, and one that is self-contained (it's a stereo system that comes with its own speakers). Both are wireless bridges, which means they can connect to a wired system and send/receive wireless signals. If you use the device that sends music to your home stereo system, think about adding speakers so that users all over the house can listen.

If you don't collect music on your hard drives, you can send music from the Internet over the system. Don't be silly enough to try this over dial-up, though—you need broadband Internet access to make this worthwhile. Keep in mind that music isn't the only software in the world. Think about giving the kids history lessons or ask them to dig up a description of the places you're going to visit on your next family vacation. Or simply send them on a fun and educational goose chase.

### Sending Music to Different Computers

My favorite use of the self-contained music device is to use its wireless capacity to send music from one of the computers on the network to my laptop, which I use when I'm working on the deck. The laptop doesn't store music files (which is common, especially when laptops are supplied by employers!), and doesn't have good speakers.

# 5

# Network Printing
# ANNOYANCES

Another nifty advantage of a home network is printer sharing, which allows everyone on the network to use the same printer, regardless of the computer to which that printer is attached. This eliminates the printing model that computer professionals call a "sneaker net," where users copy files to a floppy disk, walk over to the computer connected to the printer they need, open the software used to create the files (of course, the software has to be installed on both computers), fetch the file from the floppy disk, and print it.

Even if you have a printer for each computer, there are great advantages to printer sharing. One is that each printer can have a different type of paper. For example, you might keep checks in one printer and paper in another, or you might want plain paper in one and a fancy bond paper in the other. If all your printers are capable of color, print documents that need color only on the printer that uses the least expensive cartridges.

In this chapter, I'll point out the workarounds for annoyances you might encounter as you set up, configure, troubleshoot, and use network printers. This chapter assumes you've already completed the installation processes for each printer.

# SHARED PRINTER ANNOYANCES

## WHAT'S IN A NAME?

**The Annoyance:** We have two HP DeskJet 550C printers, each of which is attached to a different computer. On the Sharing tab of each printer's Properties dialog box, I selected the option to share the printer. Windows gave both printers the same sharename: HPDeskJe. After I install these printers on all the computers on the network, how will users be able to tell which printer is which?

**The Fix:** Users won't be able to tell the difference, but don't worry. You don't have to use the name Windows enters on the Sharing tab; it's only a suggestion. Replace the name with something more meaningful, such as the printer's location. For example, use DJ-Blue for the printer attached to the computer in the bedroom with blue walls, or DJ-Amy if the printer is attached to the computer in Amy's room.

You can also use the name to describe the printer's use. For example, even if both printers have the capacity to print color, you might want to assign one printer for color documents and the other printer for black-and-white documents. Then name the first printer "Color" and the other one "Black." Assuming you can convince everyone in the household that most documents don't really need colored text (good luck, especially with the kids), this will save you big bucks in color cartridge expenses. (For a way to enforce these rules, see "Limit Printing Choices to Avoid Printing Errors.")

You can include comments and other information about a printer (such as its location) on the General tab of the printer's Properties dialog box (see "Display Detailed Descriptions of Printers").

---

### TO WINDOWS, PRINTERS AREN'T REAL

After you complete the installation routine for a printer, an icon for the printer appears in your Printers folder (or Printers and Faxes folder in Windows XP). The icon represents a virtual printer, not the physical printer. The virtual printer is a collection of software files called *drivers*. When you print, the software sends the file to the virtual printer, at which point your document becomes what is called a *print job*. Windows now takes over the printing process and uses a complicated set of software programs (such as drivers, software monitors, and spoolers) to guide the print job through the printing process. Windows communicates directly with the physical printer regardless of where it is located on the network, thereby providing shared printing services to multiple users while keeping each user's document intact.

## OLDER COMPUTERS MIGHT NOT FIND THE PRINTERS

**The Annoyance:** I shared two printers on our three-computer network. I named one printer DeskJet-FamilyRoom and the other printer LaserJet-Bedroom. However, I can't install these printers on my Windows 98SE computer. I used both the Add Printer Wizard and the Network Neighborhood window to search for the printers, but they're not listed anywhere.

**The Fix:** Windows 98SE, like other versions of Windows prior to Windows 2000, can't see a sharename longer than 12 characters (including dashes and other punctuation). When you shared the printers, a Windows message such as the one shown in Figure 5-1 popped up after you clicked OK.

The message doesn't explain that all versions of Windows prior to Windows 2000 are really MS-DOS-based operating systems with the Windows graphical interface running on top, and are therefore considered MS-DOS

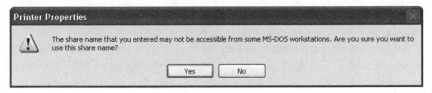

Figure 5-1. This message from Windows is so badly written that it qualifies as inaccurate.

computers. None of those versions of Windows can manage long sharenames. You probably didn't realize that you were running any of those ancient MS-DOS (text-based) computers on your network.

What makes all of this more confusing, and more annoying, is that Windows 9X supports long filenames, so it's logical to believe that a long sharename is acceptable. However, logic doesn't work here. For future reference, keep in mind that the 12-character limitation is applied to sharenames for all types of shares—printers, drives, and folders. To Windows XP's credit, when you share a folder or drive with a sharename longer than 12 characters, a cogent, precise message appears to explain the ramifications (see Chapter 2 to learn about sharing folders and drives).

To resolve the problem, open each printer's Properties dialog box, click the Sharing tab, and choose a sharename with 12 characters or less. The printers will now show up in Network Neighborhood and the Add Printer Wizard of your Windows 98SE computer. After the installation, the printers will have icons in the Printers folder.

# DISPLAY DETAILED DESCRIPTIONS OF PRINTERS

**The Annoyance:** I used the handy-dandy Comment field in the printer's Properties dialog box to provide information about our shared printers. For instance, I entered instructions for using a printer that has two trays, each containing a specific type of paper (Tray#1=plain paper and Tray#2=checks). That description isn't displayed when users select a printer, so what's the point of having the Comment field?

**The Fix:** Good question. I wish I had a good answer. Does "beats me" qualify as a good answer? You're right—if you enter information in the Comment field on the General tab, the text isn't displayed in the Print dialog box. Because you open the Print dialog box when you want to print, that's the logical time and place to show users' comments about the printer.

In Windows 2000 and XP, the General tab also has a Location field, which you can use for text such as "in the den." However, that text is also unavailable in the Print dialog box.

This text is available to users only when they're installing a printer by locating it in Network Neighborhood or My Network Places, or when they're gazing at the contents of the Printers folder. Apparently users are supposed to memorize all the information about a printer when they install it, or open the Printers folder to see if any comments exist before printing documents. Yeah, that'll happen.

To make all of this even more annoying, when you're looking at the Printers folder, or looking for printers in Network Neighborhood or My Network Places, you have to do some work to see the text that's been entered in the Location and Comments fields. If you open the Printers folder, you don't see any additional information about any printer in the default view:

- In Windows 2000, the default view is Large Icons. If you select an icon, the window's Status Bar shows any text entered in the Location field, but doesn't show text entered in the Comment field.

- In Windows 9X and Me, the default view is also Large Icons. If you select an icon, the left side of the folder displays the text in the Comment field, but not the Location field.

- In Windows XP, the default view is Tiles (same as Large Icons). If you select an icon, the Details section on the left side of the window displays the text in the Location and Comment fields.

In all versions of Windows, select View → Details to see the text you entered in the Location field (Figure 5-2).

Figure 5-2. Choose the Details view to see additional information about printers.

# INSTALL DRIVERS FOR OTHER VERSIONS OF WINDOWS

**The Annoyance:** When I shared a printer connected to a Windows XP computer, I saw an Additional Drivers button on the Sharing tab. The description of the Additional Drivers feature says that Windows XP will install drivers for other versions of Windows. This means that when I want to install this printer on computers running other versions of Windows, the drivers are available automatically. I like that this saves me the trouble of taking the original Windows 98SE CD to the computers that will share the printer. However, when I selected the option to install drivers for my Windows 98SE computer, Windows XP didn't have them. Instead, it asked me for the Windows 98SE media, which is what would happen if I installed the drivers while I was working on the Windows 98SE computer. Features that don't work "as advertised" (or, at least, as "hinted at") are really annoying.

**The Fix:** I agree that the explanation of the process of installing drivers for multiple versions of Windows isn't well explained in the dialog box, which is annoying. However, under some circumstances this is a nifty feature. (Incidentally, the same feature is available in Windows 2000.)

If you had more than one Windows 98SE computer on your network, installing the printer driver on your Windows XP computer would save you the trouble of carrying the original Windows 98SE CD to all the Windows 98SE computers. The same is true if you use printer drivers that you download from the manufacturer's web site; you only need to download the files to the computer that holds the printer.

# ATTACH MULTIPLE PRINTERS TO A COMPUTER

**The Annoyance:** We have three computers and two printers on our network. Two of the computers are squeezed into the corners of bedrooms, and there's not really enough room to add a printer. Can I attach both printers to the third computer and share them on the network?

**The Fix:** You can connect as many printers to a computer as there are ports to hold them, and share all of them on the network. If both printers require a parallel port connection and your computer has only one parallel port, you can add a Parallel PCI Card to your computer for less than $30.

Today, most printers come with two or more USB ports. If you're using your computer's USB ports for other devices (a scanner or optical mouse, for example), you can purchase a USB port extender (called a *USB hub*) to add more USB ports. One end of the hub plugs into a USB port, and the other end provides multiple USB ports for devices (usually four ports). You can even daisy-chain these hubs, using one port of each hub to connect to the next hub, providing USB connectivity to more than 100 devices.

## DECIDING ON THE RIGHT COMPUTER FOR A PRINT SERVER

**The Annoyance:** We're having an ongoing argument in our house about where to put the printer that serves all three computers on our network. One option is to connect the printer to the computer in the most convenient location, which is equally distant from the other two computers. However, that computer is old and slow (and, in fact, nobody likes to use it). I'm afraid that adding the printer will make the computer even slower.

**The Fix:** Printing services don't eat up a lot of processor power (the jargon for this is *overhead*), so connecting the printer to the older, slower computer that's in a central location is your best bet.

In fact, any computer no longer popular with users because it lacks speed, or is running out of disk space, is a great candidate for your network's print server. Uninstall software that won't be used anymore, copy the documents across the network to the appropriate computers, and you have a print server. You can put the computer and the printer on a small table without worrying about providing desk space or a comfortable chair. Another option is to leave the computer alone and add a print server appliance to the network. It's reasonably inexpensive and solves the problem handily—though it won't give your old and slow computer anything useful to do. Most manufacturers of network equipment offer print servers. You connect your printer(s) to the print server, and then connect the print server to your network. If it's a wired print server, run cable to the hub or router. If it's a wireless print server, just locate it where your wireless computers can see it (a trial-and-error task).

## PASSWORD-PROTECTED PRINTERS

**The Annoyance:** We keep checks in one of our printers, and we don't want our children to be able to access it. The printer is connected to a computer running Windows 98SE. We password-protected the printer, but the password protection doesn't work when the children are working on that computer. What's the point of password protection if you can't keep people from using the printer?

**The Fix:** Unfortunately, the password protection for shared printers, available in Windows versions prior to 2000, applies only to remote users. If your printer is attached to a computer running Windows 2000 or XP with the NTFS filesystem, you can specify permissions that cover all users, no matter what computer they use. See Chapter 7 to learn about applying user permissions.

# INSTALLING REMOTE (NETWORK) PRINTERS

## USING THE ADD PRINTER WIZARD

**The Annoyance:** I wanted to install a remote printer on my Windows XP computer. In the Printers and Faxes folder, I chose Add Printer. I clicked Next in the Welcome to the Add Printer Wizard window, and immediately became confused. The wizard window explains how to choose between a local or network printer, but the explanation doesn't make sense. I assumed I was just not technically astute enough to understand the real meaning of the message, so I followed the instructions. I never found the network printer. Am I crazy, or is the text wrong?

**The Fix:** You're sane. The text (seen at the bottom of the dialog box in Figure 5-3) is misleading—OK, it's just wrong. In fact, the instructions are backward; inside out. You use a local port when you've installed a hardware device called a print server because it creates a port on the computer for the print server. When you want to install a printer connected to a remote computer, you don't use the "Local printer" option.

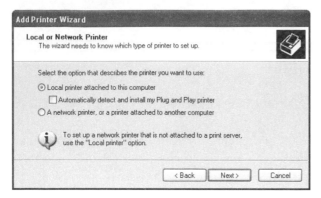

Figure 5-3. Ignore the explanation about setting up a network printer; it's wrong.

Personally, I think adding a printer through the Add Printer Wizard is too much work. I use Network Neighborhood or My Network Places to perform this task (see the next annoyance). However, if you prefer to use the Add Printer Wizard, select the "A network printer, or a printer attached to another computer" option, and then click Next.

If you don't know the exact sharename of the network printer you want to add, select the "Browse for a printer" option and click Next. Double-click the icon for the computer connected to the printer you want to install, which will display the sharename of the printer under the computer's listing. Select the printer sharename, and click Next. If Windows XP has drivers for this printer (which is likely), the system installs the printer automatically. If no drivers are available, you must provide them either from the manufacturer's disk or from a file you downloaded from the vendor's web site. Follow the prompts to point Windows XP to the location of the drivers, then continue moving through the wizard to install the printer.

If you know the sharename of the printer and the name of the computer to which it's attached, you can save all those mouse clicks. Select the "Connect to this printer" option and enter the printer in the format shown in Figure 5-4:

1. Type two backslash characters, followed by the name of the computer that holds the printer.
2. Type one backslash character, followed by the sharename of the printer.

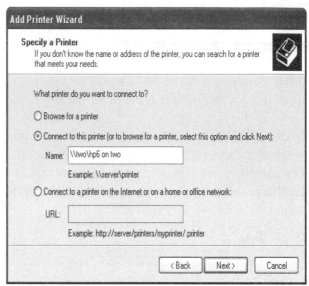

Figure 5-4. You can move directly to the printer by entering its name in the proper format.

If you're using the Add Printer Wizard in a version of Windows other than XP, the directions are similar, although some of the options might have slightly different text. The wizard windows might also look different from those for XP.

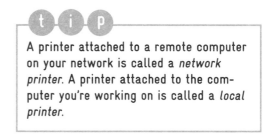

A printer attached to a remote computer on your network is called a *network printer*. A printer attached to the computer you're working on is called a *local printer*.

## INSTALL NETWORK PRINTERS FROM THE NETWORK WINDOW

**The Annoyance:** I generally try to steer clear of the wizards in Windows because they go on and on and on. Even though each new version of Windows seems to have more wizards, including some you can't avoid, I always find it faster to perform tasks manually. Can I add a network printer to a computer without clicking Next a zillion times?

**The Fix:** I agree with you, and I eschew wizards whenever there's a way to perform the same task manually. The manual workarounds are almost always faster and more efficient. To install a network printer on a computer without invoking the Add Printer Wizard, open Network Neighborhood or My Network Places (depending on the Windows version) and view the workgroup. Double-click the computer that holds the printer you want to install to open a window that shows all the shared objects on that computer (see Figure 5-5). Shared folders have icons that look like folders, and shared printers have icons that look like printers, so it's easy to spot the printer.

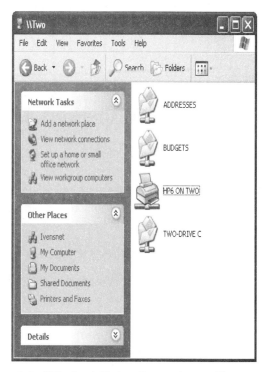

Figure 5-5. All the shared objects on the computer named Two are displayed in the window.

Right-click the printer object and choose the appropriate command from the menu that appears:

- In Windows XP and Windows 2000, choose Connect.
- In Windows 9X and Windows Me, choose Install.

Windows XP and Windows 2000 include a set of printer drivers for most printers, so the installation is immediate, and no dialog boxes or messages appear. Open your Printers folder, and the printer is there.

If no drivers are available, Windows might ask you to insert the original Windows CD so that the drivers can be copied. If Windows doesn't have drivers for this printer, a dialog box appears so that you can go through the steps of installing a driver from the manufacturer.

### Universal Naming Convention

The format \\*ServerName\ShareName* is called the *Universal Naming Convention* (UNC), and it's used to access resources on a network. In this case, the ServerName is the name of the computer that holds the shared printer. Any computer that has a shared printer connected to it is a *print server*.

## QUICKER WAYS TO INSTALL A NETWORK PRINTER

**The Annoyance:** I've found many ways to complete tasks in Windows without going through all the graphical menus, submenus, windows, dialog boxes, and wizards. Instead, I use commands, which is great for someone like me who hates taking her fingers off the keyboard to mess with a mouse. There must be some similarly quick methods for installing printers.

**The Fix:** I'm a command-line junkie myself, mostly because I'm old and I've been around computers a long time—since the days of MS-DOS—and have never gotten over my love affair with the speed of DOS commands. I have some quick tricks for skipping submenus, windows, and excessive mouse clicks.

Open the Run command on the Start menu, and type the UNC for the remote computer that holds the printer you want to install. For example, on my network, working on the computer named One, I enter `\\two` to access the computer named Two. The system opens a window displaying all the shared objects on the computer. I can simply right-click the printer object and select Connect or Install, depending on the version of Windows I'm using.

> **tip**
>
> To avoid using the mouse, press the Windows key followed by `r` to open the Run command.

Here's another method: in the Address Bar of your browser, enter the UNC to the remote computer that holds the printer you want to install. When the shared resources of the computer appear in the browser window, right-click the printer object and choose Connect or Install.

## INSTALL A PRINTER ATTACHED TO A MAC

**The Annoyance:** One of the computers on our home network is a Macintosh, and it has a terrific Post-Script printer. There must be a way to use this printer from the Windows-based computers on the network.

**The Fix:** Unless you're running OS X on the Mac, you probably can't get there from here, at least not directly. If your network includes a computer running Windows 2000 Server (not the same as Windows 2000 Professional), you can install print services for Macintosh. You'll find this option in the Windows Components section of

the Add/Remove Programs applet in the Control Panel. Enabling this component lets you find and install printers attached to Macs.

However, I suspect it's highly unlikely you're running Windows 2000 Server on your network, so the solution is a third-party software application. I've had numerous clients say good things about PC MACLAN from Computer Associates (*http://ca.miramar.com/Products/PC_MACLAN/*) and DAVE from Thursby Software Systems (*http://www.thursby.com/*), but you might find, or hear about, other Mac-PC sharing applications. These programs provide bidirectional printer sharing for PostScript laser printers, non-PostScript laser printers, and inkjet printers. Most of these applications also support file sharing between Macs and PCs.

# MANAGING NETWORK PRINTING

## CHANGE THE ORDER OF PRINT JOBS

**The Annoyance:** We often have printing traffic jams. At any given moment, the kids send documents filled with graphics and color to our shared printer. A few seconds later, my wife prints a humongous report that contains charts and has to be on her boss's desk the next morning. A few seconds after that, I print an important document that I need immediately. I have to wait forever for my document to come out of the printer, which often holds up my dinner, prevents me from watching my favorite TV shows, or keeps me up late. The printer is attached to my computer. Can I force the printer to print my stuff first?

**The Fix:** You can try, but it doesn't always work. Windows has tools to help you manipulate the order in which print jobs are completed, but stuff moves through the printing process so quickly that sometimes your actions are just too late.

If you want to try anyway, open the Printers folder (Printers and Faxes folder in Windows XP) and double-click the printer's icon to open its window, which looks something like the window in Figure 5-6.

Figure 5-6. The printer's window displays the jobs in the print queue in the order in which they were received, which is, by default, the order in which they print.

You have several choices for getting your document to print right away:

- Pause each print job that isn't yours by right-clicking each listing and choosing Pause Printing.
- Pause all the print jobs at once by choosing Printer → Pause Printing from the Menu bar. Then, right-click your own print job and choose Resume.
- Drag your print job to the top of the queue, right behind the job currently printing. (When I was a kid, waiting in line at the movie theater, we called this "cutting in," and everybody yelled at the miscreant.) You can't change the queue position of a job already in the process of printing.

- Change the priority of your own print job by right-clicking its listing and choosing Properties. On the General tab, raise the job's priority so that it prints immediately after the current print job (see Figure 5-7).

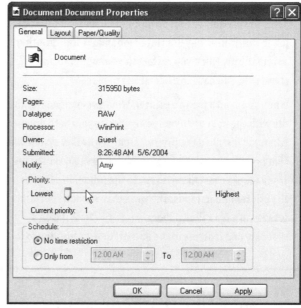

Figure 5-7. Move the slider bar to the right to raise the priority of the selected print job.

## USING THE PRINTER WINDOW

When you open a printer by double-clicking its icon in the Printers folder (Printers and Faxes folder in Windows XP), the printer's window shows all the jobs in the queue, along with information about each job (document name, size, owner, and so on). You can perform the following tasks:

- ☒ Pause a print job by right-clicking its listing and choosing Pause. A check mark appears next to the Pause Printing command to indicate that the job status has changed. The next job in the queue starts printing.

- ☒ Resume a paused print job by right-clicking its listing and choosing Resume.

- ☒ Restart a print job stopped by the system because of a

printer problem (a paper jam or out-of-paper error) by right-clicking its listing and choosing Restart.

- ☒ Drag a print job's listing up or down to change its place in the queue. You can't move the job currently printing.

- ☒ Pause, cancel, or restart all the print jobs in the queue by using the commands available in the Printer menu on the window's Menu bar.

You can also change the priority of a job so that it prints before all other jobs of a lower priority, or prints after all jobs of a higher priority. You can't change the priority of the job currently printing. By default, print jobs have a priority of 1, which is the lowest priority.

## PAUSING A PRINT JOB DOESN'T STOP THE PRINTER

**The Annoyance:** When I pause (or cancel) the current print job, the printer keeps printing, and printing, and printing. Often, the whole document prints, so pausing it didn't accomplish my goal—stopping the print job to let the next one in the queue print right away.

**The Fix:** Commands are sent to the virtual printer, not the physical printer (see the sidebar "To Windows, Printers Aren't Real" earlier in this chapter). The Pause command (or the Cancel command) stopped the printing system from sending data to the printer. However, data already sent to the printer is in the printer's memory, which is physical hardware (memory chips). No application can go there, and therefore the document continues

to print. Some printers have lots of memory; in fact, they have enough memory to store an entire large document. The only way to remove data from a printer's memory is to turn off the printer. Push the power button if the printer has one, or unplug the printer if it has no power button.

## TURNING OFF A PRINTER CAUSES A PAPER JAM

**The Annoyance:** Sometimes a user sends a large document to the wrong printer. For example, one of the children sends a long book report to the printer that has checks in its tray. If I don't want to wait for the large document to print, I pause or cancel the print job, and then I turn off the printer to stop the printing. When I turn on the printer again, there's invariably a paper jam. Sometimes I have to disassemble the printer to get to the jammed paper. What's the secret to avoiding a printer jam when you turn off a printer churning out paper?

**The Fix:** The secret is to pick the exact nanosecond between the time the printer feeds the current page to the out tray and the time that it grabs the next page. If you figure out how to tell when that nanosecond occurs, please let me know because I've certainly never figured it out. My solution is to try to avoid the jam by yanking the paper out of the printer. For a laser printer, pull the tray out of its slot. For an inkjet printer, remove all the paper. When paper isn't available, the printer stops to wait for more paper, and that's when I power down the printer to erase its memory. This almost always works, but sometimes I remove the paper after the printer has started feeding the next sheet of paper. If I can see that paper, I just pull it out. If it's already entered the interior of the printer, sometimes this causes a printer jam, as I tug and the printer refuses to release the paper. I guess this means the fix for this annoyance is "good luck."

> **t i p**
>
> I think we should all start a campaign to ask every printer manufacturer to include a button on the printer marked "Erase data in memory immediately and eject any paper currently in the paper path."

## MANUALLY FED FORMS HOLD UP PRINTING

**The Annoyance:** Sometimes another user sends an envelope or some other manually fed form to the printer attached to my computer. If I send a document to the printer, it won't print until the first user brings the envelope to the printer, inserts it, and lets it print. Meanwhile, I have to watch the printer blink its lights at me, as if it's saying, "ha-ha, you have to wait for your document until Clyde shows up to print his envelope." Clyde's working on a different floor, and it takes him a while to get to the printer. Sometimes he even forgets he sent the job to the printer. Isn't there a way to overcome this problem?

**The Fix:** You have two methods available to you for resolving this annoyance:

- Find a way to enforce a rule that says "when you send a manually fed document to a printer you must run to the printer to insert the form to avoid holding up the rest of us."

- Configure the printer so that all print jobs that require manual feeding wait until the print spooler is empty of "regular" documents (meaning documents that use the paper type available in the printer's paper trays).

The first method works only if the dynamics of your household or office operate in a way that causes threats to work. 'Nuff said.

The second method requires changing the configuration of the printer to enable an option designed specifically to prevent this annoyance. To make the change, open the Printers folder, right-click the printer, and choose Properties. Click the Advanced tab and check the "Hold mismatched documents" box (see Figure 5-8).

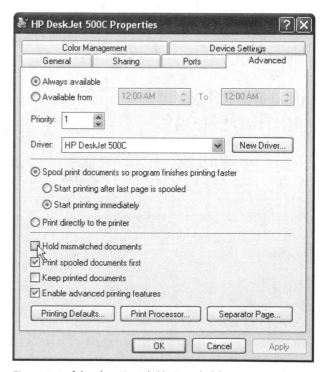

Figure 5-8. Select the option to hold mismatched documents, i.e., documents that require manual feeding of paper.

A *mismatched document* is one in which the codes for the print job going to the printer don't match the printer's configuration. For example, if the target printer doesn't have an envelope tray, an envelope will be flagged as a mismatched document because it requires the user to manually feed an envelope to the printer to complete the print job.

By enabling the option to hold mismatched documents, you configure the spooler to move other documents that are not mismatched ahead of the document that requires special handling. Eventually, when the spooler is empty except for the mismatched document file, that document is sent to the printer. Most printers blink some lights at that point to indicate that a manual feed is required to print the job.

By default, the option to hold mismatched documents is not enabled because in the business world (and in some households) printers rarely have empty spoolers. Users are constantly sending print jobs to the printer. Enabling this option means a user waiting for the mismatched document might have to wait until late in the evening, after everyone has left, for her document to be sent to the printer. Of course, some of us think this is proper punishment for a user who doesn't immediately go to the printer to insert the needed media.

## LIMIT PRINTING CHOICES TO AVOID PRINTING ERRORS

**The Annoyance:** We have a printer with two trays, one containing blank paper and the other containing the letterhead for my business. Users are supposed to select the correct tray in the Printer dialog box, but they forget more often than they remember. Is there a way to force users to select a tray before they print a document?

**The Fix:** Yes and no. You can't force users to remember to take an additional action before sending their document to the printer. In fact, it's probably true that you can't force anybody to remember to do anything. However, you *can* create a scenario in which they (or you)

don't have to rely on their memory by creating a printing environment customized for your needs.

The solution is to have network printers that permit printing from only a single tray. This doesn't mean you have to buy more printers. Instead, it means you take advantage of the fact that printers are virtual devices (see the sidebar "To Windows, Printers Aren't Real" earlier in this chapter). Simply create as many printers as you need, with each printer limited to using a specific tray. Because you print to a virtual printer rather than a physical printer, you can create multiple virtual printers for the same physical printer. This makes it easier to use specific features in the printer.

To create a separate virtual printer for each feature, you must install the same printer multiple times. You can use the same Add Printer Wizard you used to install the original printer. Go through all the steps, selecting the same printer and the same port (usually LPT:1). Windows is perfectly happy to let you connect multiple printers to the same port.

> **Warning . . .**
> During the installation process, Windows 2000 and XP ask if you want to share the printer. *Don't* share the printer at this point—you're going to rename the printer later, which removes the share. Share all the printers after you've completed the configuration process.

The wizard asks if you want to use the same driver you used when you installed the printer the first time. Say yes—why take the time and trouble to install the same files from the Windows CD? The wizard adds the printer to your system with a parenthetical number after the printer model name, such as HPLaserJet (Copy 2). The next duplicate has (Copy3) in its name, and so forth.

Install as many copies of the printer as there are features you want to isolate. For example, if you want to set up a printer for Tray 1 and another printer for Tray 2, install two copies of the printer. If the printer also has a manual feed tray you use frequently (perhaps to print envelopes or labels), create a third instance of the printer.

After you install all the printers, configure each printer for a single setting. Right-click the printer's icon and choose Properties from the shortcut menu. Move to the tab that holds the configuration settings for the printer, which differs depending on the printer—there might be a Settings tab or a Devices tab. Configure the printer to reflect a single set of default options.

For example, to create a printer that accepts only print jobs destined for Tray 1, configure the first virtual printer to use Tray 1 for the right paper size, and then select Not Available for the remaining trays (see Figure 5-9). For the next virtual printer, make Tray 1 unavailable and select the appropriate paper size for Tray 2.

The selections for each tray in the dialog box represent the paper size, not the type of media you insert in the tray. So, although each tray you configure is probably marked "letter" to represent letter-size paper, you can fill it with any media of that size (plain paper, letterhead, or checks).

Rename the printer to reflect its settings. For example, if you put plain paper in Tray 1, name the printer that has only Tray 1 available "Paper." If Tray 2 holds checks, name the printer that offers only Tray 2 "Checks." To rename a printer, right-click its icon and choose Rename from the shortcut menu.

Share each printer using a sharename that reflects the settings (in fact, it's easiest to use the new printer name as the sharename).

If you have a color printer, you can create a virtual monochrome printer and urge users to select the color printer only when absolutely necessary. This means you won't have to replace the color cartridge as frequently, which results in substantial savings.

## FIND THE MONOCHROME OPTION ON INKJET PRINTERS

**The Annoyance:** I want to configure a color printer for black-and-white printing, but I can't for the life of me figure out how to do this. I've looked at every tab on the printer's Properties dialog box, but the option for black–and–white printing doesn't exist anywhere.

**The Fix:** To perform this task you must go on a treasure hunt. To make matters worse, each printer model has its own maze, with entrance holes in different places. It's no wonder you're confused.

I can give you some general directions to get you started. Most of the time, the tabs available when you open the printer's Properties dialog box don't offer the option you're looking for. You probably have to click a button on one of the tabs to open another set of dialog box tabs.

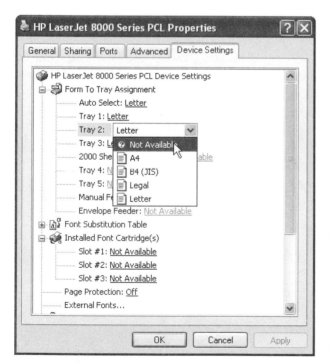

Figure 5-9. Making a tray unavailable means users can't inadvertently pick the wrong tray (and therefore the wrong paper) when they print documents.

For example, on my Lexmark inkjet, I click the Printing Preferences button and choose the Print in Black and White option. That was easy! On my HP DeskJet, I click the Paper/Quality tab and choose the Black & White option (see Figure 5-10).

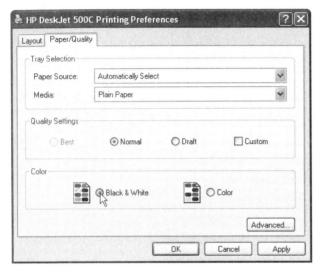

Figure 5-10. Turn one copy of your color printer into a black-and-white printer to save money on color cartridges.

> **t i p**
> Your inkjet printer might use the term *monochrome* instead of black and white.

## PRESERVE COLOR CARTRIDGES

**The Annoyance:** Before we created a network for our two computers, anyone who worked on the computer that had a black-and-white printer had to go to the computer with a color printer if they wanted to print color documents. After we shared the two printers on the network, my costs for color cartridges zoomed. I've tried to convince people to print to the black-and-white printer unless color is absolutely necessary, but my arguments fall on deaf ears. Home networks have hidden costs that are really annoying.

**The Fix:** Isn't it amazing how necessary color becomes when users don't have to copy a document to a floppy disk and walk it over to a computer that has a color printer? Maybe it's a coincidence.

You can save money by cutting down on the amount of color ink print jobs use. Most color printers offer color quality options, such as Best, Normal, Draft, and so on. The differences are the depth of color—the more depth, the more ink you use.

You can create multiple virtual printers for different qualities of color depth so that users can select the quality they need (see "Limit Printing Choices to Avoid Printing Errors"). You'll probably have to remind everyone that very few personal documents or homework assignments really need deep color saturation.

Even better, share only the color printer you configure for Draft quality. You'll be amazed at how few complaints you'll get. Most users glance at the document, see color, and are happy. If your son complains that the color quality isn't good enough for an important document, you can offer to print it for him. Tell him you're an expert in "tweaking" color printers. Of course, when you print the document, you'll just use the printer set for Normal or Best color quality.

Isn't this sneaky? Don't you love it? You'll save money on cartridges, and you'll develop a reputation for being a color printer geek.

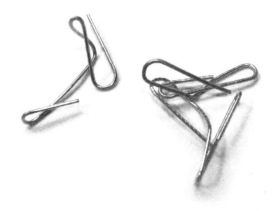

# TROUBLESHOOTING NETWORK PRINTERS

## WINDOWS 9X CAN SHOW A PRINTER AS READY WHEN IT ISN'T

**The Annoyance:** I'm working in a software program on my Windows 98SE computer, and I select a network printer to print a document. Sometimes the Print dialog box says the printer is ready to print, but then I get an error message saying there's a problem with the printer. It almost always turns out that the computer that holds the network printer I selected isn't turned on. How am I supposed to tell whether a printer is available if Windows doesn't even know?

**The Fix:** If you want accurate, up-to-the-minute information about a printer's availability when you're printing from a software application, upgrade to Windows XP. Seriously. Windows XP does a much better job of tracking the network's resources than Windows 98SE.

Windows 98SE, like all versions of Windows prior to 2000, is slow to catch on to what's happening with network printing. When a network printer is unavailable (usually because the computer to which it's attached has been shut down), it can take a long time for Windows 98SE to recognize the problem. The Print dialog box in Figure 5-11 appeared about four minutes after the computer named One was shut down. Of course, selecting OK to print the document produces an error message.

## WINDOWS 9X PRINTER STATUS MESSAGES CAN CONFUSE YOU

**The Annoyance:** While working on my Windows 98SE computer, I needed to use a network printer. The Print dialog box showed the printer's status as "User intervention." What does that mean, and how do I fix it? The status also indicates the number of documents waiting to be printed. If the printer isn't available, how does Windows 98SE know the size of the print job queue?

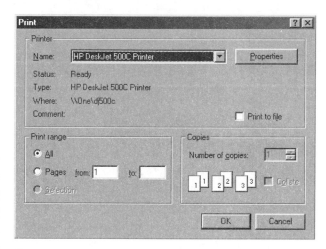

Figure 5-11. Windows 98SE says this printer is ready, but the computer that holds the printer isn't running.

**The Fix:** A status of "User intervention" (see Figure 5-12) means that Windows 98SE has recognized the fact that the printer isn't available, probably because the computer to which the printer is connected isn't running. I guess the programmers who wrote this error message are trying to tell you to intervene by walking to the computer that holds this printer and turning it on, or, if it's on, to check it for problems. Of course, I'm only guessing.

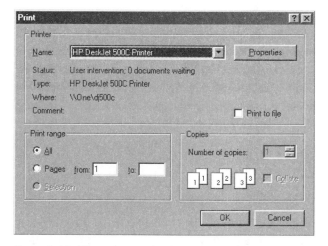

Figure 5-12. What am I supposed to do in response to the request for my intervention?

The number of documents waiting for printing refers to the number of documents stored on the local computer waiting to be sent to this printer. Windows spools print files to the local computer's spooler, and then copies them to the print server's spooler (unless the printer is local, in which case the local computer and the print server are the same machine). (See the sidebar "Understanding the Spooler" earlier in this chapter.)

Incidentally, 10 minutes after the print server was turned on, the same "User intervention" status was displayed on the Print dialog box. I clicked OK to print the document, which printed successfully. When I was ready to print the next document, the printer status was "Ready," so I guess printing to a not-ready-to-print printer is the appropriate intervention when the status doesn't reflect current conditions.

## WINDOWS XP PRINTER STATUS MESSAGE CAN DISAPPEAR

**The Annoyance:** When I open the Print dialog box in the application I'm using on my Windows XP computer, sometimes the word "Ready" isn't displayed on the Status line for the network printer I select. In fact, the line is blank. What does that mean?

**The Fix:** It means Windows XP is unable to contact the printer, so the printer isn't "ready" to accept your print job. Usually this indicates that the computer to which the printer is attached isn't running, but it could mean the printer isn't plugged in, has died, etc.

In addition to missing information about the printer's status, any text available about the printer in the Location and Comment fields is also missing, as you can see in Figure 5-13. That, too, is the result of a connectivity problem. Unlike older versions of Windows, XP contacts remote resources when you select them to make sure they're available. This means you can count on the information being current. Of course, the best thing about the

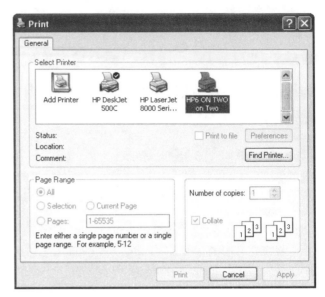

Figure 5-13. The absence of information about a network printer means it's not available.

Print dialog box is that Windows XP has made the Print button inaccessible, which spares you a long wait followed by an error message.

## CHECK THE PRINT SERVER'S STATUS

**The Annoyance:** I tried to print a document to a network printer, but I got an error message telling me the printer wasn't available. The printer is on a different floor, and instead of walking upstairs I'd like to know how I can find out what the problem is, and hopefully fix it, without leaving my computer.

**The Fix:** I'm lazy too, so I understand why you want to stay where you are to identify and fix the problem. Unfortunately, without leaving your computer, you can only find out whether the print server is down. If it is, you have to walk over to it and fix the problem. If the print server is up and running, but there's a problem with the printer, you also must make a personal visit.

To see if the computer that holds the printer is running, just try to access it. The quickest way is to open the Run command from the Start menu and enter two backslashes followed by the computer's name (e.g., \\kitchen).

Another quick way is to open your browser and enter the same thing in the Address Bar.

If the print server is available, a window opens and displays all the shared resources on that computer. At that point, you need to go to the printer and make sure it's working properly. Check the power supply and cabling. If you're still stuck, crack open the printer's manual to see what those blinking lights mean.

If the print server isn't available, an error message says that either the network name or the network path can't be found (depending on your version of Windows and whether you're using the Run command or your browser). You still have to travel because you have to go to that computer to see what's up. Most of the time, the problem is that the computer isn't turned on—so, turn it on. Because you don't have to wait for the logon screen, you can go back to your computer and print your document (see the next annoyance for an explanation).

## PRINT SERVER LOGON STATUS DOESN'T MATTER

**The Annoyance:** The computer that holds our printer is rarely used. We remember to turn it on, but sometimes the person who turns it on doesn't wait to log on to the workgroup. Can we automate the logon so that we can print?

**The Fix:** It doesn't matter whether anyone logs on to the computer because the printer is available as long as the computer is on and Windows is running. This is an intelligent way to design network printing. Incidentally, you can automate logons, but it's a security risk, so I don't advise it. (For information about automatic logons, see Chapter 7.)

## WHAT HAPPENED TO MY DEFAULT PRINTER?

**The Annoyance:** The printer attached to my computer is configured as my default printer. I spend most of my time at the computer working in Microsoft Word. I don't use the Print dialog box to print; instead, I just click the Print icon on the toolbar. When I need to print a color document, I use the Print dialog box to select a network printer (my printer is a black-and-white laser). After that, when I click the Print icon on the toolbar, the print job goes to the network printer. Obviously, "default" doesn't mean anything to this software, which is really annoying.

**The Fix:** Microsoft Word, like a number of other software applications, automatically prints to the currently selected printer. When you first launch the software, it uses the default printer as the currently selected printer. When you select a different printer, it becomes the currently selected printer. In other words, the software uses the default printer to prevent you from having to open the Print dialog box and select a printer the first time you print a document. To make your local printer the default printer again, open the Print dialog box and select it. After that, Word will print to your local printer when you use the Print icon on the toolbar.

> **t i p**
>
> Software that continues to use the currently selected printer behaves that way only for the current session. When you close the software and reopen it, the default printer becomes the currently selected printer again.

# NOTEPAD CAN'T CHANGE PRINTERS

**The Annoyance:** I print a lot of text files, and it's easy and fast to open the files from Windows Explorer. However, if my default printer isn't available or has checks loaded in its tray, I can't change printers. Choosing File → Print in Notepad doesn't open a Print dialog box, so I can't select another printer. This means I have to open my word processor, open the text file, and then open the Print dialog box to choose a network printer, which is really annoying.

**The Fix:** Change the default printer, which forces Notepad to change printers. Open the Printers folder (Printers and Faxes folder in Windows XP), right-click the icon for the printer you want Notepad to use, and choose "Set as default printer." Now you can use Notepad. Don't forget to change the default printer back when your usual printer is available again. Or, find another text editor to use instead of Notepad—one that opens a Print dialog box so that you can select a printer.

# MOVE PRINT JOBS TO ANOTHER PRINTER

**The Annoyance:** Our four-computer network has two printers, both of which are the same model. Recently, right after four large print jobs were sent to one of the printers, that printer broke. All the print jobs had to be sent to the other printer, which meant users had to open the software and the documents again, and select a different printer. Because both printers are the same model, it's really annoying that there isn't a Move command to move the print jobs to the working printer.

**The Fix:** There might not be a Move command available in the Printers folder, but you *can* move the print jobs using a nifty feature called *printer redirection*. This allows you to move the print jobs waiting to print on one printer to another printer (as long as the other printer uses the same print driver). The new printer can be on the same print server or on another print server.

Open the Printers folder (Printers and Faxes folder in Windows XP) and double-click the icon of the printer that isn't working. The list of print jobs waiting to go to the printer displays in the Printer window. The first print job is either marked as Printing or has an error message in the Status column. That print job can't be moved because it's in progress, but all the other print jobs can.

Choose Printer → Properties from the Menu bar to open the broken printer's Properties dialog box. Click the Ports tab and use one of the following actions to move the queue to another printer:

- Move the print jobs to another printer on the same print server by selecting the port to which the working printer is connected, and then click OK.

- Move the print jobs to a printer on another print server by choosing Add Port → Local Port → New Port. Then enter the UNC for the remote printer as the new port, using the format *\\PrintServer\PrinterShareName*.

Now cancel the document currently printing, and notify the person who owns the document to resend the print job. Notify everybody else that their print jobs will be coming out of the new printer.

# TOO MANY USERS CONNECTED TO THE PRINT SERVER

**The Annoyance:** My network has six computers that share one printer. The printer is installed on a computer running Windows XP Home Edition. Frequently, users who try to print receive an error message that says no more connections can be made to the print server. Sometimes, users get the same message if they try to access a file from the print server.

**The Fix:** Microsoft designed Windows to limit the number of connections any computer can accept from other computers on the network:

- For Windows XP Home Edition, the limit is five.
- For Windows XP Professional, 2000 Professional, 9X, and Me, the limit is 10.
- For Server versions of Windows 2000 and 2003, the number of licenses you purchase determines the limit.

A connection exists whenever a computer connects to a resource on another computer on the network. The resource can be a folder, file, or printer. Connections are computer-based, not resource-based. This means a computer accessing both files and printers on a remote computer uses only one connection.

There isn't any workaround, but the good news is that the limit refers to simultaneous connections, not the total number of computers on your network. Any user who receives an "over the limit" message can wait and try again, hoping that another user has disconnected.

## NEW CONNECTION NOT AVAILABLE WHEN ONE USER STOPS PRINTING

**The Annoyance:** We have six computers on our network, and we understand the five-user limit for the Windows XP Home Edition print server. However, when the limit is reached and one user stops printing, the printer doesn't become available for another user. How do I force Windows to notice that only four users are connected to the print server?

**The Fix:** Windows doesn't keep an eye on what you're doing—it only notes whether the remote computer is actively using a connection it made. If there isn't any activity, the connection is deemed to be idle. When a connection is idle for 15 minutes, the session is disconnected. Therefore, the sixth user needs to wait 15 minutes to access the printer.

You can reduce the amount of idle time required for disconnection, but every time I've done this, the system experienced negative side effects. A reduced idle time setting makes it difficult for users to work steadily, and results in chaos and angry users. You might consider buying another printer.

> The command for reducing the amount of idle time required for disconnection is `net config server /autodisconnect: X`. Substitute the new time, in minutes, for `X`.

# USING PRINT FILES

## PRINT FILE PRINTS GARBAGE

**The Annoyance:** I needed to print a report from our accounting software application at work. The printer was down, and I didn't want to wait for the repairs to be completed, so I chose the Print to File option on the Print dialog box. I emailed the print file to my home email address. When I got home, I sent the file to my printer using the correct copy command. The printer spewed out pages and pages of garbage characters, along with a small amount of text from the report. Why doesn't this work properly?

**The Fix:** Your work printer is a different model than the one you have at home. Print files don't work unless you send them to the same printer model you selected when you opened the Print dialog box. The codes in the print file are specific to, and proprietary for, the printer you selected when you created the file.

To create a print file that you can successfully print at home, install your home printer on your computer at work. Make it a local printer and assign LPT1 as the port. Then, select that printer when you print the document to a file. Don't worry, Windows doesn't peek through the monitor and say, "Hey, I don't see an inkjet printer, so I'm not going to install this driver." If a local printer already exists on your work computer, it's OK to install two printers to LPT1; Windows won't blink an eye. At home, copy the *.PRN* file to LPT1 with the `/b` parameter (see the sidebar "Understanding Print Files").

PRN files are not the best way to transfer information. They're enormous (all those codes!) and they're printer-specific. Sometimes, however, they seem to be the only choice you have if the software you used to produce the document isn't installed on the computer from which you want to print the document.

# PRINT FILES THAT WORK EVERYWHERE

**The Annoyance:** I used some software at a friend's house to analyze my financial position. The software (which I don't own and don't want to purchase) displayed a very interesting report that I wanted to keep so

that I could refer to it in the future. I couldn't print it because my friend's printer was broken. Is there a solution to this dilemma?

**The Fix:** There's a nifty solution, and it's a great solution for the previous annoyance about print files, too. Use a plain-text print file, so you can use it on any printer and any computer. You'll lose any formatting in the document, but you'll retain the information. Of course, because print files are matched to specific printers, this means you have to install a printer that prints plain text.

Guess what? Windows has a plain-text printer. To install it, open the Printers folder and start the Add Printer Wizard. Step through the wizard, using the following guidelines (the order in which the wizard windows appear might be different, depending on your version of Windows):

1. Specify a local printer.

2. *Uncheck* the "Automatically detect and install my Plug and Play printer" box (because there isn't a text printer plugged into any of the ports).

3. Select FILE: (Print to File) as the port.

4. In the Manufacturer list, select Generic.

5. In the Printers list, select Generic/Text Only.

6. Use the default printer name (Generic/Text Only).

7. Don't make this printer the default printer.

8. Don't share the printer.

9. Don't print a test page.

To print a document, select the Generic/Text Only printer in the Print dialog box. You don't have to check the Print to File box because the printer is already configured to print to a file. Just click the Print button (or the OK button, depending on your version of Windows).

The Print to File dialog box opens, allowing you to enter a filename. The dialog box differs among different versions of Windows. However, all versions of Windows save the file either to your My Documents folder or to the subfolder you're currently working in.

In Windows XP, the Print to File dialog box merely asks for the filename (see Figure 5-14). I usually add an extension, so that when I copy it to my own computer I can double-click the file in Windows Explorer or My Computer and have it open automatically in the software of my choice. For example, if I know I want to use Notepad to view and print the file, I add the extension *.txt* to the filename. If I'm planning to open the file in Microsoft Word, I add the extension *.doc* to the filename.

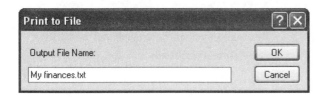

Figure 5-14. Name the text print file to suit your needs.

In earlier versions of Windows, the Print to File dialog box assumes this is a standard print file and automatically enters the file extension *.prn*. Enter a filename and replace *.prn* with a different extension, or delete the *.prn* extension and use a filename without an extension.

You can load this file into any word processor or WordPad (and format it, if you like), or into Notepad (if you don't mind keeping it unformatted). You can also copy it directly to the printer from the command line using the following command: copy *filename* lpt1. You don't need the /b parameter for the copy command because this isn't a binary file (it has no printer codes).

It's a good idea to install the generic text printer on every computer on your network. It's surprising how often it comes in handy.

# NETWORK PRINTING AND MS-DOS

## PRINT TO A NETWORK PRINTER FROM MS-DOS SOFTWARE

**The Annoyance:** I have a favorite MS-DOS program that I can't live without. I install it on every computer I buy. If the program is running on a computer with a printer attached to LPT1, there's no problem. If the computer relies on a network printer, I can't print.

**The Fix:** Yes you can, and I do this all the time. I, too, have a favorite MS-DOS program that I can't live without. It's a small shareware database in which I've been storing information since 1984. It has my address book, family birthday and anniversary dates, credit card information, PINs and passwords, and other vitally important information. The computer I use most often doesn't have a printer, so network printers are my only resource. To print from MS-DOS, you must redirect printing using an MS-DOS command. To open a command window in Windows XP, select Start → All Programs → Accessories → Command Prompt. (The menu names and sequence vary depending on your version of Windows.)

Enter the following command:

```
net use lpt1 \\PrintServerName\PrinterShareName
```

Notice the space between the port and the UNC. The system returns the following message: "The command completed successfully."

Specifying LPT1 works if the MS-DOS software is configured to use LPT1. If the software is configured for LPT2, change the command accordingly. Now you can use the print features in the MS-DOS software as if a printer were connected to the port you specified. The software never knows it's printing to a network printer.

The printer is redirected until you shut down the computer. If you don't want to enter the command every time you start the computer, you can make the redirection permanent. Add the parameter /persistent:yes to the command. For example, to use a printer with the sharename HP6P connected to a computer named Larry, enter net use lpt1 \\larry\HP6P /persistent: yes. Notice the space between the UNC and the parameter.

## REDIRECT A NETWORK PRINTER WITH SPACES IN THE NAME

**The Annoyance:** I tried to redirect a network printer to my local printer port, but when I entered the command, the system displayed the Help file for the net use command. I'm sure I entered the command correctly, so why didn't this work?

**The Fix:** I suspect either the computer name or the printer sharename has a space. In that case, you must enclose everything from the double-backslash (\\) to the end of the command in quotation marks. For example, you'll need to type net use "\\sam\deskjet one" instead of \\sam\deskjet one.

### UNDERSTANDING PERSISTENT CONNECTIONS

If you don't use the persistent parameter, MS-DOS automatically assigns connections as persistent or temporary using whichever option you used to make the last connection. In other words, MS-DOS remembers the last parameter you used and uses it as the default until you change it. So, if you use the persistent: yes parameter when you're working at the command line, the next time you redirect a connection you don't have to add the parameter because Yes is now the default.

A mapped drive is also a redirected connection—it's a network share that is assigned a local device name and drive letter. When you map a drive while working in My Network Places or Network Neighborhood, you can select the option to reconnect when Windows restarts. That's a persistent connection, and choosing that option sets the current state for persistent connections as Yes. This applies whether you use the command line or Windows interface to redirect a shared resource to your computer. (See Chapter 4 for information about mapping drives.)

To see whether the current state of a connection is persistent or temporary, enter net use at a command prompt. The first line of the display gives you the information you need:

- ☒ **"New connections will be remembered"** means the current state is persistent.
- ☒ **"New connections will not be remembered"** means the current state is temporary.

## FIND A REDIRECTED PRINTER

**The Annoyance:** I redirected a network printer to LPT1 on my computer. However, when I open the Printers folder, the network printer isn't configured for LPT1. Instead, the port is still listed as the remote computer.

How can I tell whether the redirected printer is active and will work when I need it?

**The Fix:** Redirecting the network printer to the local port has no effect on printing in Windows. To Windows, the network printer still looks like a network printer. You redirected the printer through an MS-DOS connection. To see whether the redirected printer exists, open a command prompt and enter the command `net use`. The system displays your current connections (see Figure 5-15).

Figure 5-15. Entering the net use command lets you see all your local connections, including redirected printers and mapped drives.

## PERSISTENT CONNECTIONS ARE USER SETTINGS

**The Annoyance:** I've set up persistent connections on every computer in the network, both for printers and for mapped drives. Sometimes the connections disappear when a computer is turned on, and sometimes they're there.

**The Fix:** Well, it's tempting to say that Windows boots in a whimsical way, deciding arbitrarily whether it will cooperate with your configuration efforts. But it's not so, and there's a logical explanation for this annoying behavior you're seeing. Persistent connections are user-based configuration settings. I'll bet your household, like most households, has more users than computers, so users have to share computers.

The persistent connections you established are linked to the person who was logged on to the computer when you set up the connections. When another user logs on, those connections aren't reestablished. You must reconfigure them for this user, and for each user of every computer.

## PRINT TEXT FROM THE COMMAND WINDOW

**The Annoyance:** I've learned to appreciate the power of the command line, and I'm trying to learn as much as I can. I use the help text available in the command window, but I can't memorize each command's help. Isn't there a way to print the text?

**The Fix:** You can print the help text (or any responsive text in a command window) by redirecting it to a printer port, such as LPT1. If a printer is attached to LPT1, the print job is sent there. If LPT1 is a redirected resource pointing to a network printer, the print job is sent to the network printer.

Responsive text is anything that appears after you enter a command. For example, if you enter `net use`, the system responds with a list of all your connections, and if you enter `ipconfig`, the system responds with information about your TCP/IP settings. If you want to preserve this information, the redirection feature lets you capture it.

To redirect the text to a printer, enter the following at the command line: `command /? > lpt1`. Use the actual command instead of the word "command"—for example, `print /? > lpt1`.

> You can redirect the responsive text in a command window to a file in the same manner by substituting a filename for LPT1. Open the file in a word processor if you want to work on it, or save it in your My Documents folder.

# REDIRECTING HELP FILES TO THE PRINTER FAILS

**The Annoyance:** I tried to redirect the help files for Net Use to my printer, but it didn't work.

**The Fix:** Redirecting the output of help files doesn't work for commands that are two-part tools. Net Use is part of the Net command system, which includes other commands such as Net Time, Net Accounts, and many more. A number of other two-part commands also exist. The only way to print their help files is to access the Windows Help system.

# PRINT THE CONTENTS OF A DRIVE OR FOLDER

**The Annoyance:** I want a list of all the folders on my C drive, but there's no command named Print Contents on Windows Explorer or My Computer. I'd also like to print the names of all the files in specific folders, but I can't do that either.

**The Fix:** This missing ingredient in Windows is really annoying. Luckily, the command line provides a fix. MS-DOS has a command named `DIR`, and you can redirect its output to a printer or to a file. Open a command window and navigate to the drive or folder whose contents you want to record. Then enter either of the following commands:

- `dir > lpt1` to print the list.
- `dir > `*filename* to send the list to a file that you can open in a word processor (substitute a real filename for the word "filename").

## Shared Internet
# ANNOYANCES

In most homes with an Internet connection linked to a single computer, the walls reverberate with amazingly similar cries. See if these sound familiar: "Mom, tell Billy to get out of the chat rooms and let me have the computer for my homework research," or "I have to check my email for an important message, so disconnect right now." Families try to make schedules for Internet access, but they rarely work, and the yelling continues.

Sharing an Internet connection is a way to avoid squabbles, expensive family therapy, frayed nerves, and a host of unsettling household disturbances. In this chapter I'll go over some of the setup annoyances you might face, especially as you add computers and connection types to your network. I'll also cover the configuration annoyances you encounter as you try to match your Internet Service Provider's settings with your network's settings.

# ISP RULES: CUTTING THROUGH THE CONFUSION

## LEARN WHETHER MULTIPLE ACCESS IS PERMITTED

**The Annoyance:** I can't find anything on my ISP's web site that says I can have multiple users signed in at the same time. They don't address the issue at all.

**The Fix:** Unless you have AOL, you can almost certainly take it for granted that you can share your Internet connection. All of the ISPs I'm familiar with (except, as I've said, AOL) permit multiple users to have simultaneous access. (See the AOL annoyances later in this chapter.)

---

### JUST CALL AND ASK!

Many people are reluctant to call their ISP support lines to inquire about multiple access permissions. They feel they're alerting the ISP to the fact that they plan to share their Internet connection, and if the ISP doesn't permit multiple simultaneous access, or charges extra fees, their account will be "watched." It doesn't work that way. The technology at the ISP either blocks access if more than one person logs in to an account, or it doesn't. No human being can "set" or "block" multiple access on a particular account.

---

## MAILBOXES ARE SINGLE-USER ACCESS POINTS

**The Annoyance:** Sometimes I get an error message about the mailbox being in use when I try to collect my email. This happens only if somebody else on our network is on the Internet at the same time. I can use my browser, but I can't get my mail.

**The Fix:** You need to get your own mailbox because obviously you and the other person online are using the same mailbox. The only "multiple-user block" ISPs enforce is on a particular mailbox. If someone is getting email from the mailbox assigned to *Amy@MyISP.com*, nobody else can be in that mailbox at the same time.

---

**t i p**

Some people set up family mailboxes so everyone gets email at one address, such as *Myfamily@MyISP.com*. Family mailboxes are not a good idea—they're inefficient (distributing the mail among computers is almost impossible, so you have to print messages and hand-deliver them) and they eliminate any chance of privacy. And once you move to a network and a shared Internet connection, family mailboxes are a pain! Your ISP should have a mailbox management web page you can use to set up each user's individual mailbox.

---

## ADDING MAILBOXES

**The Annoyance:** Our ISP permits three mailboxes with our account, but we have four family users who want mailboxes. I can't figure out how to let two people share a mailbox, surf the Internet, and get their mail all at the same time.

**The Fix:** It can't be done, so give it up. Go to your ISP's web site and check the fee schedule for an additional mailbox. I bet you'll find it costs less than you thought.

## CHANGING YOUR ISP MEANS CHANGING YOUR EMAIL ADDRESS

**The Annoyance:** We're changing our ISP so that we can share our Internet connection. Of course, the email address for our old ISP won't work anymore. How do we let people know our new address in an efficient way, so we still get our email?

**The Fix:** If you don't have your own web site (which gives you an email address that never changes, no matter who your ISP is), you're going to have to change your email address when you change your ISP. This is a pain! Some people have done this numerous times, and it never gets easier. However, it must be done.

The big problem is that once your old ISP is canceled and your mailbox is closed, anyone sending email to that mailbox receives a "bounce" message that says the mailbox doesn't exist or the recipient doesn't exist. Bounced mail provides no information about how to find you now that you've moved. Here are some guidelines to help you make this less confusing for your correspondents:

- Sign up with your new ISP and create all the mailboxes you need before you cancel your old ISP.

- Delay canceling your old ISP for at least a month—two months is better. You'll be spending money on two ISP services for that period, but consider that money well spent in pursuit of an easy transition and no lost email.

- Send a message notifying every email correspondent of your new email address.

> **Warning. . .**
> Some ISPs limit the number of recipients in a single message as a way to make sure nobody uses it for spam. You might have to email several small groups of recipients.

- Use the Signature feature in your email software to create a message saying that the recipient should change his records to reflect your new email address. Add the signature to every message you send.

- See if your current (old) ISP will forward email that arrives in your previous mailbox. Some ISPs are generous enough to provide this service.

> **t i p**
> When you send your new email address to your email correspondents, always use the new email address for those messages. Nothing is more annoying than getting email from *MyName@AOL.com* telling you that his new email address is *MyName@MYNewISP.com*. It's confusing. Also, many email software applications have a feature that automatically creates an address book entry for the sender's email address. You want that email address to be your new one, not your old one.

called "caching information" to fill in the login name and password automatically. When another user attempts to use the connection, the "cache" is empty, so the information has to be entered manually. That new information is then stored in the user's profile, so in the future dialing out becomes an automated process for each person.

# DIAL-UP CONNECTION-SHARING ANNOYANCES

## DIAL-UP CONNECTION DOESN'T REMEMBER LOGIN INFORMATION

**The Annoyance:** Dialing out to my ISP has been very easy. I set up the connection on my Windows Me computer, and now everything happens automatically—even my password is filled in for me. However, I set up a second user on the same computer, and when she launched the dial-up connection, she had to fill in the login name and the password manually.

**The Fix:** In all Windows versions except XP, the dial-up settings are saved in the user profile of the person who configured the connection. (See "Windows XP Dial-Up Connections Are for All Users".) Windows uses a feature

## DIAL-UP CONNECTION DOESN'T OPEN AUTOMATICALLY

**The Annoyance:** I work at the Windows XP computer that has the modem for our shared connection. Every time a user wants to dial out, I have to open the connection and connect to the ISP. If I'm not at the computer, users have to come to the computer and make the connection. This is a really annoying way to share an Internet connection.

**The Fix:** This is a *maddening* way to share an Internet connection, so you should fix it. You can configure the connection to open and dial out automatically whenever any user wants to connect to the Internet. Right-click the icon for your dial-up connection and choose

Computer professionals have developed a lot of jargon for the components involved when a network shares an Internet connection via a telephone modem. Take a minute to go over some of this jargon before you continue reading this chapter.

☒ *ICS* stands for Internet Connection Sharing. This is a shared connection model in which one computer has a modem (either telephone, DSL, or cable) and shares that modem with the other computers on the network. (The other connection model is a router, in which each computer independently connects to the Internet. Routers are available only with DSL and cable modems.)

☒ *ISP* stands for Internet Service Provider, which is the company that provides your Internet access. When you dial out to the Internet, you're really dialing into a computer maintained by that company. The computer has modems that answer your modem's call.

☒ The software configuration for connecting to your ISP is known as your *connection*. When you set up a connection, Windows creates an icon. In Windows 98SE, the icon is in the Dial-Up Networking folder in your My Computer folder. In later versions of Windows, the icon is in the Control Panel.

☒ *Login data* for a connection is the login name and password your ISP assigned you to access its servers. This is unrelated to the login data required to log on to your computer.

☒ *Host* is the computer that holds the modem.

☒ *Client* is a computer that accesses the modem over the network.

---

Properties. Click the Advanced tab and check the "Establish a dial-up connection whenever a computer on my network attempts to access the Internet" box (see Figure 6-1). Hereafter, the connection will open automatically and connect to your ISP whenever a network user opens Internet-based software (such as a browser, an IM window, or an email application).

# WINDOWS XP FIREWALL AND DIAL-UP CONNECTIONS

**The Annoyance:** My Windows XP computer has the modem for our shared Internet connection. I have two icons for connections in the Control Panel: one for my ISP and one for our home network. I'm confused about using the built-in firewall. Do I need to enable it on both connections?

**The Fix:** It's confusing until you get a good mental picture of what the firewall does and where it does it. A firewall is a barrier that protects your computer from

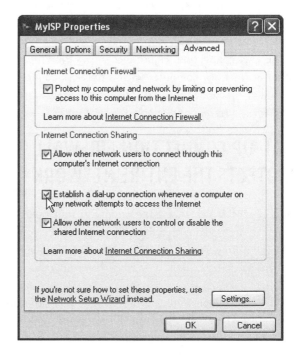

Figure 6-1. Automate the dial-up process for all network users.

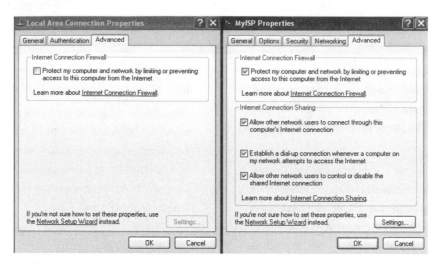

Figure 6-2. Protect the modem (the point of entry to the Internet) with a firewall, and turn off the firewall on the network connection.

unauthorized access from the Internet. This means the firewall has to be erected around the point of entry between your computer and the Internet. In your case, the point of entry is your dial-up connection (or modem), so you need only enable the firewall on that connection.

If you have a network, the Windows XP firewall prevents network communications (unless you're running Windows XP Service Pack 2), so you must disable the firewall on the LAN connection. Figure 6-2 shows the Properties dialog boxes for a computer with a network connection and a dial-up connection. Notice that the firewall is disabled for the former and enabled for the latter.

## DIAL-UP CONNECTION FIREWALL PROTECTS THE ENTIRE NETWORK

**The Annoyance:** The computer that holds the modem is protected with a firewall. I was told I also have to install a firewall on every computer on the network. Is this true?

**The Fix:** Nope, you've protected the point of entry between your network and the Internet and you don't need to bother with firewalls on the other network nodes.

A firewall blocks traffic coming from the Internet, and the modem is the only device connected directly to the Internet. Because the firewall protects the gateway to the Internet, all the computers behind the firewall are protected.

### Windows XP SP2 Firewall Is Better for Networks

If you're running Windows XP Service Pack 2, you can configure the firewall. One important configuration option is the ability to let network traffic through the firewall. Before SP2, the built-in firewall stopped network traffic, and it couldn't be used in a network environment. Instead, you had to install a software firewall, such as Zone Labs' ZoneAlarm or Symantec's Norton Personal Firewall.

# PUT A DIAL-UP CONNECTION ICON ON THE TASK BAR

**The Annoyance:** I use the computer that has the modem, which automatically dials out to make a connection whenever a network user opens a browser or email program. How can I configure the dial-up connection to put an icon on my task bar, so I know when a user connects to the Internet?

**The Fix:** The steps required to put a dial-up connection icon on the task bar vary, depending on the version of Windows your computer is running:

- In Windows XP and 2000, right-click the icon for your dial-up connection. Click the General tab and check the "Show icon in notification area when connected" box.

- In Windows 98SE and Me, open the Dial-Up Networking folder in My Computer. Select Connections → Settings, click the General tab, and check the "Show an icon on taskbar after connected" box.

# CLOSE THE CONNECTION FROM CLIENT COMPUTERS

**The Annoyance:** We have a network of two Windows XP computers. When I use the computer that has the modem, I'm asked if I want to disconnect after I close the Internet (browser or email) software. When I use the other computer on the network, the connection opens automatically and dials out as soon as I open Internet-based software. When I close the software, I'm never asked if I want to disconnect. Instead, I have to yell "you can close it down" to the person working at the other Windows XP computer, which is annoying.

**The Fix:** You can configure the Windows XP connection to communicate with client computers and close the connection after you close the Internet-based software. On the host computer, right-click the connection's icon in the Control Panel and choose Properties. In the Properties

dialog box, click the Advanced tab and check the "Allow other network users to control or disable the shared Internet connection" box (see Figure 6-3).

Figure 6-3. Let client computers disconnect the modem.

However, the client computer won't prompt the user to close the connection in the same way as the host computer. Instead, this configuration option merely empowers the user to disconnect the connection in either of the following ways:

- Right-click the icon for the connection in the Control Panel and choose Disconnect.

- Right-click the icon on the task bar (if one exists) and choose Disconnect.

To enable Windows 98SE and Me ICS client computers to control the connection in this manner, you must use the Windows XP Network Setup Wizard floppy disk to configure these computers for ICS. (During the configuration of the connection in Windows XP, you're offered the opportunity to create a disk for client computers instead of performing the setup manually.)

# CONNECTION TERMINATES UNEXPECTEDLY

**The Annoyance:** Sometimes our modem connection shuts itself off. Nobody on the network claims responsibility; in fact, all users deny doing anything to disconnect.

**The Fix:** Your connection didn't shut itself off; your ISP terminated it. Most ISPs have an "idle time" counter that tracks the time that the connection is not actively used—nobody is collecting email, and nobody is using a browser to travel to web sites. After a certain amount of idle time, the modem on the ISP's server automatically hangs up. This makes the modem line available for other customers.

## TERMINATE AN IDLE CONNECTION

**The Annoyance:** Our family uses my Windows XP computer as the ICS host. I don't spend a lot of time on the computer, but I keep it on so that other people on the network can get to the Internet. The connection is configured to autodial whenever a network user opens a browser or email software. However, nobody bothers to disconnect and we get charged for extra hours.

**The Fix:** If your ISP isn't automatically disconnecting you after a certain period of idle time, you can perform that function locally. The configuration settings are

in your Windows XP Internet Options dialog box, which you can reach in either of the following ways:

- Double-click the Internet Options applet in the Control Panel.
- If you use Internet Explorer, select Tools → Internet Options from the menu bar.

In the Internet Options dialog box, click the Connections tab. Your dial-up connection should be listed, along with the settings you configured for dialing the connection (see Figure 6-4).

Figure 6-4. Your dial-up connection and its settings are displayed in the Internet Options dialog box.

Click the Settings button to open the Settings dialog box for the connection, and then click the Advanced button. Check the "Disconnect if idle for X minutes" box, and specify the number of minutes you want to allow before automatically disconnecting (see Figure 6-5).

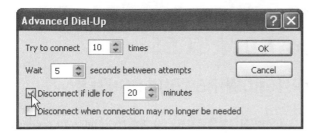

Figure 6-5. Set your own specification for disconnecting when nobody's using the Internet.

The Advanced Dial-Up dialog box also offers a "Disconnect when connection may no longer be needed" box. This means that when all Internet-based windows are closed (browsers, IM, chat windows, email software, etc.), the connection automatically disconnects. If you select this option, some user will probably open an Internet-based window as soon as you disconnect and the modem will dial out again.

# NETWORK TCP/IP SETTINGS CHANGED AFTER ENABLING ICS

**The Annoyance:** After I set up ICS on my computer (which has the modem), I noticed the TCP/IP configuration on my Local Area Connection changed. I originally configured it to obtain an IP address automatically, but now it has a static IP address.

**The Fix:** The ICS host becomes the DHCP (Dynamic Host Configuration Protocol) server, which means it provides IP addresses to the client computers. DHCP servers must have fixed IP addresses. When you shared your dial-up connection, ICS automatically provided a fixed IP address to the network adapter that connects the computer to the network. That IP address is 192.168.0.1, and the subnet mask is 255.255.255.0. The other computers on the network must be set to obtain an IP address automatically, and it's the host computer that automatically provides those IP addresses. (See Chapter 2 for more information about DHCP.)

In fact, ICS makes another change to your computer. Because your computer is now a DHCP server, it must maintain a file that maps the names of the computers on your network with the IP addresses assigned to those computers. This file is called a *hosts file*, and it's stored in the *C:\Windows\System32\Drivers\Etc* folder. Don't mess with it.

---

### STARTUP ORDER MATTERS WITH ICS

When you use ICS, you assign the role of DHCP server to the host computer. When that computer boots, it has an IP address because the network adapter is configured for the static IP address 192.168.0.1. However, when the other computers on the network boot, they have to look for a DHCP server because their TCP/IP configuration setting is set to "Obtain an IP address automatically."

When you start your computers, make sure the ICS host (the DHCP server) boots first. Once you see that the computer has begun booting the Windows operating system, turn on the other computers. This way, the host computer is available to fulfill requests from the client computers for IP addresses. The host computer only needs to have Windows up and running to fulfill these requests; it doesn't matter whether you log on. The client computers look for the DHCP server early in the Windows startup process, before you see a user logon dialog box.

If a client computer can't find a DHCP server, eventually it assigns itself a private IP address, but this lengthens the startup and user logon process. The private IP address allows network communications, but won't let the computer access the Internet. (See Chapter 2 for information about private IP addresses.)

The client computer continues to search for a DHCP server. When it finds one, it replaces the private IP address with the IP address assigned by the DHCP server. The periodic search for a DHCP server slows the computer's response time, so any work you're doing on the computer moves at a slower-than-normal pace.

---

# SHARED BROADBAND ANNOYANCES

## OUTGROWING YOUR ROUTER?

**The Annoyance:** Our Ethernet network shares a DSL connection with a router. The router has four ports, but now we're adding a fifth computer to the network. Do we have to buy another router?

**The Fix:** When it comes to routers, it's one to a customer—one router plugged into one DSL modem. Your solution lies in a hub or a switch, which connects computers together. The hub or switch, having collected the connections of multiple computers, can in turn be connected to the router. To connect the hub/switch to the router, use one of the ports you're currently using for a computer. Plug the computer you're removing from the router into the hub/switch. In fact, you could connect all the computers to the hub/switch. (See Chapter 1 to learn the differences between hubs and switches.)

## WIRELESS ROUTER IN A WIRED NETWORK?

**The Annoyance:** My husband won a door prize—a wireless router. We have a wired network (two computers and a hub), and we share a telephone modem. It's annoying to think we have this free device that would let us switch to a cable modem for Internet access, and we can't use it unless we buy the equipment to change our network to wireless.

**The Fix:** Hold it! You don't have to change a thing. Wow, a freebie for the most expensive device on the network. Good job! You can use a wireless router without moving your network topology to wireless communication because all routers, wireless or wired, have Ethernet ports.

Take a peek at the back of the router. You should see one port labeled WAN, and that's the port you use to connect to the cable modem (WAN stands for wide area network, and it's a reference to the Internet). Then look for one or more ports labeled LAN. Those are the ports you use to connect your computers to the router (LAN stands for local area network).

If you find one LAN port, run Ethernet cable between that port and your existing hub. Read the documentation that came with the hub and the router to see which port on the hub you should use for the connection (usually, it's the hub's Uplink port).

If you find two LAN ports, plug your two computers into those ports and sell the hub (or save it for the day when you expand your network with more computers).

## CABLE MODEM SPEED VARIATIONS

**The Annoyance:** We have cable access and we've noticed that during the early evening, when the whole family is usually on the network, our transmission speed is markedly slower. A friend told me that it's because the network is crowded with users sharing bandwidth. It's annoying that four people accessing the Internet could cause this slowdown. It's also annoying to spend this much money each month to get speeds that don't seem much faster than our previous telephone modem provided.

**The Fix:** Your friend is correct, but he is rather imprecise. The network referred to is the cable access provider's network, not your home network. Cable access works more or less like your network, with a number of computers attached to a single network. The network "hub" (I'm using the term metaphorically) is at your cable company's Cable Modem Termination System (CMTS), the jargon for which is the *head end*. The head end has a certain amount of bandwidth, which is divided among the current users.

Most cable companies have plenty of bandwidth, and although you might notice a slower speed when the kids are out of school and the parents are home from work all over the neighborhood, it should never be as slow as your telephone modem. If it is, call tech support.

To test your broadband speed, check out CNET's Bandwidth Meter at *http://reviews.cnet.com/Bandwidth_meter/7004-7254_7-0.html.*

## CABLE ACCESS UPLOAD AND DOWNLOAD SPEED DIFFERENCES

**The Annoyance:** My cable company provides high-speed download capacity, but the upload speed is a fraction of the download speed. For this monthly fee, why don't I get equal speed?

**The Fix:** The upload speed is always much slower than the download speed for several reasons. The slower upload speed lets the cable company save some bandwidth, which keeps the system robust when lots of users are online. Also, this is a way for cable companies to discourage users from running big, busy servers (such as a business would run) for the price of residential service. In truth, you don't really need a lot of upload speed unless you're running an Internet site from your home, or you use your computer for videoconferences.

Incidentally, when data is sent at a slower speed, data loss is usually less, and the cable system can manage any problem with signal quality. When data loss occurs at high speed, many data packets have to be sent again, which effectively reduces the speed of the data transfer. As a result, your download speed isn't necessarily what it's advertised to be, but the upload speed is usually right on target.

Some cable companies now offer "business packages" in which the upload speed is slightly higher than the normal residential upload speed. These packages are not designed to let you run business web servers, but they can be useful for workers who telecommute and upload a significant amount of data. If upload speeds are important to you, switch to DSL.

The technology behind the uncapping function exists only for cable Internet access; DSL systems operate on a totally different technology that can't be tampered with.

## UNCAP CABLE MODEM SPEED

**The Annoyance:** I heard about a way to pay for one speed, and then change the way the cable modem operates to get the real maximum-possible speed. It's called uncapping, and it's annoying that it's apparently a secret known only to computer engineers.

**The Fix:** Information on uncapping is available all over the Internet, and unfortunately, many of the web sites that describe it (or offer software to uncap your cable modem) don't explain the important features:

- It's illegal, and cable companies have prosecuted people who try uncapping.
- It's really close to impossible to do with today's cable modems.
- If you do manage to uncap your modem, your cable company will discover your trick quite quickly, and then you're in biggggg trouble.

> **Warning. . .**
> Many of the software downloads offering uncapping features are really viruses.

### UNCAPPING CABLE MODEMS: AN URBAN MYTH IN THE MAKING

Cable data transmissions can be blazing fast, but all cable companies cap the transmission speed to make sure multiple users get a fair share of the bandwidth. The cap is imposed on the modem, not the wires. Today's cable modems operate under a technology called DOCSIS (Data Over Cable Service Interface Specification) to manage the modem's behavior. DOCSIS controls the way the modem communicates with the cable company's head end. When the modem checks in, the head end matches the modem's MAC address (a unique number assigned to the modem during manufacturing) against the specifications for this connection (the package you purchased). The head end downloads a configuration file to the modem. The file contains the IP address, the settings for the speed cap, and other communications instructions. The cable modem begins communicating once it receives the configuration file.

You can't stop this process, so you can't uncap the speed. Some people think that if they can learn the MAC address of a modem belonging to a customer who's allowed to transmit at higher speeds, they can use known technology to change the MAC address of their modem to get a different configuration file from the head end (one with a higher-speed cap). This doesn't work because the head end won't let two MAC addresses on the network at the same time, just the way your home network won't let two computers with the same IP address participate on the network.

## BUY YOUR OWN CABLE MODEM AND SAVE MONEY

**The Annoyance:** My cable company will either rent or sell me a modem. Is it possible to buy a cable modem from a source other than the cable company?

**The Fix:** Yes, you can now buy cable modems, so you're no longer locked in to your cable company's rates. A few years ago, the cable companies had a monopoly and forced you to either buy or rent a modem from them. Today, Linksys, Netgear, D-Link, and other manufacturers all offer cable modems.

> **Warning. . .**
> Make sure the cable modem you purchase is DOCSIS compliant.

## ENHANCE YOUR DSL SPEED

**The Annoyance:** I have residential DSL service, but it seems a little slow. How can I increase the speed of my DSL modem?

**The Fix:** There are two ways to get faster DSL transmissions:

- Move closer to the telephone company's central office (CO).
- Pay more.

The maximum speed available for DSL services depends on your location relative to the telephone company's CO. The further away you are, the lower the maximum attainable speed. When you sign up for DSL services, the telephone company tells you the maximum speed available for your house. If you live too far from a CO, you can't get DSL service for any price.

---

### OVERVIEW OF DSL TECHNOLOGIES

A wide range of DSL technologies is available today, although some are specific to certain providers and some are available only in certain countries. However, a few are common enough to be available through any of the DSL service providers who serve your neighborhood. Your distance from the telephone company's CO can affect the maximum speeds mentioned here.

*ADSL* (Asymmetric Digital Subscriber Line) is the common form of DSL for residential subscribers. The signal is asymmetric because most of the bandwidth is devoted to the downstream direction. A small portion of bandwidth is available for upstream communication. ADSL generally offers speeds up to 6.1 Mbps for downloading and up to 640 Kbps for uploading. When you subscribe to ADSL, the telephone company splits your phone line to separate the DSL data signals from your regular telephone services (telephone, fax, and telephone modem).

*DSL Lite* (sometimes called GLite, splitterless ADSL, or Universal ADSL) is a way to provide ADSL without sending a technician to split the line at the user end (the split is at the telephone company's CO). DSL Lite provides speeds up to 6 Mbps downstream and up to 384 Kbps upstream (slightly slower than ADSL, but very few people notice the difference).

*SDSL* (Symmetric DSL) offers speeds up to 1.544 Mbps (higher in Europe) in both directions (that's why it's called symmetric). SDSL doesn't use an existing telephone line split for DSL services. Instead, the telephone company runs a line specifically for the service. Many DSL providers call this "Business DSL." The service usually includes a number of fixed IP addresses.

The general rule of thumb is that you must live within 18,000 feet (about 3.5 miles) of the CO. However, other factors can extend this distance. If your phone company uses 24-gauge wire instead of the older 26-gauge wire, the data signal can be carried a couple hundred feet further. If your phone company uses fiber-optic cable (not a common scenario), you gain several hundred feet more.

DSL services are priced by speed. If you live close enough to the CO to have plenty of choices, your maximum speed is a matter of how much you're willing to pay each month.

# DSL UPLOAD AND DOWNLOAD SPEED DIFFERENCES

**The Annoyance:** My DSL service has a pretty fast download speed, but a much slower upload speed. I maintain web sites and need to increase the upload speed.

**The Fix:** You can buy DSL services with high upload speeds, as long as you're willing to pay the price—and it can be a rather hefty price. You might have to change the type of DSL service you subscribe to, and that, in turn, can change the way your telephone lines are used (see the sidebar "Overview of DSL Technologies").

**tip**

Unlike users of cable services, DSL users don't compete for bandwidth with their neighbors. Each DSL line is independent, which makes it easier to custom-design your upload and download speeds.

## DSL LINE FILTERS

**The Annoyance:** I was told that the DSL signal uses a totally different part of my telephone line than my telephone. However, my DSL provider said I had to put a filter on every telephone jack in the house. Why don't they warn you that DSL messes up your telephone service?

**The Fix:** You have it backward. Your DSL provider isn't using filters to protect your phone lines from DSL interference; the filters protect the DSL frequencies from telephone frequency interference. Telephone equipment is always "listening in" on the phone line, so the telephone knows when to ring and the fax machine knows when to pick up. The circuitry that performs these tasks isn't "high tech," and can cause a short circuit in the DSL signal and interfere with data communication.

The filters (see Figure 6-6) provide a way to stop the telephone frequency from moving into the DSL frequencies— frequencies it has no business occupying. Plug one end of the filter into the phone jack, and plug your telephone or fax machine into the RJ11 connector (which should have a marking, such as the word "phone" or an icon that looks like a telephone).

Figure 6-6. Filters protect your DSL signal from your telephone signal.

If you have more than one telephone line coming into your house, you have to filter only the telephone jacks that serve the line your DSL uses.

## DSL AND HOME SECURITY SYSTEMS

**The Annoyance:** Our home security system dials out when security is compromised. It uses the same telephone line as our DSL modem and telephones because we have only one line. After experiencing all kinds of trouble with our DSL Internet access, we learned that the security system is interfering with the DSL frequencies. We're told we have to bring in a second telephone line and use it for either the security system or the DSL service.

**The Fix:** You wouldn't have encountered this problem if your DSL system had been professionally installed—and your line was split at your house and the DSL frequencies were delivered to the telephone jack for your modem. Unfortunately, DSL providers usually ignore this whole subject, and don't inquire about security systems when you're asked if you want to self-install your system. If you have a security system, tell your DSL provider you need a professional installation.

## BUYING DSL SERVICE FROM THIRD-PARTY PROVIDERS

**The Annoyance:** My local telephone company offers DSL services, but I'm really not a fan of their service and response time for my telephone service. Can I buy DSL services from somebody else?

**The Fix:** Yes, unlike cable companies that usually have exclusive franchises for an area, the services available over telephone lines are open to competition. DSL services are included in that paradigm. But before you get excited, remember that no matter who provides your DSL service, they have to use your telephone company's lines. So, in a way, you're still locked into your local telephone company.

## ROUTERS ARE NOT SPECIFIC TO MODEM TYPES

**The Annoyance:** I went to a local store to buy a router to share our DSL connection. How can you tell whether the router is for a DSL modem or a cable modem? Is there some technical code in the model number that I don't know about?

**The Fix:** Routers talk to both DSL and cable modems because the router's technical job is unrelated to the type of broadband communication your modem provides. Your modem connects your home network to your broadband provider, which in turn sends your communications on to the Internet. Your router's job is to merge the multiple components of your network (your computers) so that they can address the modem. The router just delivers the data; the modem translates the data signal into the proper technology for your broadband provider.

## ROUTERS AND FIREWALLS

**The Annoyance:** Our network shares a DSL connection with a router. The router doesn't have a built-in firewall, and I'm not sure how to protect the network.

**The Fix:** If your router doesn't have a firewall, you must run a firewall on every computer on the network. The router sits between your network and the Internet, and if an Internet intruder can get past the router (which he can if the router isn't protected with a firewall), he can get to every computer connected to the router (even if the computers are connected to a hub or a switch, which in turn are connected to the router). Look at Zone Labs' ZoneAlarm firewall, which you can download for free at *http://www.zonelabs.com*.

## WIRELESS ACCESS TO A WIRED ROUTER

**The Annoyance:** We have a wired network and share our broadband connection with a wired router. My laptop from work has a wireless network adapter. How do I join this computer to the network so that I can get to the Internet?

**The Fix:** You have two choices for mixing a wireless computer with a wired network:

- Buy an Ethernet network adapter for the laptop and plug directly into the hub, switch, or router.
- Buy an access point.

An *access point* is a device that connects to both wireless and wired devices. It has an antenna (to communicate with wireless devices) and an Ethernet port. Use an Ethernet cable to connect the access point to your wired router.

## CONNECT PHONELINE AND POWER-LINE DEVICES TO A ROUTER

**The Annoyance:** Our home network is growing into a mix-and-match configuration. The original network, two computers and a router, is located on the second floor. On the first floor, we want to network two computers using either phoneline or powerline connections so that we don't have to run Ethernet cable to the first floor. How do we get the first-floor computers on to the Internet?

**The Fix:** You need a *bridge*, which is a device that connects to both an Ethernet device (your router) and a phoneline or powerline device. Locate the bridge on the second floor, near the router. Use an Ethernet cable to connect the bridge to the router. Then, plug the bridge into the appropriate connector (a phone jack for a phoneline network or a wall plug for a powerline network). All manufacturers of networking equipment sell bridges.

# BROADBAND TECHNICAL SUPPORT ANNOYANCES

## NO ROUTER SUPPORT FROM YOUR SERVICE PROVIDER

**The Annoyance:** We lost our Internet access and the support technician said she could "see the modem," so nothing was wrong with our cable service. She said, "If you're using a router, it's your problem because we don't support the use of routers." I don't know if she meant the cable company didn't help with router problems, or the cable company didn't permit me to share the service with a router.

**The Fix:** It's hard to tell what the support technician meant without knowing the rules of service for your cable provider. Some cable companies have a "loose" rule that you can't share the connection without notifying them and paying extra. By "loose" I mean they look the other way when you share the connection. Regardless of the rules, if you didn't buy your router from the cable company, you won't get technical support for that device.

## RECYCLE THE MODEM

**The Annoyance:** I go crazy being on hold for a half-hour or more when I call tech support. It's annoying that broadband service providers don't supply users with diagnostic tools and instructions.

**The Fix:** It's dangerous to give inexperienced, untutored users the ability to mess around with complicated hardware equipment. However, one procedure might help you regain Internet access without calling for support. In fact, statistics show that about 50% of the time, this trick will fix your problem.

Recycle the modem. If your modem has an On/Off button, press it to turn off the modem, wait about 20 seconds, and press it again to turn on the modem. If the modem lacks an On/Off button, unplug it, wait 20 seconds, and plug it in again.

It takes a while for the modem to go through its self-testing procedures (in fact, it could take a full minute or more). You'll see lights blinking slowly, then flashing rapidly, and finally just glowing. When all the lights are glowing (for most modems, that means four glowing lights), try getting to the Internet again. Half the time you'll be successful, and the other half the time you'll have to call technical support. But always try recycling the router first.

On the whole, cable companies have a terrible reputation for support (for both cable television and Internet access services). Here are some hints to improve your support problems:

☒ Cable companies often send a technician out faster for cable television problems than for cable Internet access problems. Perhaps they just have more technicians assigned to the television business, but apparently most cable technicians can find and cure both television and Internet signal problems. Some people call the cable television support line and report that their television cable is down, affecting all sets in the house (which points to the cable as the source of the problem). The technicians are dispatched immediately, they find the bad cable and fix it, and the Internet access returns. This is what you call a creative workaround!

☒ If you have frequent outages due to cable problems, you need to see whether there's an area-wide problem with the cable. Find out whether any neighbors have cable Internet access, and if so, whether they have frequent outages due to the cable. If you can't find anyone with cable Internet access, see if anyone has subscribed to digital TV services. If so, ask if they have frequent outages (digital TV transmissions are apparently more sensitive to cable signal problems than plain old analog cable TV transmissions).

☒ If you find that the frequent outages are area-wide, get everyone to call the cable company and demand an inspection of all the cable in the neighborhood.

## HOW CAN IT BE A CABLE PROBLEM IF THE TELEVISION WORKS?

**The Annoyance:** Sometimes we lose our cable Internet connection. When we call for support, we're told the problem is in the cable (the wires) and that it will take several days for a technician to come out to fix the problem. If the problem is in the cable, why does our cable television continue to work?

**The Fix:** It doesn't seem logical, but it is possible to have a problem with data transmission on the cable and still keep your television signal. Data is generally more sensitive than the television transmission to a cable that's having signal problems.

## CABLE MODEMS THAT DIE TAKE FOREVER TO REPLACE

**The Annoyance:** Our cable modem dies about twice a year. The cable company always replaces the modem for nothing, so the price is right. But it takes days for them to ship or deliver the new modem, while we live without Internet access. This is truly annoying! Do you have any hints about getting the cable company to move faster?

**The Fix:** Anyone who can figure out how to make cable companies more responsive to problems will be rich and famous overnight, and might even be nominated for sainthood. I agree that it's hard to walk away from a "no questions asked" free replacement for equipment, but you need to decide what your priorities are. If you really miss (or need) your Internet connectivity, perhaps it's a good idea to buy your own cable modem. Even if you buy an inexpensive modem (for less than $50), how bad could it be? It's almost certainly going to last longer than your cable company's modem.

> **tip**
>
> Sometimes the problem with ever-failing modems is with you, not your manufacturer. Is the modem plugged into an outlet that might be delivering low voltage (which destroys chips)? Make sure no laser printer, air conditioner, or other "amp pig" is operating on the same circuit.

## TELEPHONE LINE PROBLEMS WITH DSL

**The Annoyance:** Whenever I lose Internet access and call for support, it seems that most of the time the problem isn't with my equipment or the DSL equipment at the telephone company, it's with the telephone lines.

**The Fix:** That's true for almost everyone who has DSL. Telephone lines are in sorry shape in most places, and as they deteriorate, the signal is affected. Unfortunately, data signals are much more sensitive to line problems than voice signals (and it's amazing how we all just accept a minor amount of static on the telephone line).

Telephone line problems are usually caused by the deterioration of the external sheathing, which squirrels love to chew on (when the lines are running above the street), and other, more disgusting, rodents enjoy gnawing at (when the lines are running under the street). Lines below the street also tend to sit under water if there's been a lot of rain.

When the sheathing deteriorates, the lines are exposed to weather and touch other unshielded lines, both of which cause short circuits. Your solution is to force the telephone company to install and maintain lines that are trouble-free (see the sidebar "Solving Telephone Line Problems").

---

**SOLVING TELEPHONE LINE PROBLEMS**

Telephone companies don't do a good job of maintaining lines; they replace them only when they have to. More often, they'll just "shunt" a line that's in trouble to another line until they run out of spare lines. Then they'll install a few new lines so that they can continue this patchwork repair paradigm.

My neighbors and I took our complaints about the condition of the lines to our state's public utility commission. After an exchange of documents and a hearing, the telephone company was told to install new cable. We found the public utility commission to be extremely consumer-oriented and helpful. All states have similar organizations, and if you're having a constant problem with telephone lines, contact them.

---

# EMAIL ANNOYANCES

## EMAIL SETTINGS REMAIN THE SAME

**The Annoyance:** Now that we share our Internet connection, how do we set up our email? The instructions from the ISP regarding settings for the router (or for Internet Connection Sharing) are quite detailed. It's annoying that they aren't as specific about email settings.

**The Fix:** Your email settings don't change when you share the Internet connection throughout the network. The configuration settings you need to retrieve mail from your mailbox or to send mail are the same whether you're working on a standalone computer or on a network.

# USE OUTLOOK EXPRESS ON MORE THAN ONE COMPUTER

**The Annoyance:** I use the same computer most of the time, but occasionally I have to use a different computer on the network. I want to be able to collect and send email and have my address book, Inbox, and other mail folders available on both computers. Both computers have Outlook Express. How do I do this?

**The Fix:** It's not easy. In fact, it's so difficult that you'll be content to do just some of that. You can easily fetch and send email messages from any computer. The part that's a pain is having all your folders and messages available on more than one computer (see the sidebar "Copy Your Entire Email Installation to Another Computer").

If you just want to get and send email from the "other" computer, you have two options:

- Use the web-based mail software your ISP provides instead of using email software.

- Open Outlook Express and set up your mail account. Then, collect and send messages the same way you do on your "regular" computer.

If you choose the latter option (using Outlook Express to fetch and send email), you have a couple of methods for making sure all your email lands in one spot (your regular computer):

- Before you collect email on the "other" computer, configure the email software to keep messages on the server. Open the Properties for your email account and go to the Advanced tab. Select the option to keep mail on the server, and select the manner in which mail should be removed from the server (see Figure 6-7). Then, when you return to your regular computer, the messages will be downloaded again the next time you collect email.

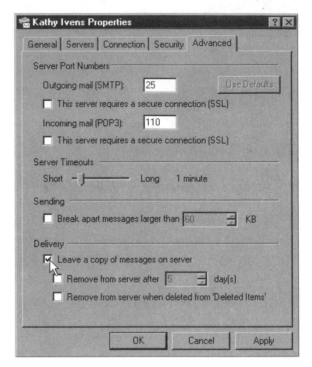

Figure 6-7. You can leave mail on the server and collect it again from the other computer.

- You can forward the messages you want to keep to yourself, and then don't collect email again until you return to your regular computer. If you send a message, add your email address to the Cc: field (or, better yet, to the Bcc: field). When you download your email, those forwarded messages are received.

> **Warning...**
> When you download the forwarded and Cc'd messages the name of the Sender is you, and your Inbox won't show the real sender's name in the message list.

# USE EUDORA ON MORE THAN ONE COMPUTER

**The Annoyance:** Every computer on our network has a copy of Eudora installed. Each copy has every email account (one for each user). I can easily get my email when I'm working on a computer that's not the one I usually use. But there must be an easy way to move the messages I receive to my regular computer. I tried forwarding mail to myself, but then the message lists me as the sender.

**The Fix:** Fortunately, Eudora keeps every component in its own discrete file, including attachments (unlike Outlook Express, which has a humongous file that holds all your mail folders and attachments).

Create a new mailbox on both computers to handle the exchange of mail between the two (I named my mailbox "Transfers"). Collect and send mail on the other computer. Then transfer all the mail from the Inbox and Outbox to the new mailbox. Copy the files for the new mailbox ("Transfers") to the other computer. There are two files:

- *Transfers.mbx* (the mailbox)
- *Transfers.toc* (the index for the mailbox)

Make sure you copy the files into the folder where Eudora keeps your mailboxes, which differs depending on your version of Eudora and the way you installed it. Look in the main Eudora folder or a subfolder named "Data" for other files with the *.mbx* extension. Windows will ask if you want to replace the existing file; say Yes.

Cut and paste all the attachments you've received from the Attach subfolder (under the Eudora folder) to the Attach subfolder of the Eudora installation on your regular computer.

After you've copied the files across the network, delete all the contents of the "Transfers" mailbox (so that it's empty for the next time).

When you're back at your regular computer, open the "Transfers" mailbox. Select all the incoming messages and transfer them to your Inbox. Select all the outgoing messages and transfer them to your Outbox. It's easy to tell the difference because when you mix inbound and outbound messages in the same mailbox, Eudora uses italic font for listing outgoing messages. When you've finished transferring the messages, the "Transfers" mailbox is empty and ready for the next round.

# AOL ANNOYANCES

## AOL DIAL-UP DOESN'T SUPPORT MULTIPLE LOGONS

**The Annoyance:** After the host computer logs on to AOL, users on the other computers get an error message that says the account is in use. What's the point of a shared Internet connection if only one person can be online at any one time?

**The Fix:** This annoyance is an AOL exclusive. However, with some versions of AOL, your client users might be able to get to the Internet after the user on the host computer has logged on to AOL. The logon to AOL establishes a network-wide Internet connection.

In this scenario, client users aren't logged on to AOL, but they are physically connected to the Internet and can surf the Web. They have to use the version of Internet Explorer that comes with Windows instead of the AOL version of IE (which is a blessing, not a curse, because the AOL version of IE isn't as good as the built-in version of IE).

See the AOL help files to see whether your version of AOL supports this. If not, you must upgrade the AOL software on every computer. Of course, client users who are on the Internet aren't logged on to AOL with their screen names, so they can't get their email.

> AOL has a plan called AOL Broadband that permits multiple screen names to log on.

## AOL MIGHT NOT WORK WITH ICS

**The Annoyance:** We use ICS for our telephone modem, and when our host computer (running Windows XP) connects to AOL, none of the client computers can reach the Internet.

**The Fix:** Some AOL versions (e.g., Version 7) can't coexist with ICS. You need to download the latest version of AOL (*http://www.aol.com*).

## AOL BROADBAND REQUIRES DOUBLE PAYMENTS

**The Annoyance:** We signed up for AOL Broadband so that our whole family can log on to AOL at the same time. AOL isn't a broadband ISP, so do we have to buy ISP services?

**The Fix:** The only thing AOL Broadband Services buys you is the ability to have up to seven simultaneous screen names, at a hefty monthly charge. You also have to pay a monthly charge to your broadband provider. There's no fix for this, so if you like AOL, you have to live with it.

## MIXING BROADBAND AND DIAL-UP AOL ACCOUNTS

**The Annoyance:** We moved from dial-up to broadband Internet access, but we want to continue to use our AOL mail accounts and participate in IMs. Is there a way to do this?

**The Fix:** You'll have to continue to pay AOL for an account and get your mail from the AOL web site. AOL offers a lower rate for users who have their own ISP. Only one screen name at a time can be logged in. Each user must open Internet Explorer and travel to *http://www.aol.com*. Log in (the Login box is on the right side of the window). Once you're logged in you can access your mail and participate in Instant Messaging.

AOL offers a free IM software application for non-AOL members. You can download the software (AIM) from the AOL web site (*http://www.aim.com*).

## DEFAULT ROUTER SETTINGS DON'T SUPPORT AOL LOGINS

**The Annoyance:** After we moved to broadband Internet access and installed a router to share the connection, we signed up for AOL Broadband Services. Now we can't log in to AOL.

**The Fix:** You need to reconfigure your router for AOL access. Luckily, you can get to the Internet through your broadband ISP, so go to the web site of your router manufacturer and search the support pages for information on AOL. Most routers require a rather complicated and convoluted configuration process to support your AOL login needs. You might have to disconnect the modem from the router and connect the modem directly to one computer's network adapter to perform the tasks involved in setting up a router for AOL.

# Security
# ANNOYANCES

7

Computer security has become such an important issue that the mainstream press regularly covers the topic, but the information is almost always incorrect. Television news writers love hyperbole (fires are "infernos," car accidents are "disasters," flooded streets are "deluges," and so on). As a result, the coverage of security threats is designed to scare you, not assist you. Pay no attention to the computer security articles on the news pages. Instead, head for the computer columnist's page.

Security is an important issue, and it's true that a security breach is dangerous and scary. But you have plenty of tools at hand to help you secure all the computers on your network. In addition to security problems caused by viruses, worms, and hackers, most home networks have other security issues. For example, you might want to keep some files private, and exclude access by a re-mote user. But then how do you get to your own files from anoth-er computer if you've made them inaccessible across the network?

In this chapter, I'll deal with general security annoyances for home networks, including the tasks you must perform to make sure your antivirus and firewall software protects you. I'll also give you some tricks to make sure you, and nobody else, can retrieve your private files across the network.

# FIREWALL ANNOYANCES

## FIREWALL? WHERE'S THE FIRE?

**The Annoyance:** I have antivirus software running on every computer on my network, so why do I need a firewall? Buying and installing all this stuff is annoying.

**The Fix:** Antivirus software and firewalls are two different animals, and they protect you from two different types of attacks. Antivirus software locates and eliminates viruses, which are destructive programs sneaked on to your computer (usually through your email). A firewall protects you from attacks by ne'er-do-wells who are trying to enter your computer while you're on the Internet. Because evildoers use both methods of attack, you need both forms of protection.

## WINDOWS XP FIREWALL HALTS NETWORK TRAFFIC

**The Annoyance:** I added a Windows XP computer to our network. The Help files tell me how important it is to have a firewall on the computer, and they explain how to enable the built-in firewall. However, friends tell me that if I use the built-in firewall, none of the other computers on the network will be able to access the Windows XP computer. Why would an important tool such as a firewall not work on a network?

**The Fix:** Your friends are right. The firewall built into Windows XP stops network communications (unless you're running Windows XP Service Pack 2). Isn't that an interesting way to design an operating system feature? Maybe Microsoft doesn't know about the explosive growth of small networks.

---

### WHAT'S AN INTERNET ATTACK?

Internet attackers use software that randomly selects an IP address and automatically attempts to access the computer linked to that address. (They don't specifically target your computer because they think you have the instructions for finding a long-lost gold mine in a file on your hard drive.) If the attempt fails (a firewall blocks entry), the software moves on to the next IP address. However, if the attempt succeeds, the intruders have access to your computer and its contents. Everything they do occurs in the background, so you won't even notice. Some of the things intruders have done include the following nefarious acts:

☒ Sending executable files containing viruses to your computer.

☒ Renaming or removing files needed to run your computer and its software.

☒ Copying your documents back to their own systems and looking for personal and sensitive information they can use (e.g., identity theft schemes).

☒ Sending enormous files or an enormous number of small files (not necessarily dangerous in themselves) to fill all the free space on your hard drive.

☒ Accessing your computer multiple times in rapid succession, causing the computer to become so overwhelmed that it becomes nonresponsive and frozen. This is called a Denial of Service (DOS) attack.

If the firewall has been automatically enabled (which occurs frequently when you use the Internet Connection Wizard in Windows XP), you should disable it. Open the Properties dialog box for the Local Area Connection, click the Advanced tab, and make sure the box in the Internet Connection Firewall area is *unchecked* (see Figure 7-1). Then install a software firewall or a firewall-enabled router (if you're using a router to share your Internet connection).

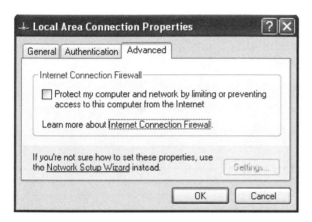

Figure 7-1. Disable the Windows XP Internet Connection Firewall if you're running a network.

# WINDOWS XP SERVICE PACK 2 OFFERS IMPROVED FIREWALL

**The Annoyance:** Our Windows XP computer is running Service Pack 2, and the advertising blurbs say the new firewall lets you have a network. I enabled the firewall, but other computers still can't access the XP machine. What happened?

**The Fix:** With SP2, Microsoft added setup options to the built-in firewall. To let network computers access this computer, follow these steps:

1. Open the Properties dialog box for the Local Area Connection and click the Advanced tab.

2. Click the Settings button to open the Windows Firewall dialog box.

3. Click the Exceptions tab and check the File and Printer Sharing box (see Figure 7-2).

Figure 7-2. Enable network communications by making an exception to the firewall's data blocking.

It's beyond the scope of this book to discuss the firewall and all the security settings available in Windows XP Service Pack 2. However, you should investigate some of the other firewall settings that allow you to use the Remote Assistance and Remote Desktop features. The Help files for SP2 provide instructions and explanations. You'll also need to configure the firewall if you want to play Internet games or take part in online conferences.

# SHARED TELEPHONE MODEMS NEED FIREWALLS

**The Annoyance:** Our network uses Internet Connection Sharing to share a telephone modem. Do I have to have a firewall on every computer on the network?

**The Fix:** Nope, you only need to protect the computer that has the modem (the *host computer*). The host is a gateway, and a firewall on the gateway guards the computers on the network side of the gateway like Cerberus guards the entrance into the underworld.

### Hound of Hell

If you're not up on mythology, Cerberus is a fierce, three-headed dog that guarded the entrance of Hell to prevent the living from entering the world of the dead. In some ancient documents, the dog's name was spelled Kerberos. Companies that run Windows 2000 or 2003 domains use a security process named Kerberos to authenticate users and prevent unauthorized entry into the network. Taking this to its logical conclusion, it means that corporate network systems are a form of Hell, a statement that some system administrators find accurate and even satisfying.

## WINDOWS XP FIREWALL FOR BROADBAND-BASED ICS

**The Annoyance:** We have a cable modem, but we didn't buy a router. Instead, we attached the cable modem to a Windows XP computer and set it up as an ICS host. Can I use the built-in Windows XP firewall to protect the entire network?

**The Fix:** Yes, but make sure you enable it on the right network adapter. The host computer has two network adapters: one connects to the hub where the other computers meet and the other connects to the modem. To share a cable modem (or a DSL modem) without a router, enable the built-in firewall on the adapter connected to the modem.

## SAFEGUARDING OLDER COMPUTERS

**The Annoyance:** The four computers on our network share a router without a firewall. Two of the computers, however, run Windows XP SP2 and use the built-in firewall. The other two computers run Windows 2000 Professional and 98SE. Do they have a version of the built-in firewall?

**The Fix:** No, you'll have to install a software firewall on the computers running Windows 2000 Professional and 98SE. I use Zone Labs' ZoneAlarm, and for most home networks the freebie version of ZoneAlarm does the job. Another well-known software firewall is Internet Security Systems' Black Ice. Symantec and McAfee, best known for their antivirus software, also offer good firewall programs.

- Zone Labs (*http://www.zonelabs.com/store/content/home.jsp*)
- Internet Security Systems (*http://www.iss.net/*)
- Symantec (*http://www.symantec.com/index.htm*)
- McAfee (*http://www.mcafee.com/us/*)

## ROUTERS CAN PROTECT YOUR NETWORK

**The Annoyance:** We use a router with a built-in firewall for shared Internet access. Do I still have to install firewall software on all the computers on the network?

**The Fix:** No, the router blocks malicious intruders at the gateway, which protects all the computers on the network.

> **Warning...**
> Most hardware-based firewalls block only incoming traffic. This approach doesn't provide bidirectional security (see "Software Firewalls Go Both Ways").

## STATEFUL INSPECTION CAN TELL WHO'S LYING

**The Annoyance:** We're considering adding a router with a firewall to our network. Some of the routers say they use "stateful inspection." Is this an important feature worth paying for?

**The Fix:** *Stateful inspection* is a firewall technique that makes sure the data coming through the firewall is truthfully describing itself. Different types of data use different virtual ports on a computer, and a firewall lets data come through some ports and closes other ports. For example, a stateful inspection firewall will make sure that the data that uses the HTTP port (the protocol of Internet web pages) is really HTTP, and not some dangerous programming code. Because Internet hackers don't announce their data packets with a reference that says "there's dangerous stuff in this data packet even though it says it's HTTP," stateful inspection is important. (If you're curious about the technical stuff, see the sidebar "Ports and Data.")

## SOFTWARE FIREWALLS GO BOTH WAYS

**The Annoyance:** Some people tell me that a software firewall is preferable to the Windows XP firewall or a firewall on a router. Isn't blocking data from the Internet the same thing no matter which type of firewall you use? I mean, either the data is allowed through or it isn't; who cares what type of firewall does the blocking?

**The Fix:** Your logic is impeccable. If you want to block unwanted data trying to get to your computer from the Internet, a firewall is a firewall is a firewall.

### PORTS AND DATA

Computers send and receive data through ports. You've already worked with ports because you've connected a printer to a parallel or USB port, or you've attached a modem or handheld device to a serial or USB port.

Besides these physical, visible ports, your computer has thousands of virtual ports. A virtual port is a software service. However, all ports, both physical and virtual, exist to accept and send data.

Virtual ports are numbered from 0 to 65536, and the ports between 0 and 1024 are reserved for use by certain services. For example, Hypertext Transfer Protocol (HTTP), which is the protocol you use when interacting with a web page, usually uses port 80. Ports work by "listening" for data and will automatically accept data if it's the right type of data for that port.

Internet intruders use ports to send and receive data between their computers and your computer. They use software that tests certain ports by pretending to send data of a type supported by that port. This practice is called *port scanning*, and it's the most popular method of testing whether a computer is vulnerable to attack. The intruders scan the ports on computers and determine the services currently *listening* for connections and the specific ports they're listening on. (A port that is *listening* is deemed open and willing to accept data.) The Internet hacking software uses that information to make the data stream they send resemble the appropriate type of service for the listening port. Virtual ports are dumb, and they'll accept the incoming technical information that says the data stream is of a certain type.

Firewalls that use stateful inspection check the data passing through ports to catch data packets that identify themselves as being appropriate for the port, but really aren't. When the firewall discovers that the data packets are faking the datatype, they stop the transmission.

But hold on a minute. You talked about blocking data trying to get into your computer. What about data trying to get out? Can you think of times that you don't want to send data to another computer on the Internet? No? Well, suppose you pick up a virus that gathers your files and sends them to some hacker's computer? Suppose you download a really nifty software program or game and you don't know that it's programmed to send sensitive and private information to some punk who will use it to steal your identity, or use your cookies to gain access to a web site that has your credit card numbers.

Most hardware firewalls worry only about incoming data streams; they don't give a hoot about stuff moving from your computer to the Internet. Software firewalls ask your permission before letting any software send data from your computer to the Internet.

> You can configure some hardware firewalls to protect you from unwanted outward-bound data transmissions. However, you usually have to know a lot of technical gunk to get the configuration right. Play it safe and go with a software firewall.

## STOP FIREWALL POP-UP NOTIFICATIONS

**The Annoyance:** The software firewall I installed on all the computers on our network drives everyone crazy. A pop-up appears every few minutes to announce that the firewall has blocked access to the computer from the Internet. I would rather risk an intruder than have to click OK to clear the pop-up window every couple of minutes.

**The Fix:** Don't worry; you can stop the pop-ups. But aren't you amazed at how often somebody tries to access your computer? The thought that some or most of those attempts are attacks is scary.

All software firewalls offer an option to suppress the pop-up notifications about incoming data streams, and you usually have the option to save the information to a log file. Check the Help files to learn the exact steps.

## DON'T BLOCK OUTGOING FIREWALL POP-UP NOTIFICATIONS

**The Annoyance:** Every so often, my firewall software opens a pop-up message to ask me whether some program can send information to the Internet. It's always OK because the program needs to get to the Internet (for instance, the Microsoft Help Files program). Is there a way to turn off the notifications?

**The Fix:** Your firewall asks for permission when it doesn't know how you feel about a specific program. By default, most software firewalls assume you want to let your browser access the Internet, so they configure themselves to permit the browser to send data without asking your permission. Any other program that isn't on the list requires your permission.

When you give permission for a program to access the Internet, always select the option to give the program permanent permission. Then you'll never be asked again. You can also preconfigure your firewall with the names of programs (in addition to your browser) that should automatically be allowed to send data from your computer. Check the Help files to learn how to add programs to the list of preapproved data senders.

## APPROVED OUTGOING PROGRAMS ASK FOR PERMISSION AGAIN

**The Annoyance:** My antivirus and accounting software both check the vendors' web sites periodically for updates. I configured the firewall to let these programs access the Internet, and selected the option to make it a permanent permission. Today, the firewall asked me if the accounting software could access the Internet. Doesn't the firewall have the same definition of "permanent" that I do?

## The Fix: The program changed and your firewall is asking permission again to make sure it's OK to let the changed program send data from your computer to the Internet. In fact, you can probably find a note on the pop-up that says the program has changed since the last time you gave it permission to send data to the Internet.

Programs change when you download upgrades to the software, and for both antivirus and accounting software programs, this is a frequent event. The firewall's approach is a good protection scheme because it prevents the possibility that some virus or other maleficent program is using the name of an existing software program to accomplish some horrific deed. If you didn't recently upgrade the software, don't give permission.

## CHECK THE PROGRAM BEFORE YOU GIVE PERMISSION

**The Annoyance:** Sometimes my firewall pop-up tells me that some program is trying to exchange data with another computer—not with the Internet. In fact, sometimes the pop-up warns me that the program is asking for server rights. This sounds very scary.

## The Fix: Some programs, mostly utilities built into Windows, are designed to implement network tasks. For example, you might see a pop-up reference to Generic Host Process for Win32 (which lets computers on the network access each other) or to the Spooler Service (which lets you send data to a remote printer). Most of the program names contain a reference to Microsoft or Windows, but do some homework (search the Internet or Microsoft's web sites) before you give permission.

## WHICH COMPUTERS SHOULD HAVE A SOFTWARE FIREWALL?

**The Annoyance:** We've decided on a software firewall for our network. Do I have to install a copy on every computer on the network?

## The Fix: Maybe yes, maybe no. If your computers directly access the Internet through a router (without a built-in firewall), each computer needs a copy of the firewall. If you're using ICS, only the computer that hosts the Internet connection needs a firewall.

## TEST THE FIREWALL

**The Annoyance:** How can you tell whether the firewall works properly?

## The Fix: Test it. Several web sites exist for testing firewall effectiveness. One of the best is from Gibson Research Corporation (*http://www.grc.com/*). To test your firewall, click the Shields Up! link on the home page, and then scroll down the page and click the Shields Up! link. Click the Proceed button to begin the test. Select the tests you want to run (File Sharing and Common Ports are the most important). GRC attempts all sorts of tricks to break into your computer and then posts its results. You can see the results of my File Sharing test in Figure 7-3, and the results of my Common Ports test in Figure 7-4. If you don't see similar results when you test your computer, you need to reconfigure your firewall.

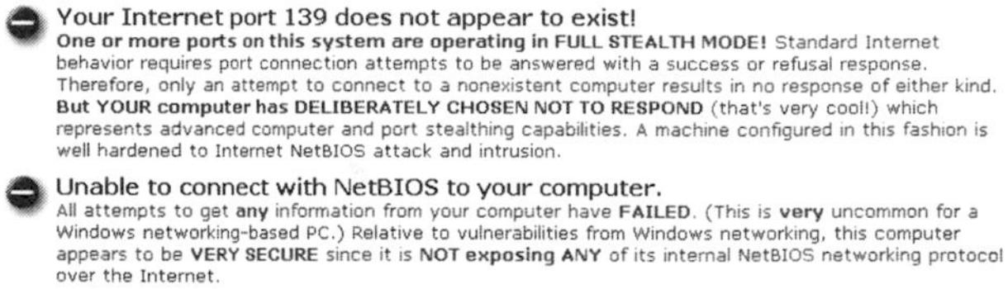

**Your Internet port 139 does not appear to exist!**
One or more ports on this system are operating in FULL STEALTH MODE! Standard Internet behavior requires port connection attempts to be answered with a success or refusal response. Therefore, only an attempt to connect to a nonexistent computer results in no response of either kind. **But YOUR computer has DELIBERATELY CHOSEN NOT TO RESPOND** (that's very cool!) which represents advanced computer and port stealthing capabilities. A machine configured in this fashion is well hardened to Internet NetBIOS attack and intrusion.

**Unable to connect with NetBIOS to your computer.**
All attempts to get **any** information from your computer have **FAILED**. (This is **very** uncommon for a Windows networking-based PC.) Relative to vulnerabilities from Windows networking, this computer appears to be **VERY SECURE** since it is **NOT exposing ANY** of its internal NetBIOS networking protocol over the Internet.

Figure 7-3. My firewall is taking care of file security.

**Unsolicited Packets:** PASSED — No Internet packets of any sort were received from your system as a side-effect of our attempts to elicit some response from any of the ports listed above. Some questionable personal security systems expose their users by attempting to "counter-probe the prober", thus revealing themselves. But your system remained wisely silent. (Except for the fact that not all of its ports are completely stealthed as shown below.)

**Ping Echo:** PASSED — Your system ignored and refused to reply to repeated Pings (ICMP Echo Requests) from our server.

| Port | Service | Status | Security Implications |
|------|---------|--------|-----------------------|
| 0 | <nil> | Stealth | There is NO EVIDENCE WHATSOEVER that a port (or even any computer) exists at this IP address! |
| 21 | FTP | Stealth | There is NO EVIDENCE WHATSOEVER that a port (or even any computer) exists at this IP address! |
| 22 | SSH | Stealth | There is NO EVIDENCE WHATSOEVER that a port (or even any computer) exists at this IP address! |
| 23 | Telnet | Stealth | There is NO EVIDENCE WHATSOEVER that a port (or even any computer) exists at this IP address! |
| 25 | SMTP | Stealth | There is NO EVIDENCE WHATSOEVER that a port (or even any computer) exists at this IP address! |
| 79 | Finger | Stealth | There is NO EVIDENCE WHATSOEVER that a port (or even any computer) exists at this IP address! |
| 80 | HTTP | Stealth | There is NO EVIDENCE WHATSOEVER that a port (or even any computer) exists at this IP address! |
| 110 | POP3 | Stealth | There is NO EVIDENCE WHATSOEVER that a port (or even any computer) exists at this IP address! |
| 113 | IDENT | Closed | Your computer has responded that this port exists but is currently closed to connections. |

Figure 7-4. Secured ports keep intruders out of my computer.

# VIRUSES, WORMS, AND OTHER SLIMY CREATURES

## ANTIVIRUS SOFTWARE SLOWS ME DOWN

**The Annoyance:** Since I installed antivirus software on my computer, it takes longer to collect my email. The messages used to pop into my Inbox as fast as lightning, but now that my antivirus software is checking each message, it seems to take twice as long, or longer.

**The Fix:** Yeah? So? And your point is?

## YOU DON'T NEED EMAIL TO GET A VIRUS

**The Annoyance:** One of the three computers on our network has no email. We use it only for Internet access, and most of that work is for the children's homework and school research. Because of the lack of email, I didn't install an antivirus program. But my 12-year-old son tells me no computer should be without antivirus software.

## NOT THAT IT MAKES A DIFFERENCE TO THE VICTIMS...

As a technical exercise, here's a brief overview of the different types of destructive, slimy creatures that can destroy your computer.

A *virus* is a program, even if it appears not to be (for instance, it might look like a screensaver). The programming is designed to cause an unanticipated, and usually harmful, occurrence. In addition, virus code is designed to reproduce itself on other drives on your computer, on other computers on your network, and on other computers throughout the world (via your email software).

A *Trojan horse* behaves just as maliciously as a virus, but by strict definition it's not a true virus because it doesn't replicate itself (self-replication is part of the technical definition of a virus). The damage to the receiving computer is similar to, and as dreadful as, the damage caused by a virus.

A *worm* is a self-contained program and must be manually opened to do its damage. Like a virus, a worm replicates itself (frequently by mailing itself to recipients in a Microsoft Outlook or Outlook Express address book). One of the characteristics of a worm is its incredibly powerful ability to propagate itself across drives and networked computers. Sometimes, as a worm clones itself across the network, each clone has a slightly different assignment. As a result, when all those worms go into action, they can do an incredible amount of damage to a network. Worms almost always arrive as email attachments.

**The Fix:** In many families, the 12-year old is the resident computer geek, and your household is no exception. Your son is right. You can get viruses from other computers on your network, or from a web site.

# A VIRUS DISGUISED AS A DOCUMENT

## The Annoyance: If viruses can exist only as programs, how come I picked up a virus from a Microsoft Word document?

## The Fix: The virus got into the document because the document contains Visual Basic Script (VBS) programming code used to create a macro. The macro is part of the document file, and because VBS produces executable code just like any other programming language, a macro qualifies as a program. Such viruses are called *macro viruses*. Be sure you configure your Microsoft programs to enable Macro Virus Protection. For example, in Word, select Tools → Macro → Security and choose a security level.

If you don't use VBS and don't have to run VBS files, change the file association for *.vbs* files to Notepad. Then, if you open a document file that also contains a VBS file (which might contain a macro virus), it will open as a text file in Notepad (instead of executing its malicious code). Check your Windows help files to learn how to change file associations.

# VIRUS SCAN TAKES FOREVER

## The Annoyance: I follow the advice of my anti-virus software and run a complete scan once a week. It takes forever. Is there a way to speed this process?

## The Fix: You can shorten the time it takes to scan your system by preparing for the scan with the following steps:

- Delete the contents of the Recycle Bin.
- Delete temporary Internet files. In Internet Explorer, select Tools → Internet Options. In the Temporary Internet Files section of the General tab, click the Delete Files button.
- Delete document backup files from software that creates backup files. To quickly delete all your document

backup files in Windows XP, select Start → Search → For Files or Folders. Click the "All files and folders" link in the left pane, enter *.Ext* in the top field, and click the Search button. Substitute the file extension your software applies to backup files for *.ext*. For example, to remove Microsoft Word backup files, enter *.wbk* (see Figure 7-5). When the backup files appear, press Ctrl-A to select them all, and then press the Delete key.

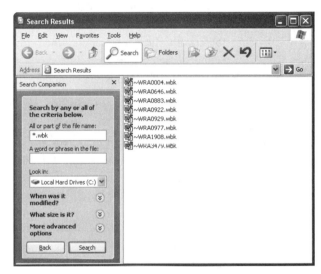

Figure 7-5. Get rid of unneeded files before scanning your computer for viruses.

> **t i p**
>
> If you hold the Shift key while you press the Delete key, the files are deleted instead of going to the Recycle Bin. If you forget to hold the Shift key, don't forget to empty the Recycle Bin after you remove the backup files.

## SELECT MAPPED DRIVES FOR A VIRUS SCAN

**The Annoyance:** My computer has several mapped drives linked to shared folders on other networked computers. If I select Entire Computer as the target of my virus scan, those mapped drives are scanned, too. This increases the time it takes to scan the computer.

**The Fix:** Because you certainly installed antivirus software on the other computers, it's a waste of time to scan individual folders on those computers when you scan your own computer. Select the local hard drive as the target of the scan, instead of the entire computer.

> If you map drives to remote drives, you can scan the entire network from one computer (see "Scan the Entire Network").

## SCAN TWO DRIVES

**The Annoyance:** My computer has two hard drives and several mapped drives to remote folders. I don't want to scan the remote folders, but my antivirus software doesn't let me select both hard drives.

**The Fix:** Isn't that annoying? The only solution is to scan the first hard drive, and then scan the second hard drive in a separate action. Of course, depending on the way you use the second drive, you might be able to skip the scan (or perform the scan less often). Many people use the second drive to hold documents (which makes backing up documents much easier). In that case, you don't have to scan it as often because you rarely find a virus in a document you created.

## SCAN THE ENTIRE NETWORK

**The Annoyance:** Even though I installed antivirus software on every computer, it's very time consuming to scan each computer. Can I scan the entire network from one computer?

**The Fix:** Good thinking! Your antivirus software probably doesn't have an option labeled "Scan Entire Network," but you can manually set up such a scan. Share every drive on every computer on the network, and then map drives to those shared drives on the computer that does the scan. Selecting the entire computer in the scanning options includes all mapped drives—ergo, you scan the whole network. If you don't want to share drives on your network, just create the shares and map them for the virus scan, then disable the drive sharing until the next time you want to scan the whole network.

## WHAT'S HEURISTIC SCANNING?

**The Annoyance:** My antivirus software has an option to use heuristic scanning techniques. I have no idea what that means, but I read a tip that says it takes longer to scan with this option, and it's not absolutely foolproof.

**The Fix:** Heuristic scanning analyzes an executable file that does not contain a known virus to try to identify whether it's a potential threat. This is a way to catch viruses new to the computer community. Each antivirus program has its own method for defining "suspicious" code during heuristic scans. Heuristic scanning is a guessing game, but at least it uses educated guesses. It slows the scanning process and sometimes produces false alarms. For example, a perfectly safe program can contain programming code that the antivirus software thinks is related to the way a virus acts. Still, it's better to be safe than sorry.

## SCHEDULE SCANS FOR THE MIDDLE OF THE NIGHT

**The Annoyance:** I'd like to schedule my weekly scan for the overnight hours, so it doesn't interfere with my computer use. But what happens if the scan finds a virus and I'm not there to take care of it?

**The Fix:** Scheduling scans at night is an excellent idea. The software, and any viruses it finds, will wait patiently for you to return to the computer and deal with the problem. In fact, programs such as Norton AntiVirus will automatically remove the virus or quarantine the file so that it can't infect your computer. Make sure you check the quarantined files (if your antivirus software performed that action) and delete them.

## WHAT'S WITH THIS CONSTANT UPDATING?

**The Annoyance:** Almost every time a computer on the network dials out to the Internet, the connection is slowed for a while because the antivirus software is checking for updates. Do they bring out updates of the program every day?

**The Fix:** It's not the program that changes daily; it's the virus information file. Antivirus software has two parts:

- The program, which is the engine that drives the work.
- The virus information file, which contains all the information about known viruses. The program uses this information to find viruses.

Because new viruses, or variants of known viruses, are discovered almost daily (in fact, sometimes hourly), the only way to ensure that virus checking is performed with up-to-date information is to keep a current copy of the virus information file on your computer. When you go online, the software checks the manufacturer's web site to see if either the virus information file or the software

program has changed. If it has, the new file or files are downloaded to your computer.

## ANTIVIRUS PROGRAM UPDATE REQUIRES A REBOOT

**The Annoyance:** My antivirus software checks for updates constantly because we have an always-on Internet connection. Sometimes all the computers on the network see a pop-up that says an update has been downloaded, and clicking OK makes the pop-up go away. Other times, however, the pop-up says the computer has to be rebooted. Why?

**The Fix:** Usually you need to reboot because the software program itself has been updated (the frequent downloads of updated virus information files are responsible for the regular pop-ups). When you're asked to reboot to incorporate the new features, it means your antivirus software is disabled, so you should restart the computer as soon as possible.

## TURN OFF AUTOMATIC UPDATING

**The Annoyance:** Because we use a telephone modem to connect to the Internet and often have more than one person online at a time, the automatic updates of our antivirus software really make us less productive. Can we turn it off?

**The Fix:** Yes, you can turn off automatic updates, but I'll tell you how to do this only if you promise to check for updates manually every day. Promise? OK.

Your antivirus software used your Windows Task Scheduler to automate checking for updates. You can delete the task, and then use the menu bar in the software window to check for updates manually. Here's how to delete the scheduled task:

1. Select Start → Programs → Accessories → System Tools → Scheduled Tasks (see Figure 7-6).
2. Right-click the update task for your antivirus software and choose Delete.

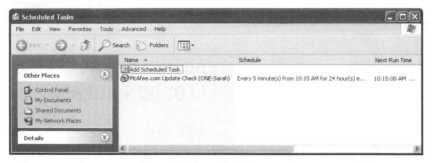

Figure 7-6. Your antivirus software schedules regular checks to see if updates are available. For an always-on Internet connection, the task occurs very frequently.

## MY ISP SCANS FOR VIRUSES, WHY SHOULD I?

**The Annoyance:** My ISP has virus blocking enabled on mailboxes. Why should I buy and run antivirus software?

**The Fix:** First of all, your ISP can't scan your drives and find viruses that have come into your system over the network, or over the Internet. Second, the only way to know that the antivirus activity is using up-to-date information is to run your own antivirus software, which is updated whenever new viruses are discovered.

## ANTIVIRUS SOFTWARE WON'T INSTALL

**The Annoyance:** We added a third computer to our network several days ago, and today I went to the web site of our antivirus software vendor and tried to download the program. The download failed about halfway through, and I tried again with the same result. The other computers never had a problem downloading the files. Why am I suddenly not able to install the software?

**The Fix:** I'll bet big bucks that the computer has a virus. You waited too long to install the antivirus software. An existing virus is one of the primary causes of installation failure. In fact, many viruses are programmed to prevent antivirus software installations.

Luckily, you have a network, so you can cure this—something people who run standalone computers can't do easily. Use the following steps to check for a virus on the computer:

1. Share the hard drive of the computer that has the problem.

2. On a computer running antivirus software, map a drive to the shared drive you created.

3. Open the antivirus software and select the mapped drive as the drive to scan.

4. Start the scan.

If the scan discovers a virus, delete the virus-laden file(s). Then go to the software company's web site and search for the virus by name to see if there are additional removal tasks (such as deleting additional files the virus installed, or removing registry items added or changed by the virus). Then download the antivirus software. If the scan doesn't discover a virus, something else is going on, and you should call the vendor for support.

If you can get to the Internet, you can use the free, web-based virus scan available at *http://www.mcafee.com*. It cleans your computer and then asks if you'd like to purchase McAfee virus protection software.

## CLUES TO VIRUS HOAXES

You can usually spot a virus hoax email message because it contains multiple clues. First of all, the sender is not a computer expert (for example, your brother-in-law, who is an IT professional, would never send you a message like this). In fact, often the sender isn't even a polite emailer because he includes all the previous forwarded messages that crossed the Internet, forcing you to scroll through a million recipient names and a thousand iterations of the message body. Doesn't that annoy the heck out of you?

Second, the message includes screaming demands to warn everyone you know about this dangerous virus. "Screaming" in email is USING ALL CAPITAL LETTERS TO REINFORCE THE NEED TO PANIC.

Third, the information that no antivirus software company has been able to get a handle on the virus is a big clue that this is a hoax. That's ridiculous. A "troublesome" virus is one that takes more than an hour to pinpoint—usually it takes only minutes to figure out what a virus is doing and how it is doing it.

Finally, the message usually contains some kind of long, complicated story with a protagonist who is a computer expert. For example, somebody was warned by his cousin who is an engineer at IBM/Microsoft/Oracle/Intuit/<insert name of any other major computer company here> that this virus will destroy computers within five minutes.

## DON'T GET FOOLED BY VIRUS HOAXES

**The Annoyance:** Occasionally I get email from people I know warning me that some horrible virus has emerged, and the antivirus software companies can't seem to find a fix. Most of the time, the instructions in the email tell me to delete files from my Windows folder, which makes me nervous.

**The Fix:** Why do perfectly reasonable, intelligent people broadcast a zillion emails to warn their friends without checking the facts first? Don't remove any files from your Windows folder—you'll probably stop some important feature from running. Instead, check the veracity of the information yourself.

The email message probably contained a name for the virus. Enter that name in the Search box at your antivirus software company's web site. You'll almost certainly see an article explaining that the virus warning is a hoax. You can also check one of the following web sites, which keep up with virus hoaxes:

- *http://www.vmyths.com/*
- *http://hoaxbusters.ciac.org/*

# WIRELESS SECURITY ISSUES

## WIRELESS SECURITY LIMITATIONS

**The Annoyance:** I'm a total security freak. In fact, I approach paranoia when I configure security for my computers and network. For my wireless network...

**The Fix:** STOP RIGHT THERE! If you're that serious about security, you don't want wireless technology on your network. A wireless network has an "intrusion possibility" factor that's much higher than any wired network (Ethernet, phoneline, or powerline). To get into a wired network, an intruder needs to come into your house and connect to the wired network. You'd probably notice that. Getting into a wireless network is much easier because it can be accomplished without anyone noticing. The security features available for wireless networks don't overcome that security gap. Keep your network hardwired or you'll probably have a nervous breakdown!

### WIRELESS TRANSMISSION ENCRYPTION SCHEMES

Encryption is an essential tool for wireless communications because without it, any intruder can intercept and read your transmissions. For wireless home networks, two encryption schemes are available: Wired Equivalent Privacy (WEP) and Wi-Fi Protected Access (WPA).

All wireless network equipment manufacturers offer WEP. To use WEP, you enter a key of 10 or 26 characters into all the devices involved in the wireless network (each computer, access point, and wireless router), following the instructions from the manufacturer. The devices use the WEP key to identify each other (it's essentially a password). They also use the key to encrypt and decode the data they send and receive. The key isn't "friendly," which means it's not words or plain characters. It's a complicated series of hex characters, which means you have to enter text such as 64B7XACAC9104B0 X98841R9545 on every device without any typos (if one character is wrong or missing, the key doesn't match the other devices).

A newer encryption system called WPA is more secure and easier to use. The key you enter can be regular text. In addition, the key you enter is only the starting point of encryption and password protection. The devices use that key to create a series of extremely complex keys. All the wireless devices generate new keys periodically, secretly exchanging the information among themselves automatically.

## WEP DISABLED BY DEFAULT

**The Annoyance:** I want to set up my WEP key, but I can't figure out where or how to perform this chore. Why is it so hard to find?

**The Fix:** By default, wireless device manufacturers disable (hide) WEP. To turn it on, you need to read the instructions that came with the device. Isn't this annoying? I asked representatives of two manufacturers about this decision and received similar answers from both of them: "Configuring WEP is complicated and prone to errors, so we decided to disable it as the default mode." Right, I see, so it's better to let your customers send data that can be intercepted by anyone in the vicinity who has a wireless adapter.

> **Warning. . .**
> Most manufacturers with devices that support WPA encryption hide it (just like they hide the WEP feature). Currently, only Linksys (not Belkin, D-Link, or Netgear) lets you enable WPA during the setup wizard. Hopefully, the others will change their approach soon.

## WPA SUPPORT IN WINDOWS XP

**The Annoyance:** I want to use wireless technology for my Windows XP laptop. I'm interested in using WPA encryption, but Windows XP doesn't appear to support it. I'm really annoyed because I was told that Windows XP provided the best support for wireless security.

**The Fix:** You haven't been keeping up with Windows updates. WEP support was introduced in Service Pack 1. Service Pack 2 is now available, which incorporates all the enhancements in SP1, and adds even more robust support for wireless communications and wireless security.

## WIRELESS DEVICES DON'T SUPPORT WPA

**The Annoyance:** I installed a wireless network about six months ago, but the adapters and router don't support WPA. It's really annoying to have to replace practically brand-new equipment just to have better security.

**The Fix:** You don't have to replace the equipment because most (probably all) manufacturers provide free hardware upgrades. A hardware upgrade is called a *firmware* upgrade, and the file is downloaded to the device. Go to the support section of the manufacturer's web site and look for a link to "downloads." You'll be asked for your model number and operating system. The downloaded file is compressed (it's usually a zip file). If the file package doesn't include installation instructions, look on the web site.

> **Warning. . .**
> Manufacturers offer firmware downloads to enhance many hardware features in most versions of Windows. For firmware that includes WPA support, you'll probably find that only Windows XP is supported.

The Wi-Fi Alliance web site (*http://www. wi-fi.org*) has a list of the equipment certified for WPA support.

## USING DEFAULT SETTINGS IS A BAD IDEA

**The Annoyance:** I added a wireless computer and an access point to my wired home network. I set up the computer for infrastructure mode. When I booted my computer, Windows XP announced it had found the wireless network, which is really nifty (and now I know why people say Windows XP has great built-in support for wireless networks). Unfortunately, the computers on the network aren't in my house. I finally found out I was accessing my neighbor's wireless network. How is this possible?

**The Fix:** Scary, huh? Have you thought about the fact that your neighbor can get to your network, too? You and your neighbor are using the default network settings and Windows XP found your neighbor's signal first. Are your computer and access point near a window that faces your neighbor's window?

Your workgroup is probably still named MSHOME, your SSID is the default identification string, and you're using the default wireless channel for the signal. Each part of that statement represents a mistake you made. Reconfigure your network immediately! Create a unique setting for each network and security setting.

> ### Warning. . .
> Wireless hackers go down streets and through buildings (apartment houses and business structures) with their wireless computers configured for default settings. That configuration gets them into more than half of the existing wireless networks. Change the default settings, people!

Access points and routers require passwords to enter the setup feature to change the settings. Don't forget to change the default password.

## WIRELESS SECURITY SETUP ISN'T SECURE

**The Annoyance:** To establish the connection between a wireless adapter and the access point for the first time, it's necessary to enable broadcasting of the access point's SSID, which is usually not broadcast for security purposes. In other words, to enable security, you first need to make the connection insecure. That makes no sense.

**The Fix:** I agree, and I wish I had an easy workaround for this problem. All I can say is "work fast." Or, bring all the computers and access points (including the wireless router) into a room that has lead walls, and then set up your security.

## SECURITY FOR LAPTOP COMPUTERS

**The Annoyance:** I read an article about someone who lost his laptop at a convention. The computer was filled with secret information about his company's plans and financial situation. I take my laptop to client offices, meetings, airports, and so on. I have a lot of sensitive, private information in the documents, which I need to conduct business. Do I have to chain the laptop to my neck to make it secure?

**The Fix:** Laptop security is an enormous problem because the risk of loss or theft is very high. In addition to sensitive documents, many laptops have cookies to web sites where you store credit card numbers and passwords. The trick is to make sure the information on the laptop can't be read by anyone except you. Here are some guidelines:

- Don't save passwords on web sites.
- Use a complicated logon name and a more complicated password to log on to the computer. The logon name and password should contain both numbers and letters.
- If you have to step away from the computer, even for a couple of seconds, log off.
- Laptops should be running Windows 2000 or Windows XP with the NTFS filesystem, so you can take advantage of the Windows Encrypted File System (EFS) feature.
- Use EFS to encrypt all the documents in all the folders that hold documents.
- Never take your laptop on the road without first backing up the encrypted files and encryption key.

EFS encrypts files using a complicated, hard-to-break encryption algorithm. When a file is encrypted, all reads and writes to the file are decrypted and encrypted transparently to the user who encrypted the file (the logged-on user). If another user logs on to the computer and tries to open an encrypted file, an Access Denied error appears because the user does not possess a key to decrypt the file.

You can copy your EFS key to a floppy disk and keep it in your office or at home. If your laptop goes missing, you can use the key to work on the backup files you made before you took the laptop out. You can learn more about EFS on Microsoft's web sites.

# FILE AND FOLDER SECURITY

## USER-LEVEL CONTROLS IN WINDOWS 98SE/ME

**The Annoyance:** I want to protect some of the folders on my Windows 98SE computer so that only certain users can access them. The Access Control dialog box offers the option of user-level controls, and has a field for entering the location of the user list. I'm not sure whether to enter the name of the computer or the name of a file. If it's a file of usernames, how do I create it?

**The Fix:** I'm assuming your network is a workgroup, not a domain. If you were running a domain (usually found only in business environments), the name of the domain would have been entered automatically in the "Obtain list of users and groups from" field (see Figure 7-7). For workgroups, only the share-level access control option is available.

Here's what's *really* annoying about this. Even though user-level access controls aren't available for workgroups, Microsoft doesn't make this option inaccessible when a computer is part of a workgroup. And wait, I'm not done.

Figure 7-7. Windows 98SE and Me computers that log on to a domain instead of a workgroup can limit access to specific users or groups.

Not only is the option available, but also, you can enter anything in the field and the system will accept it (and make you reboot the computer to put the new setting into effect). However, after you go through all that, no users will ever be able to access the folder across the network because, of course, the option isn't really available.

Your network is a workgroup, so you're limited to share-level access controls. To protect the files, password-protect the folder and give the password only to those people you want to let into the folder.

## DEFAULT PERMISSION OPTIONS FOR SHARE-LEVEL CONTROLS

**The Annoyance:** I shared a folder on my Windows 98SE computer. Anyone on the network can open the files in that folder, which is what I intended when I shared it. However, if anyone working on a remote computer, including me, tries to save that file, the system displays an error message. What did I do wrong?

**The Fix:** You didn't look carefully at the Sharing dialog box when you created the share. By default, Windows 98SE and Me impose a Read Only access restriction on shared folders. This means files can be read (opened) but not written (saved). If you want remote users to be able to save files, right-click the folder icon and choose Sharing, then select the Full option under Access Type (see Figure 7-8).

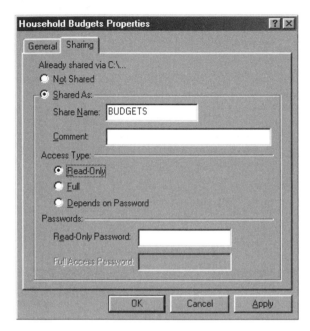

Figure 7-8. By default, remote users can see, but not save, files in this folder.

**Warning...**

If you configure a shared folder for read-only access, the restrictions aren't limited to saving a file when you're working in software. Network users can't move or copy files into the folder, either, because there's no write access.

# LOCAL USERS DON'T NEED A PASSWORD TO ACCESS A PROTECTED FOLDER

**The Annoyance:** On my Windows 98SE computer, I password-protected a folder and didn't give anyone the password. I use the password to work on the files in that folder from another computer on the network. However, anyone who works on the Windows 98SE computer can get into the folder and open the files. The system never asks for a password. What kind of security protection is this?

**The Fix:** That's the kind of security protection you have in Windows 98SE and Me. The password-protection feature is only for users who access files across the network. Local users can access anything, anywhere, at any time. If you want to protect files, use the password-protection features in your word processor.

# DEFAULT PERMISSION OPTIONS FOR SHARED FOLDERS IN WINDOWS XP

**The Annoyance:** I shared a folder on my Windows XP computer by checking the "Share this folder on the network" box. Everybody on the network, including me when I'm working on a remote computer, can open the files in the folder. But nobody can save the files.

**The Fix:** By default, when you share a folder for network access, the system makes the folder read-only, which means nobody can write (save) to the folder. If you want to write to the folder, right-click its icon and choose Properties. Click the Sharing tab and check the "Allow network users to change my files" box (see Figure 7-9).

Figure 7-9. You must specifically choose the option to let users change files if you want network users to be able to save files to the folder.

## SHARE THE WINDOWS XP SHARED DOCUMENTS FOLDER OVER THE NETWORK

**The Annoyance:** I put some documents into the Shared Documents folder for the express purpose of letting everyone share those documents. That way, I can keep all my other folders private. But nobody, not even me, can find the Shared Documents folder when working on another computer on the network.

**The Fix:** The Shared Documents folder is designed to let multiple users of the local computer access the documents it contains. It's not a network-based sharing scheme. However, you can share it across the network by right-clicking its icon and selecting Properties from the shortcut menu. Click the Sharing tab and check the "Share this folder on the network" box. To let users make changes to files, check the "Allow network users to change my files" box.

## FIND THE SHARED DOCUMENTS FOLDER ON THE NETWORK

**The Annoyance:** I shared the Shared Documents folder on the network, but when I'm working on another computer, I can't find it.

**The Fix:** This folder has a different name when you access it over the network; it's named Documents.

## PRIVATE FOLDER FEATURE IN WINDOWS XP REQUIRES NTFS

**The Annoyance:** I want to make some of my folders private, but the "Make this folder private" option isn't available.

**The Fix:** Making a folder private is a security feature, and your computer must be running NTFS to have security features available. Apparently, your computer is running the FAT (or FAT32) filesystem. To see which filesystem was used to format your hard drive, right-click My Computer and choose Manage. In the left pane of the Computer Management console window, select Disk Management. The right pane displays information about your hard drive(s), including the filesystem (see Figure 7-10).

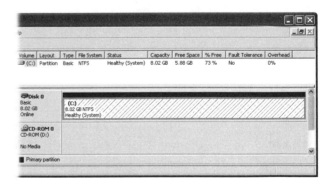

Figure 7-10. Only drives formatted with NTFS offer security features.

A filesystem controls the way an operating system manages files and folders. The filesystem is installed when you format a hard drive, a step that must take place before you can install an operating system. The Windows operating system can run on any of three filesystems: FAT, FAT32, and NTFS.

FAT (along with its slightly more powerful cousin, FAT32) derives its name from the structure the filesystem uses to manage files and folders—the File Allocation Table. It's a lot easier to say "FAT filesystem" than "file allocation table filesystem." The file allocation table is an index that tracks the name and location of every file and folder on the drive.

NTFS is called NTFS, and whatever it stood for when it was named has been lost in history. If you ask the people at Microsoft who should know these things, you get the answer "I don't know" quite frequently. Some people say NTFS stands for NT File System because the filesystem was introduced with Windows NT. (Microsoft people can't agree on what the "NT" in Windows NT stands for, but the most say New Technology.) NTFS tracks file and folder information using a much more complicated database than the file allocation table. One of the additional sets of data in this database is security information, such as user permissions. This is what gives NTFS its ability to provide security options to users.

## SOME FOLDERS CAN'T BE MARKED PRIVATE

**The Annoyance:** I have some folders that contain software, and I want to keep some of them private. However, Windows won't let me check the "Make this folder private" box.

**The Fix:** Your computer is running Simple File Sharing, which is the default security mode for Windows XP (see the sidebar "Simple File Sharing Simplified" for an explanation). With Simple File Sharing, you can make folders private only if they exist as part of your personal folders hierarchy (called your user profile). To see the folders in your user profile, follow these steps:

1. Open My Computer or Windows Explorer.

2. In My Computer, click the Folders icon on the toolbar to change the My Computer window so that it shows drives and folders in the left pane, and the contents of drives and folders in the right pane (Windows Explorer automatically presents the two-pane view).

3. In the left pane, click the plus sign next to Local Disk (C:) to expand its contents.

4. In the left pane, click the plus sign next to the Documents and Settings folder to expand its contents.

5. In the left pane, click the plus sign next to your logon name.

6. The folders you see in the left pane, under your logon name, are your personal folders (see Figure 7-11).

If you're running Windows XP Professional, you can turn off Simple File Sharing. If you're running Windows XP Home Edition, you can't turn off Simple Fire Sharing, but you have some other workarounds to make files private. Both of these options are discussed in the annoyances that follow.

Figure 7-11. Your personal folders are subfolders of your logon name folder, and some of the subfolders have additional subfolders, indicated by a plus sign.

## TURN SIMPLE FILE SHARING OFF IN WINDOWS XP PROFESSIONAL

**The Annoyance:** I'm running Windows XP Professional with NTFS and I want to be able to decide which folders are private and which can be accessed by other users of my computer. How do I get rid of Simple File Sharing?

**The Fix:** Open any Windows system folder (My Documents, Windows Explorer, My Network Places, etc.), and select Tools → Folder Options. Click the View tab and uncheck the "Use simple file sharing (Recommended)" box.

After you disable Simple File Sharing, the Properties dialog box for every folder displays the classic Security and Sharing tab. You can use that tab to specify user permissions for shared folders.

## INSTALL SOFTWARE AND MAKE IT PRIVATE IN WINDOWS XP HOME EDITION

**The Annoyance:** I want to install QuickBooks on my computer, and I don't want anyone who logs on to the computer to be able to use it. However, the folder in which QuickBooks is installed can't be made private. It's annoying that Windows XP won't let me keep software private.

**The Fix:** To keep a software installation private, install the software in your user profile because any folder in your user profile can be made private. To accomplish this, you need to create a subfolder for the software in your user profile, and then change the installation process so that the software is installed into that folder.

To create a folder for the software in your user profile, open My Computer or Windows Explorer, expand the hard drive, expand the Documents and Settings folder, and select the folder bearing your user logon name. Select File → New → Folder to create a new subfolder in your user profile. Name the new folder for the software (in this case, QuickBooks).

Install the software, but instead of accepting the default location for installation (commonly a subfolder under the Program Files folder), select the option to customize the installation process. Then select your new subfolder as the target folder for the software.

After the software is installed, open My Computer or Windows Explorer and navigate to the folder you created for this software. Right-click the folder and choose Sharing and Security from the shortcut menu, then check the "Make this folder private" box. If any other user tries to open the software, an error message appears.

## MAKE SOFTWARE DATAFILES PRIVATE IN WINDOWS XP HOME EDITION

**The Annoyance:** I installed Quicken on my computer and now I want to make sure nobody can get to my datafile. I can't make the installation folder private, but it's OK if other users use the software as long as they can't see my datafiles. However, Quicken automatically saves the datafile in the installation folder. What can I do?

**The Fix:** You have two ways to make software datafiles private: password-protect the file, or move the datafiles into a private folder (almost all software applications offer both of these features).

If you want to move the datafiles to a private folder, first create the folder within your user profile. Then copy (don't move) the datafiles to the new location. Open the software. Most database software applications, such as Quicken, automatically open the datafile you were working on when you last closed the software (which is why I told you not to move the datafiles—that would confuse the software, and it could hang for a long time trying to find the file). Open the datafile that exists in the private folder (using the File → Open command). Then close the software to make sure the datafile located in the private folder is the last used file, which is the file that is opened the next time you use the software.

To make sure it worked, rename the original file (add a letter or number to the beginning of the original filename). Open the software again to make sure the datafile in the private folder opens automatically. If it does, you can delete the original file. If it doesn't, check the software's documentation or call the support line to find a solution.

> **Warning...**
> Some software applications create multiple files that combine to comprise a datafile. In this case, you must copy all the files related to your datafile to the private folder.

> Check to see if your software has a feature that lets you move or copy datafiles. For example, Quicken offers a Copy File feature. The software then asks if you want to use the copy (the file in the new location) as your datafile. Nifty feature!

## SHARE SOME, BUT NOT ALL, OF YOUR DOCUMENTS

**The Annoyance:** I save all my documents in My Documents and many of them are private. However, I want to share some documents with other users on the same computer and across the network. I use Windows XP Home Edition, and it's annoying that I can't specify shared or private status on a file-by-file basis.

**The Fix:** It would be easier to set security permissions on individual files. However, you have several ways to work around this limitation:

- Make your My Documents folder private and move public files into the Shared Documents folder. Enable the option to make the Shared Documents folder available to network users.

- Keep your My Documents folder public, and password-protect the private documents using the password features available in your software applications.

- Keep your My Documents folder public. Create a subfolder for private documents in your My Documents folder and make the subfolder private. Save private documents to the subfolder.

## WORK ON PRIVATE DOCUMENTS FROM A REMOTE COMPUTER

**The Annoyance:** The computer I use most frequently is also used by other household members, so I created a private subfolder under My Documents. However, sometimes I work from a different computer and need to access my private documents. Of course, the system doesn't let me into the private folder, which is really annoying.

**The Fix:** Private means private, and when you're working on a remote computer, you're a guest on the computer that holds your private files. Because you're not the same person who made the files private, you can't access them.

The only solution is to use your software's password-protection feature and save the files in a folder you configured as public and accessible across the network. When you open the software on the remote computer and then open the file across the network, entering the password makes the file available.

## HIDE SHARED FOLDERS

**The Annoyance:** I want to be able to work on my own documents from a remote computer. I'm really annoyed at all the stuff I have to go through to make folders private, public, password-protected, and so on. Is there an easier way?

**The Fix:** You can create shared folders and then hide them. When users view the computer from My Network Places or Network Neighborhood, they see all the shared resources. They don't see shared folders that are hidden. The person who created the hidden folder is the only person who knows it exists.

To create a hidden, shared folder, create the folder (use some innocuous name), share it across the network, specify that users can change the files, and make the last letter of the sharename a dollar sign (see Figure 7-12).

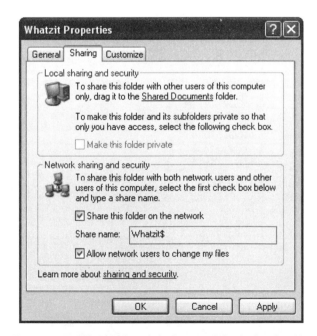

Figure 7-12. Adding $ to the end of a sharename hides the share from My Network Places and Network Neighborhood.

Of course, now you're asking how to get to the files in your hidden share when you're working on a remote computer. Opening My Network Places or Network Neighborhood doesn't help because the share doesn't show up. Here's the trick: select Start → Run and enter \\*ComputerName*\\*Sharename* (don't forget the $ at the end of the sharename). For example, in Figure 7-13, you can see the command I enter to open the hidden share I created on the computer named One.

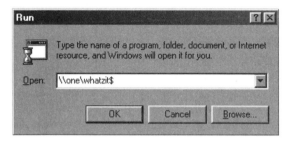

Figure 7-13.   Go directly to the hidden share; do not stop at My Network Places or Network Neighborhood.

Click OK to open the hidden share's folder (see Figure 7-14). Go to work!

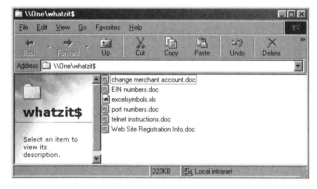

Figure 7-14.   Ta-da! Here are my hidden files.

> ### Warning...
> A hidden folder isn't a "private" folder. If anyone else learns the name of the folder, they can get to it.

# HIDDEN SHARES WITH SHARED PARENT FOLDERS AREN'T REALLY HIDDEN

**The Annoyance:** I created a hidden share as a subfolder under My Documents. I share the My Documents folder on the network so that I can work on files from any computer. When I open My Documents, I see the hidden share listed. It has a dollar sign at the end of the name, but it still shows up. This is really annoying.

**The Fix:** Unfortunately, when you share a folder, you share all its contents. Anyone who can see the share can see all the contents. If those contents include shares with a dollar sign at the end of the name, that's tough nuggies.

The best way to create a hidden share is to use a folder on the C drive, not a subfolder of an existing folder. If you want to use a subfolder, never share the existing parent folder. And of course, avoid sharing the drive because that becomes the parent of all folders, hidden or otherwise. If the parent is shared, so are all its contents.

# WHO'S VISITING MY COMPUTER?

**The Annoyance:** I wish there were a way for me to know whether network users are in my computer, and what they're doing there.

**The Fix:** You can track remote users easily, but the process depends on your version of Windows.

### View network visitors in Windows XP/2000

In Windows XP and 2000, you can keep an eye on network connections in the Computer Management console. Right-click My Computer and choose Manage. When the console window opens, click the plus sign next to the Shared Folders object in the left pane to display the following objects:

- Shares, which lists all the shares on the computer, including hidden and administrative shares

- Sessions, which displays the current network sessions for remote users (see Figure 7-15)

- Open Files, which lists each local file opened by network users, and the name of the user

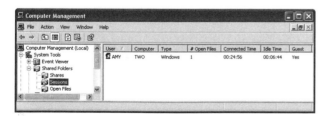

Figure 7-15. You can see who's on your computer, and which remote computer they're using.

### View network visitors in Windows 98SE/Me

In Windows 98SE and Me, your network spy is Net Watcher. Select Start → Programs → Accessories → System Tools → Net Watcher. The Net Watcher window opens with a view of the current remote connections (see Figure 7-16).

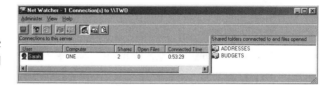

Figure 7-16. Net Watcher tracks information about remote users.

To change the view so that you can see the names of open files and the shares on the computer, use the options in the View menu.

# INSTALL NET WATCHER

**The Annoyance:** Net Watcher doesn't appear on my System Tools menu.

**The Fix:** Net Watcher is not always included when you install the operating system (it depends on the settings for installation). If you don't see Net Watcher on the System Tools menu, use the following steps to install it (you'll need your Windows CD because the system has to copy the Net Watcher files):

1. Open the Control Panel and double-click Add/Remove Programs.

2. Click the Windows Setup tab.

3. Scroll through the listings to select System Tools and click Details.

4. Check the Net Watcher box.

5. Click OK twice.

The system copies the files from your Windows CD and installs Net Watcher on the System Tools menu. This is one of the few times you don't have to reboot Windows 98 and Me after making a change to the system.

## DISCONNECT REMOTE USERS

**The Annoyance:** Can I get rid of remote users if I want to?

**The Fix:** Yes, you have a way to get rid of remote users. (Well, "get rid of" seems harsh—the technical term is "disconnect," which sounds less vicious.)

In Windows XP and 2000, right-click My Computer and choose Manage to display the Computer Management console. Select the Sessions object in the left pane, and then take the appropriate action:

- To disconnect a user, right-click the user's name in the right pane and choose Close Session.
- To disconnect all users, right-click the Sessions object in the left pane and choose Disconnect All Sessions.

In Windows 98SE and Me, select the user you want to disconnect and choose Administer → Disconnect User from the menu bar.

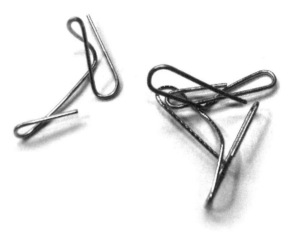

# Maintenance
# ANNOYANCES

# 8

Network maintenance is an ongoing chore, like housework. And network maintenance is just as annoying and boring as housework. (Can you tell I have an attitude about housework? I hate doing things that I get to watch come undone, do them again, watch them come undone again, do them again...).

Some maintenance jobs need to be done with relentless frequency, while others are intermittent. The only way to manage the job of maintaining your network is to prepare for the task properly. You must have the information and tools you need at hand. Information that you keep on a computer might not be accessible when you most need it—drives die, controllers that run the drives get terminally ill, power supplies fail, and so on.

In this chapter, I'll discuss some of the annoyances you'll face as you work to keep your networking running smoothly (or sometimes, just running). I'll cover ways of documenting your equipment, network settings, and other important data so that you'll have a reference when you have to update or replace equipment. I'll present some methods of making the backup process easier and more convenient, which makes it more likely that backups will be performed every day. And, I'll talk about the need to upgrade equipment and operating system files.

# DOCUMENTATION AND RECORD KEEPING

## DOCUMENT COMPUTER SETTINGS

**The Annoyance:** Every time one of the computers on my network has a problem, I have to check the settings. I keep a file of each computer's settings in a file cabinet because keeping it on the computer seems dangerous. I'll need the settings if the computer won't boot or if I can't get to the drive. However, keeping paper-based information is a pain because I have to leaf through all types of information to get to what I need.

**The Fix:** The annoying thing about paper is that you can't change the way it's sorted, nor can you perform a search operation. The solution is to keep both computer-based and paper-based information. On my network, every computer has a document on the root directory named "ComputerName settings". If I need to replace or reconfigure a network adapter, I just open the document and search for the data.

I also print the document and file it. Every time I make changes to the document, I print it again and toss the old copy. The document is a table with the structure described in Table 8-1. The data represents everything I need to know to reconfigure a component, update a driver, or rebuild the computer in case of a hard-drive failure. Tracking manufacturers of components lets me grab the appropriate driver disks when I have to reinstall those components. On my own computer, I have an additional master document that holds all the settings of all the computers on all the networks. (I have two networks—one is a domain and one is a workgroup.) I also print the master document and keep copies of it on a few other computers on the network in case my machine dies.

Table 8-1. Sample computer information data.

| | |
|---|---|
| Computer name | One |
| Domain/workgroup name | Ivensnet (workgroup) |
| Windows version | XP Home SP1 |
| Filesystem | NTFS |
| Drive C | 80GB |
| Drive D | None |
| CD #1 | HL-DT-ST CD-ROM GCR-8523B |
| CD #2 | HL-DT-ST CD-RW GCE-8525B |
| Administrator password (during installation) | Blank |
| NIC | Linksys LNE100TX |
| IP address | Automatic |
| DNS IP address | Automatic |
| Gateway address | None |
| SMTP server | *mail.speakeasy.net* |
| POP server | *popmail.ivens.com* |
| Wireless SSID | N/A |
| Warranty | Ends 8/05 - store warranty-Mantis Computer Co. |
| Notes | power supply replaced 6/04 - 1 year guarantee |

Create the same type of document for your router, and record every setting you made. The document is useful if you have to replace the router, but I've also used it when I had to reset a router to clear a problem. Resetting a router returns all configuration settings to the original defaults, so you have to go through each dialog box and set each field.

## TRACK INSTALLED SOFTWARE

**The Annoyance:** I want to track the installed software for each computer, including operating system patches. The Add/Remove Programs window displays all the installed software, but it has no Print icon or menu item. In fact, there's no menu at all. It's annoying to have to sit in front of each computer and write down what you see on the screen.

**The Fix:** Actually, you can print the list of installed software programs. When the window is open, press Ctrl-P to open the Print dialog box. Click Print to create a hard copy of the list of installed applications.

> Years ago, driven by frustration, I tried pressing Ctrl-P for any window that held data but lacked a Print command. It's amazing how often it works. Try it yourself.

## A PICTURE IS WORTH A THOUSAND WORDS

**The Annoyance:** I want to maintain information about the devices displayed in the Device Manager. I expand each device type to see the specific information about each device. However, printing a report from the Device Manager means using a lot of paper filled with detailed technical stuff that doesn't matter for the purpose of rebuilding a computer or tracking manufacturer model numbers.

**The Fix:** Take a picture. I don't mean that literally, as in "stand in front of the monitor with a camera" (although that might work; I've never tried it). I mean take a digital snapshot of the window.

The quick and easy way to do this is to use the built-in screen capture feature called PrintScreen. When you press the PrintScreen button on your keyboard, Windows copies an image of the screen to the clipboard. Open any software application capable of managing graphic images (such as the built-in Paint program located on the Accessories submenu) and choose Edit → Paste to insert the contents of the clipboard into the software window.

When you press the PrintScreen button, it captures a picture of the entire screen. To grab a screen dump of a particular window rather than everything on the screen (all the open windows, the task bar, etc.), select the window's titlebar to make it active. Then, hold the Alt button while you press the PrintScreen button. Only the active window is sent to the clipboard.

Save the graphic image so that you can access it easily from the computer if you need any of the information it contains. Also, print the image so that you have a hard copy to refer to in case of computer failure.

**Warning. . .**
You must open the software, paste the image, and save it before you can use the PrintScreen button again. The clipboard holds only one image at a time.

You can also install screen capture software, which gives you more flexibility in cropping the screen image and offers a variety of file formats. Use your favorite search engine to find screen capture software sites on the Internet.

# BACKING UP INFORMATION

## BACKING UP ENTIRE DRIVES ISN'T NECESSARY

**The Annoyance:** With three computers on our network, finding a way to back up all those hard drives is becoming a financial problem. I thought about buying another computer with two enormous hard drives just to hold the backups.

**The Fix:** Why do you need to back up the entire drive? You have the CDs for the installed software, so you can reinstall all the programs if you have to replace the hard drive or the computer. Restoring the entire drive doesn't work unless you've also backed up the registry (millions and millions of bytes). Just back up the data—that's the only priceless, irreplaceable stuff on the drive.

If you're using software you downloaded from a web site, copy the original download file to a CD.

Backing up an entire drive, including the registry, is a luxury that few of us can afford. The amount of space it takes is unbelievable, and it's such a time-consuming process that most users are tempted to skip it. It's a bit more work to reinstall the software when you have to replace a computer or a drive, but in the end, most people who have tried both ways agree that it's more efficient and economical to back up just the user data.

## INSTALL BACKUP EQUIPMENT ON ONE COMPUTER

**The Annoyance:** Buying backup equipment so that we can back up the data from each computer is expensive. Each computer needs a tape unit or a separate drive (such as a zip drive). At work, our documents are saved on a network file server, which is backed up every day. But our home network doesn't have that type of setup, and each user saves data on the local computer. I hate having to spend all that money to make sure nobody loses important files.

**The Fix:** You have a network, so take advantage of it to create the same environment you have at work. If each user copies datafiles to one computer every day (a mini backup), you only have to back up that receiving computer to save all the data on the network. Now you've created a file server, although your file server is also a regular computer used by household members. (Pick the computer with the largest amount of disk space for your file server.)

Create a folder named UserBackups on the computer you routinely back up. Next, create and share a subfolder for each user, then make sure each user copies his or her My Documents folder to the appropriate shared user subfolder. Every night, back up the UserBackups folder.

> Don't forget to create a subfolder for users who work on the computer acting as the file server, and make sure users copy their My Documents folder to that subfolder. When the UserBackups folder is backed up, so is all the network data inside it.

# CHOOSING A BACKUP DEVICE

**The Annoyance:** One of the computers on our network has a zip drive, and that's the only computer we back up. I want to copy all network user documents to this computer every day and back all of it up, but the zip drive isn't large enough. At work they use tape to back up our servers, but I hear that tape isn't a good idea if experts aren't keeping an eye on the tapes. What are my options?

**The Fix:** Tape has a number of disadvantages, not least of which is the fragility of the media. Many manufacturers offer alternative devices that are useful for backups, or you can sign up for an Internet-based backup system.

### Hardware backup devices

For hardware solutions, a good backup device uses removable media, which you can take offsite. (It's always a good idea to keep a copy of your backed-up data in a separate location.) Your zip drive is an example of a removable drive. You could consider a zip drive for each computer. In fact, if that decision doesn't break the bank, it's the best solution. Make sure each zip device has at least two disks.

Iomega makes the zip drive in addition to several other devices you should investigate. The Iomega REV holds 35GB of data and comes with a compression utility that doubles the amount of data it can hold. It's like a zip drive on steroids.

Iomega also offers a series of external drives that are perfect for backup chores. Called Iomega HDD, these drives come in a variety of sizes. They don't have removable media, so you should copy the contents to CD periodically for offsite storage.

Most manufacturers of networking devices offer stand-alone hard drives that are good for backups (although they're removable, you should occasionally copy the contents to CDs). These devices are called *Network Attached Storage* (NAS) because they're designed to plug right into your network (just like a computer). Once they're plugged into your hub, switch, or router, you can access them from any computer on the network. Linksys and D-Link, among others, offer NAS devices, some of which are wireless.

Key chain drives are a new technology. They're nifty devices—basically miniature hard drives. Some of them have a key ring at one end so that you can attach the drive to a key chain or a necklace, if you wish. The hard drives attach to your USB port. The models I've seen have storage capacities that range from about 5MB to 2GB.

Online backup services let you upload your files to a server on the Internet. These are subscription-based services, and they use servers that are maintained by computer professionals. I know of three services, but no doubt there are others:

- Connected Corporation (*http://www.connected.com/*)
- NovaStor Corporation (*http://www.novastor.com/*)
- LiveVault Corporation (*http://www.livevault.com/*)

# ROTATE BACKUP DISKS

## The Annoyance: I have a zip drive on each computer on my network. One of the disks produced an error message when I was doing a backup yesterday. Now the disk won't read or write, so I can't access the contents. Luckily, whatever caused the disk to die didn't affect the computer, but it's scary to think you could lose your data on the hard drive and disk at the same time.

## The Fix: It's scary indeed, and that's why there's a rule about using disks. The rule is (write this down, OK?): *never back up over the last backup*. Ideally, you should have a disk for every day of the week, but that's expensive—probably too expensive for a home network, though not for a business network. Regardless, you should have at least three backup disks:

- One for the odd dates
- One for the even dates
- One for the 31st day of the month and the leap year day, February 29th (so that you don't back up to the odd disk the next day)

If you have large, external drives, you can create folders for multiple computers or users and share the drive, but everyone must adhere to the odd/even/last-day-of-months-with-odd-numbers-of-days rule.

# USING BACKUP SOFTWARE

## The Annoyance: I use backup software on each network computer because it's fast and easy. The software came with the removable drives I installed. I recently had to restore a single file because my son deleted a really important document by accident. It took forever to find that particular file. Apparently the backup software creates one big file instead of copying all the files individually. It's annoying that it's probably just as fast to restore the whole backup as it is to search for a single file.

## The Fix: That is definitely the chief annoyance you encounter when you use backup software. Unfortunately, there's no workaround.

# AUTOMATE BACKUP SOFTWARE

## The Annoyance: Every night at my house we have an argument about backing up the computers because there's always some user who says, "I'm not finished working on the computer, so don't start the backup." Sometimes the last user doesn't remember to start the backup, which makes me nervous.

## The Fix: It would make me nervous, too. I have a theory, based on the experience of many clients, that the day you fail to back up a computer, the computer fairies will notice the lack of a backup and destroy your hard drive. It goes without saying that on that day you will have created an incredibly important file, or entered a month's worth of transactions into your financial software, which is now gone.

The solution is to automate the backup and configure the program to run automatically during the night, when nobody is likely to be working at the computer. Most backup software has the ability to do this; in fact, I've never seen backup software that couldn't schedule an automatic backup.

## CAN'T FIND WINDOWS BACKUP SOFTWARE IN WINDOWS XP HOME EDITION

**The Annoyance:** I want to use the backup software that comes with Windows XP Home Edition, but there's no menu item for the software in the System Tools submenu.

**The Fix:** Isn't that annoying? Microsoft automatically installs the backup software when you install Windows XP Professional, but not when you install the Home Edition. To make matters worse, you can't even add the backup software to your system with the Add or Remove Programs feature. Microsoft doesn't even list it in the Windows Components list (which is the way you add components not previously installed). The only logical conclusion to reach is that Microsoft doesn't think home users have files worthy of backing up. Amazing, huh?

Find your Windows XP Home Edition CD, because you're going to have to transfer some files. If Setup automatically starts when you put the CD in your CD-ROM drive, cancel it. Open Windows Explorer or My Computer, right-click the listing for the CD-ROM drive, and choose Explore. Navigate to the *\ValueAdd\Msft\Ntbackup* folder and double-click the *Ntbackup.msi* file. Follow the prompts and instructions to install the software.

## MY COMPUTER DIDN'T COME WITH A WINDOWS CD

**The Annoyance:** We bought our computer with Windows XP Home Edition preloaded on the hard drive, and we didn't get a Windows CD. Instead, we have a CD labeled Recovery Disk. I searched the disk, but no files named *Ntbackup* exist.

**The Fix:** This is a common scheme used by computer manufacturers that sell computers with Windows pre-loaded. It's beyond annoying—in fact, it's enraging that they don't provide a real copy of the operating system on a CD. The price of the computer included the cost of a Windows license, but do you get Windows? Nooooo.

You can call the manufacturer, or visit the web site, and ask for (or even demand) a full copy of Windows. However, you have a rather slim chance of getting it. You can try to get them to send you a copy of all the files needed to install the backup software, but I hear that doesn't work very often either. Find a friend who has a real copy of Windows on a CD, and install the backup software from that disk.

### Some Manufacturers Hide the Windows Files

Some computer manufacturers that sell machines with Windows preloaded actually include the files on the hard drive. If your computer's drive was partitioned into drive C and drive D, you might have Windows files on drive D. The files are packed into cabinets, but you can't find the files you need. Call the manufacturer and ask a support technician to walk you through the process of extracting files from the cabinets.

# USE THE SEND TO COMMAND FOR COPYING USER DATA

**The Annoyance:** I'm trying to make it easy for everyone to back up their My Documents folder. Some users find it too much trouble to navigate to the remote backup computer and use the Copy and Paste commands to copy their files. As a result, they don't back up every day.

**The Fix:** To make it easier, add the backup device to the user's Send To shortcut menu (the menu you see when you right-click an object and choose Send To). For example, if all your users back up to one computer on the network (which is in turn backed up to a removable device), map a drive to the user's server-based backup folder. Then, open My Computer and right-drag the icon for the mapped drive to the desktop. When you release the right mouse button, select Create Shortcut(s) Here. Then, make that target available in the Send To submenu:

- In Windows XP and 2000, drag the appropriate shortcut into each user's Send To subfolder in the user profile (*C:\Documents and Settings\UserName\SendTo*).
- In Windows 98SE and Me, drag the shortcut into the *\Windows\SendTo* folder. Make sure each shortcut contains the user's name, because all users see the same Send To menu.

When the user right-clicks the My Documents folder and chooses Send To, the target folder is on the list. It doesn't get much easier than that!

# MY DOCUMENTS HAS NO SEND TO COMMAND ON THE SHORTCUT MENU

**The Annoyance:** When I right-click the My Documents folder on the desktop, no Send To menu item appears.

**The Fix:** The desktop icon is a shortcut, not a folder. Shortcuts don't have all the right-click menu commands that folders have. You need to right-click the real folder, which is in your user profile:

- In Windows XP and 2000: *C:\Documents and Settings\UserName\My Documents*
- In Windows 98SE and Me: *C:\Windows\Profiles\UserName\My Documents*

# BACKUP DATA NOT KEPT IN MY DOCUMENTS

**The Annoyance:** Our financial software keeps the datafiles in the same folder as the software, not in My Documents. We used to back up the datafiles to floppy disks, but now the files have grown so large that it takes multiple floppy disks. It's so inconvenient that nobody bothers to back up anymore.

**The Fix:** Tell the software to back up to your hard drive, and make the location of the backup your My Documents folder. Then, when you back up your My Documents folder, your financial datafiles are backed up, too.

> **Note. . .**
> Some financial software displays a warning when you back up to the same hard drive as the original files. It's OK to tell the financial software to accept your backup location because you're backing up to My Documents, which in turn is backed up.

# BACK UP FAVORITES AND COOKIES

**The Annoyance:** A friend of mine backs up his computer religiously. His hard drive crashed recently, and after he installed the operating system and software, he restored all his datafiles. However, he had to rebuild his Internet Explorer Favorites list. Also, he lost all the cookies he had in IE that let him get into password-protected web sites (such as his web-based email).

## The Fix: Your Internet Explorer Favorites list is an important datafile, as are the cookies you've enabled for those web sites that require you to log on or that have your credit card information so that you can shop quickly. You can put your Favorites list and cookies into My Documents, so they're backed up every day.

Whenever you add an item to your Favorites list or add a cookie to your system, transfer that data to your My Documents folder. Here's how to do this in Internet Explorer (check the help files of your browser if you don't use Internet Explorer):

1. Choose File → Import and Export to open the Import/Export Wizard, then click Next.

2. Choose either Export Favorites or Export Cookies, then click Next. You can't select both at the same time, so after you export one file, repeat the steps to export the other file. By default, Internet Explorer saves the file in My Documents. (Isn't that handy?)

3. Click Finish.

> The export file for cookies is named *cookies.txt*. The export file for Favorites is named *bookmark.htm*.

If you have a hard-drive crash or you buy a new computer, use the Import Favorites and Import Cookies wizards in Internet Explorer to restore your data.

## USE A BATCH FILE TO BACK UP DATA

## The Annoyance: I've set up one computer to be the file server for backups from the other two computers on our network. I back up the file server to an external hard drive. I showed everyone in the family how to copy their My Documents folder and other datafiles to the file server, but they frequently forget to copy over the data-

files not located in My Documents. In fact, once in a while, somebody actually copies the wrong folder.

## The Fix: You can control the copying process with a batch file, if you're comfortable writing batch files (or if you have a geeky friend who can help you create one). A batch file is a text file that contains a series of commands, one command to a line. Batch files use the *.bat* extension, which indicates an executable file.

A batch file that copies documents to a shared folder on another network computer has to have the following components:

- It must name the source files (the local folders and/or files being copied). If any folder or filename has a space, enclose the source file statement in quotation marks.

- It must name the target (the shared folder on the remote computer) using a mapped drive letter.

- It must issue commands with parameters that ensure the copying job doesn't encounter any difficulties.

> Because both the Documents and Settings folder and the My Documents folder have spaces in their names, it's almost impossible to avoid using quotation marks when you're creating a batch file for backing up.

Because batch files contain plain text, I use Notepad to create them. I save the document with the name *netback* and the extension *.bat* (instead of the default *.txt* extension for Notepad). I stash the file in the root directory of the computer, and I put a shortcut to the file on the desktop or in the Quick Launch toolbar.

> If the computer has multiple users, include the username in the filename for each batch file (e.g., *larrynetback.bat*).

The command I use for a batch file that backs up files is xcopy, which is a more powerful version of the copy command. Here's a sample batch file that copies the contents of My Documents and the datafiles for QuickBooks from a computer running Windows XP. The user running the batch file is named Larry, and he has a shared folder on the computer being used as a file server (or backup server). Larry's shared folder has been mapped to drive Z (see Chapter 3 for detailed information on creating mapped drives):

```
xcopy "c:\documents and settings\larry\my
documents\*.* z: /s/i/r/c/y
xcopy c:\QB\LarryBiz.qbw z: /s/h/i/r/c/y
exit
```

If Larry's folder had been on a Windows 98SE or Me computer, the source for his My Documents folder would be:

```
c:\windows\profiles\larry\my documents\*.*
```

The *.* in the first line tells the xcopy command to copy every file in the folder. (The first asterisk means every filename and the second asterisk means every file extension.) The command exit tells Windows to close the command window when the batch file has finished its work.

## XCOPY COMMAND PARAMETERS

The xcopy command offers plenty of parameters you can use to tell the command how to perform its work. For the batch file I created here, I used the following parameters:

/s copies all the subdirectories of the source folder (in this case, My Documents).

/i manages subfolders by maintaining the folder/subfolder structure you created in your My Documents folder. This means you don't have to create the My Documents folder and its subfolders on your target folder in advance. Additionally, as you add subfolders to My Documents, they're automatically kept intact.

/r overwrites read-only files (by default, you can't write over a file configured read-only).

/c continues the copying process if a minor error occurs. For example, if one of the files you want to copy happens to be open when the batch file runs, xcopy can't copy it (files in use can't be copied). Without this parameter, xcopy displays a message asking if you want to skip this file, and waits for the user to click Yes. Using this parameter makes sure nobody has to sit in front of the computer watching the batch file run, waiting to click OK to overcome a minor problem. This parameter does not prevent the command from shutting down in the face of a major error, such as not being able to find the target computer (in case it isn't turned on, for example), or encountering a problem with your network connection.

/y tells xcopy to automatically assume "Yes" to the question, "Overwrite existing file?". Because most of the files you're copying probably already exist in the target folder, this means no user has to sit in front of the computer clicking Yes a zillion times.

## CREATE BATCH FILES THAT COPY FILES FOR MULTIPLE USERS

**The Annoyance:** Two of our computers have multiple users. When one user starts the backup batch file, the other user has to wait until the backup is finished before she can log on.

**The Fix:** You can create a single batch file that backs up everyone's My Documents folder, as well as any other folders or files that contain user data. For example, here's a batch file that copies the My Documents folders for users named Larry and Sarah, then copies Larry's Quick-Books datafile and Sarah's Quicken datafiles:

```
xcopy "c:\documents and settings\larry\my
documents\*.* z: /s/i/r/c/y
xcopy c:\QB\LarryBiz.qbw z: /s/h/i/r/c/y
xcopy "c:\documents and settings\sarah\my
documents\*.* z: /s/i/r/c/y
xcopy c:\Quickenw\sarahfile.* z: /s/h/i/r/c/y
exit
```

> **Warning...**
>
> A user with administrative rights must be logged on to the computer running the batch file. Otherwise, the batch file will be denied access to other users' files. Executable files run with the permissions afforded the user currently logged on. If you automate running the batch file, make sure a user with administrative rights logs on before everybody goes to dinner (or to bed for the night).

## EXIT COMMAND DOESN'T WORK IN OLDER WINDOWS VERSIONS

**The Annoyance:** We run batch files to copy user documents from each computer on the network to the computer backed up every night. On our Windows 98SE computer, the command window stays open, even though we have the Exit command in the batch file. It's annoying to have to close the window manually.

**The Fix:** Windows 98SE doesn't interpret the Exit command as a directive to close the command window. However, you can overcome this problem by creating a shortcut to the batch file, and configuring the shortcut to close the command window.

To create the shortcut, open Windows Explorer and right-drag the file's icon to the desktop. When you release the right mouse button, choose Create Shortcut(s) Here to place the shortcut on the desktop.

To configure the shortcut to close the command window automatically, right-click its icon and choose Properties. Click the Program tab and check the "Close on exit" box (see Figure 8-1).

You must run the batch file from the shortcut, not from the original file, for this solution to work.

Figure 8-1. You can configure a shortcut to a batch file to close the command window.

# AUTOMATE BACKUP BATCH FILES

**The Annoyance:** We use batch files to back up each user's data to one computer, which is then backed up to an external drive. Half the time, users don't bother to back up their data at all.

**The Fix:** Just like the backup software, you can schedule batch files to run automatically. To accomplish this, you must create a scheduled task using the following steps:

1. On the Accessories menu, point to System Tools and select Scheduled Tasks.

2. In the Scheduled Tasks window, double-click Add Scheduled Task to launch the Scheduled Task Wizard.

3. Click Next to see a listing of installed applications. Your batch file doesn't appear in the list, so click Browse.

4. Navigate to the location of your batch file, select it, and click Open.

5. Enter a name for the task and select the frequency for running it (see Figure 8-2).

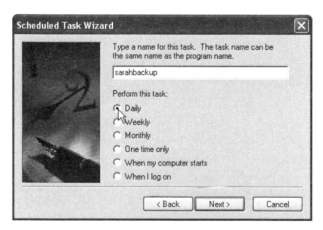

Figure 8-2. Each task must have a name and instructions to tell it when to run.

6. Click Next, select the time to run the task, and specify other details (see Figure 8-3). The detail options vary depending on the frequency you selected in the previous wizard window.

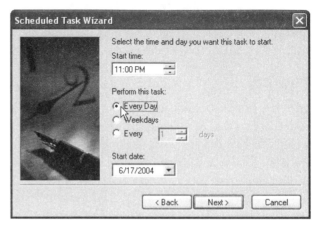

Figure 8-3. Specify the details for running this task automatically.

7. In Windows XP and 2000, enter the name of the user attached to this task. The wizard automatically enters the name of the user currently logged on (see Figure 8-4). If the logged-on user doesn't have administrative permissions on the computer, enter the name and password of a user who does. Otherwise, the files being backed up might not be accessible. (Earlier versions of Windows don't have permission levels for users, so this window doesn't appear in the wizard.)

8. Click Next, then click Finish to schedule the task.

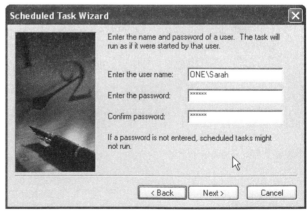

Figure 8-4. Make sure a user with administrative permissions is attached to (owns) this task.

The last wizard window has an option that allows you to view advanced properties for the task when you click the Finish button. If you select that option, you can change any of the settings you just created, and set other options (see Figure 8-5). Most of the time, the additional settings aren't needed.

Figure 8-5. Most of the advanced settings aren't needed for regular desktop computers.

## TOP-DOWN BACKUPS ARE EASIER

**The Annoyance:** We created a backup schedule for each computer to copy datafiles to the computer with an external backup device. People either don't use the schedule at all, or they use it irregularly. I'm tired of having to run around the house to start each computer's backup.

**The Fix:** Change the way the backups are performed by arranging a top-down backup paradigm. This means that instead of pushing the files from the network computers to the computer acting as a backup server, you let the backup server pull the files to it.

On each network computer, share the My Documents folder of every user, as well as any other folders that contain datafiles you want to back up. Map those drives, and then set your backup software to include those files when backing up. Or create a batch file to move the files to the server before backing up to the external disk.

## CLEAN OUT THE BACKED-UP DATA FOLDERS

**The Annoyance:** We copy files to removable disks for backup, but the disks get more and more filled as we add files to the computers. Even though we clean out old, unneeded files on the computer, the backup routine doesn't replace the contents of the removable disk with the new contents (the way backup software does).

**The Fix:** As you've noticed, when you perform manual backups by copying files, the old set of files and folders isn't automatically replaced with the new set of files and folders. Periodically, you have to clear off the target disk, regardless of whether it's a removable disk or a folder on another computer.

If you're using removable disks, just select the disk and delete the contents before performing the next backup. Then, even if something goes wrong with the target disk or computer, you have yesterday's backup on a different disk.

If you're using another computer on the network as the target, delete the folder contents just before the next backup (you have a copy of it on the removable backup media you use to back up the computer). If you're using CDs to back up the computer acting as a backup server, and you don't burn a CD every day, create a CD before emptying the folder.

## BACKING UP TO CDS

**The Annoyance:** It's really annoying that my backup software won't back up to a CD. CDs are reliable and safe, and it would save me a lot of money. Instead, I have to buy expensive external disks to hold my backups.

**The Fix:** You can use a CD for backup media, but unless you buy a backup program (such as Dantz Retrospect) that writes directly to a CD, you have to do it indirectly using two steps. Have your backup software back up to a file on the computer, and then copy the backup file to the CD.

## ENFORCE THE "BACK UP YOUR FILES" RULE

**The Annoyance:** Nobody on our network, except me, backs up regularly. Everybody thinks it's too much trouble. Eventually somebody has a corrupted file, or a file is inadvertently deleted, or the hard drive dies. Of course, there's no backup. How do you enforce backing up?

> **People who don't back up and then lose a hard drive or a computer tend to pay attention to backups for a while (in the computer consulting world, we call this "getting backup religion"). Unfortunately, it doesn't take long for them to revert to their old habits. Perhaps there's just no such thing as a permanent cure.**

**The Fix:** If I could answer the question "How do you enforce backing up?", I'd be as rich as Croesus. This is the never-ending problem of all computer networks. I've reached the point, after telling clients over and over about the need to back up, of saying "sorry, I can't help you" when they call after a crash, haven't backed up in weeks (or months), and desperately need their financial files or important contracts. In fact, I've reached the point where I no longer feel even a pang of sympathy. My only attempt at civility is to bite my tongue when I want to say "I told you so, you fool." The only solution is to automate the backup process.

# UPGRADING THE NETWORK

## INSTALL NEW HARDWARE DRIVERS

**The Annoyance:** Sometimes I read about updated drivers for network devices that will add features to the hardware, or fix a problem. To install a driver, do I have to uninstall the hardware and then reinstall it with the new driver I downloaded?

**The Fix:** No, you don't have to uninstall the hardware. All driver updates can be installed to existing installed hardware. The method differs by manufacturer. When you download new drivers, the web site should have instructions you can print, or the downloaded files will include a file named *readme.txt*. Most downloaded files are compressed into one file, which is usually a self-extracting file that has the extension *.exe*, or a zipped file with the extension *.zip*. (The latter requires WinZip software to extract—Windows XP has a zip file extractor built into the operating system.)

If the drivers are contained in a software application, running the software automatically updates the driver (follow the instructions that came with the software). If the drivers are files that have to be linked to the software, you need to use the Windows Update Driver feature. For hardware that appears in the Device Manager (which is pretty much everything except printers), right-click the hardware device and choose Properties. Then select Update Driver and follow the prompts to install the new drivers. (The process varies slightly depending on your version of Windows.)

## INSTALL HARDWARE FIRMWARE UPGRADES

### The Annoyance: We upgraded our Windows XP computers to Service Pack 2 and we want to take advantage of the additional wireless security available with WPA. It's annoying to have to buy new network adapters and a new wireless router just because our original equipment doesn't support WPA.

### The Fix: The manufacturer of your wireless devices almost certainly has free firmware updates that you can use to upgrade the equipment to support the new features you need. Check the support pages of the manufacturer's web site.

If you find a firmware upgrade, download it and follow the instructions carefully. Make sure you read the instructions on the web site or in the *Readme.txt* file that you download with the firmware. (The instruction file might not be named *Readme*, but it will have a name that indicates it's an instruction file.)

Use the following guidelines when installing firmware upgrades:

- Firmware is almost always specific to the model. Don't use a firmware upgrade file for a model that is similar to but not exactly the same as your device.
- After installation, turn the upgraded device off and then on again to test the installation.

## INSTALL OPERATING SYSTEM UPDATES ACROSS THE NETWORK

### The Annoyance: We have two Windows XP computers on our network. They frequently need to be updated to keep up with all of Microsoft's patches, security fixes, etc. We use a telephone modem for Internet access, so updating is a slow process. At times, it seems almost to be a full-time activity. Is there a way to update one computer, and then copy the update to the other computer across the network?

### The Fix: It's rather easy to install the updates from one computer to another. Instead of performing the update while you're connected to the update web site (which is the "Install the Update" option), you can download a catalog version of the update file. Then you can install the update at your convenience. If you decide to self-install the updates, you can turn off automatic updating (but don't forget to check the Microsoft update site frequently).

To turn off automatic updating, right-click My Computer and choose Properties to open the System Properties dialog box. Click the Automatic Updates tab and uncheck the "Keep my computer up to date" box (see Figure 8-6).

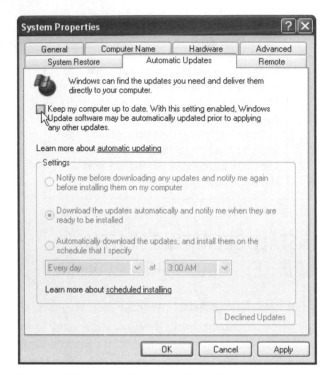

Figure 8-6. You can turn off automatic updates of the operating system, but only if you make sure to check for important updates frequently.

Use the following steps to download an update file you can run locally rather than installing the update directly from Microsoft's site:

1. Go to the Microsoft update site at *http://windowsup-date.microsoft.com*.

2. Click the Personalize Windows Update option.

3. Select the "Display the link to the Windows Update Catalog" option under See Also (see Figure 8-7).

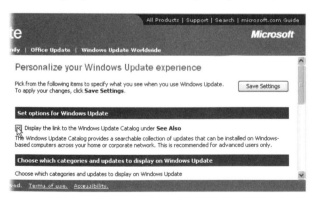

Figure 8-7. Change your Windows update settings so that you can get to the catalog.

4. Click Save Settings.

5. In the left pane of the See Also section, a link to the Windows Update Catalog appears. Click that link to go to the catalog web page.

6. Select Find Updates for Microsoft Windows Operating Systems, choose the appropriate product from the list of Windows versions, and click Search.

7. Choose Critical Updates and Service Packs, locate the update you want, and click Add. This adds the update file to your download basket. You can select multiple updates, if needed.

8. Click Go to Download Basket.

9. Enter the path to the folder on your computer into which you want to download the file(s), or click Browse to select the folder (see Figure 8-8).

10. Click Download Now.

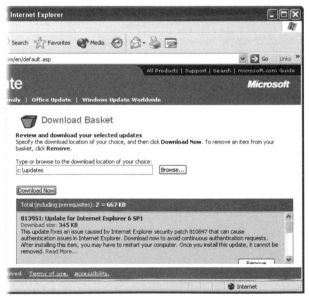

Figure 8-8. Specify the local folder in which you want to store downloaded updates.

All of the update files in the catalog are self-extracting executable files. Use any of the following methods to distribute the update to the appropriate computer (the one with the matching version of Windows):

- Copy the update file to the computer that requires it.
- Share the folder in which you stored the catalog file. Then, access the file across the network from the computer that needs the update.
- Copy the file to a CD and take the CD to the computer that requires the update.

To install the update, double-click the file's listing in Windows Explorer or My Computer.

# Expanding the
# NETWORK

Because this book is written for people who have a home network up and running, I haven't covered the basics of planning, purchasing, and installing equipment. Instead, this book focuses on the annoyances you face as you use and maintain your home network.

However, one absolute rule of thumb (can a rule of thumb be absolute, or is that an oxymoron?) is that all networks are dynamic—they grow and change. You'll add more computers and more equipment. You'll move existing equipment to make it more accessible to users or to redecorate your home.

This appendix covers the basics, the stuff you need to think about and know about as you expand, change, and tweak your network. I'll talk about the planning process and the equipment available, some of which is necessary and some of which is just luxuriously nifty.

# CREATING A BLUEPRINT

Home networks that grow haphazardly and spontaneously usually end up with problems that are difficult to diagnose and manage. You need to know the technological details of the equipment you're adding or moving, and the ramifications of changes you make to the network's layout. The best solution is to avoid problems by planning properly.

## DISTANCE MAXIMUMS

Regardless of the topology (connection method) you use for your home network, you have to understand that data doesn't travel for infinite distances. All topologies have distance limitations.

### Ethernet distance maximums

For Ethernet wiring, the maximum length of a cable run is 328 feet (100 meters). A cable run is a length of cable, which is connected at both ends to an Ethernet device. Usually, one end of the cable is connected to a computer's network adapter, and the other end is connected to a hub, switch, or router. However, you can also connect a cable between a hub, switch, or router and any of the following devices:

- An access point, if you need to add a wireless computer or an entire wireless network to your Ethernet network or router

- A powerline bridge, if you need to add a powerline network (one or more computers with powerline network adapters) to your Ethernet network or router

- A phoneline bridge, if you need to add a phoneline network (one or more computers with phoneline network adapters) to your Ethernet network or router

The distance limitation for Ethernet isn't usually a problem, but before you assume you can add a network device in the basement to your router in the attic, remember that you're not measuring "as the crow flies." You might have to cross floors or ceilings to get to walls, and then cross floors or ceilings again to get to the target devices.

For your blueprint, measure the horizontal and vertical distances your cable has to travel; you'll probably find this produces a higher distance measurement than you originally thought.

### Distance maximums between Ethernet hubs

Sometimes a network grows so large, and/or the computers on the network are located so far apart, that you're better off creating two cabled networks, each meeting in its own hub or switch. Then, you need to connect the hubs. (See the later section "Create Separate Networks and Link Them Together.")

The maximum distance for Ethernet cable between two hubs/switches is 16.4 feet (5 meters). This often presents a problem, but if you run into this situation, you don't have to redraw your blueprint. Instead, you can buy a gizmo called a *distance extender*. The distance extender is installed inside the hub and occupies a port (the occupation is virtual; you don't plug anything into the port, you just lose the use of that port for regular RJ45 connectors). When the distance extender is in place, the distance maximum becomes the same as regular Ethernet cabling—328 feet.

> **Warning...**
> Distance extenders, and their methods of installation, vary by manufacturer. You should buy your distance extender from the manufacturer of your hub or switch.

### Wireless distance maximums

Because I have more courage than brains, I'm going to talk about wireless distance maximums. My discussion is almost entirely theoretical, which means you can pretty much ignore whatever I tell you and learn from your own experience. However, I think that gaining the theoretical knowledge will make it easier for you to plan as you add or move any wireless devices on your network. Someday I hope to meet someone who has a wireless network that comes close to matching these distances.

First of all, wireless has two types of distance maximums: total distances (from one end of your network to the other end), and distances between individual wireless devices.

## Distance maximums for wireless networks

If your network is outdoors, your wireless network can extend up to 1,500 feet (457 meters). If your network is indoors, the distance limit is 300 feet (91 meters). But wait—that maximum distance is theoretical, and it shrinks as the signal travels through interior walls, ceilings, and floors. The amount of loss depends on the material inside your walls (metal and water inhibit, and sometimes even block, the signal). Other things can interfere with, slow down, or shorten the distance of the signal, such as devices competing for the same frequencies (cordless phones, microwave ovens, etc.).

## Distance maximums between wireless devices

The maximum distance between any wireless network adapter and another wireless device (two computers, one computer and an access point, etc.) is 150 feet. However, some manufacturers sell products (network adapters and antennas) that can extend the range, although not by much.

## Phoneline distance maximums

If you have a phoneline network, the maximum distance between computers is about 1,000 feet. Even for very large homes, it's hard to believe that limit would present a problem.

## Powerline distance maximums

For a powerline network, the maximum distance for the network is slightly more than 1,600 feet (500 meters). In this case, "maximum" means the distance between the two nodes that are farthest apart.

# LOCATING HARDWARE IN THE RIGHT PLACES

As home networks grow, a battle ensues between the household members who look at the "techie" side of things and the household members who care about aesthetics. Sometimes a network designed to meet optimal technical specifications can make rooms look very unattractive. Your blueprint for the network has to make concessions to the blueprint for the décor. (Or perhaps it works the other way around in your house.)

## Locating Ethernet cable runs

Ideally, cable should run inside walls, between floors, or in crawl spaces above or below the house. This is the "tidy" approach to running cable because you don't see it (except where it exits the wall), and it's less likely that somebody will trip over it.

However, installing cable inside walls is a lot of work, and many households have some exterior cable that runs across rooms. The best way to locate cable running outside the wall is to run it along the baseboard or the quarter round. Use electricians' staples to secure the cable. These are U-shaped metal staples placed around the cable and hammered into the surface.

## Locating computers

Except for computers with wireless adapters, computers should be located as close to their connectors as possible. This always means that wired computers should be against a wall, with the back of the computer close to the wall. A long stretch of wire between the back of the computer and the wall has a way of causing accidents.

> **Warning. . .**
> Make sure you have at least 6 inches of space (a foot is better) between the computer and the wall so that the air can circulate properly.

## Locating hubs and switches

Your hub or switch is "connection central" for your Ethernet network, but you don't have to locate the device in the epicenter of your network. If the majority of your computers are in the same general location (perhaps on the same floor, or on the left side of the house), place your hub there. Then you need to make long cable runs to only one or two computers.

The only time you have to access a hub or switch is when you're adding a computer to the network or troubleshooting network connectivity. This means you can place the device almost anywhere because you don't have to worry about convenient access.

In fact, the ideal location is a closet because it's a good place to terminate all that ugly cable. Unfortunately, hubs and switches need power, so unless you have a closet with an electrical outlet, this won't work. However, if there's an outlet near the closet, you can run an extension cord into the closet. Be sure to tape, staple, or otherwise secure the cord along the doorjamb or wall.

Hubs and switches get warm and need air circulation to avoid overheating (which could result in a fire). Don't place them on radiators, windowsills, or anywhere else that would expose them to heat or direct sunlight.

## Locating modems

If you're using a telephone modem, you have a limited amount of flexibility about the location. The modem has to be near the computer to which it's attached (if it's external), and of course it needs to be near the phone jack.

A DSL modem must be close to the telephone jack, but you have some leeway here because you can use a long telephone cord if you need to move the modem away from or further down the wall.

A cable modem has less flexibility because you have to connect the modem to your coax cable. Unlike telephone cords, coax cable and connectors aren't available at your local supermarket.

You lose some flexibility in selecting a location if you're using a router instead of ICS to share the modem. In that case, you need to be able to reach the router using Ethernet cable.

Follow the same environmental guidelines for modems as for hubs and switches. An external modem (telephone, DSL, or cable) must have air circulation and be kept away from heat. In addition, you should avoid interference by keeping modems away from fluorescent lights.

## Locating routers

A router sits in the middle of two networks: your LAN and the Internet. As a result, it must be able to connect to both networks.

The router must connect to the LAN using any of the following methods:

- Directly connecting the network computers to the router's RJ45 ports to use the router's built-in switch
- Using Ethernet cable to connect to a hub or switch that holds the connections for your wired computers
- Using Ethernet cable to connect to a powerline or phoneline bridge
- Using an antenna to connect to your wireless network (a wireless router)

To connect to the Internet, the router must be connected to your modem using Ethernet cable.

Obviously, your router needs to be near both the network connections and the modem connection. You have a certain amount of latitude if you use longer Ethernet cable, but you won't be able to put the router a great distance away from the devices it has to connect to.

Wireless routers should be located as far as possible from the following:

- Other wireless devices, such as the wireless network adapters of computers located in the same room
- Metal objects such as file cabinets or desks
- Devices that operate on the same frequencies, such as cordless phone equipment

Routers have to exist in an environment that provides circulating air and avoids direct heat.

### Locating access points

You can use an access point to mix an Ethernet network with a wireless network or join a single wireless computer to an Ethernet network. The antenna on your access point is almost certainly multidirectional, and the best way to take advantage of its strength is to locate the access point away from walls, ceilings, and floors.

The best location is halfway up the wall and halfway across the floor, which means hanging the device from the ceiling. That's not an attractive décor element, but it's certainly an efficient way to use an access point. If that's not feasible, place the access point on a shelf or on top of a bureau or bookcase, and put it on the front edge of the surface to take advantage of the multidirectional signal. If your device must be near a wall, think about purchasing a directional antenna.

Don't locate an access point near devices that operate on the same frequencies, such as cordless telephone sets or microwave ovens.

> **t i p**
>
> Access points are also useful in a totally wireless environment because they can extend the signal. This is useful if you want to use a wireless computer in a location too far from the router to facilitate communications.

### Locating bridges

If you're using a bridge to connect your powerline or phoneline network to a router, locate the bridge near the router. The bridge communicates with the computers via the nearest electrical outlet or telephone jack, and connects to the router with Ethernet cable.

If you're using a phoneline network and a DSL modem, you have to share the phone jack with both the bridge and the modem. You'll need a DSL filter that provides separate jacks for phone and DSL connectors. Alternatively, you can run a long phone cord from a different room to the bridge, or daisy-chain the bridge to the nearest computer, attaching a phone cord to the second RJ11 port on the computer's phoneline network adapter. Another option is to install a second phone jack in the room with the bridge and modem.

# CREATE SEPARATE NETWORKS AND LINK THEM TOGETHER

To make cabling easier, or to reach your router from any location in the house, it's sometimes easier to create two networks and link them. This is obvious if you have two types of networks operating in your house, but what's less obvious is that this is a handy blueprint design even if your entire network is operating on one topology.

If you have an Ethernet network, and it's easy to run cable vertically but not so easy to run it horizontally, separate networks are a good solution. For example, if your house has radiators, the space around the radiator pipes provides an easy way to drop cable vertically throughout the house. The problem is that all the computers might not be on the same side of the house.

Figure A-1 shows a typical blueprint for connecting two sides of the house with two hubs (or switches). You can create the same blueprint with an attic instead of a basement. Or you can put the two hubs/switches (as well as the router and modem) on one of the floors.

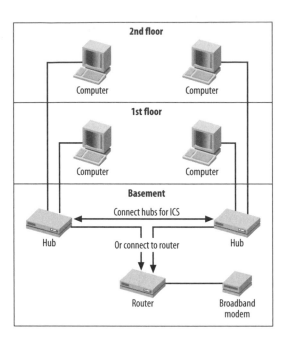

2nd floor

Computer          Computer

1st floor

Computer          Computer

Basement

Connect hubs for ICS

Hub          Or connect to router          Hub

Router          Broadband
modem

Figure A-1. Sometimes it's easier to cable two networks together than to create one sprawling network.

# MINIMUM EQUIPMENT REQUIREMENTS

As you contemplate the purchase of network devices, you need a financial blueprint as well as a physical plan. Some of the add-on equipment for networks looks really cool, but you might want to stick to the necessities for a while.

> **t i p**
>
> Unlike most other commodities, computers and computer equipment keep getting less expensive. If you can't make up your mind about buying some nifty gadget, it's fine to delay the decision because the price will certainly go down.

# ETHERNET MINIMUM REQUIREMENTS

To add a computer to an Ethernet network, you need a network adapter in the computer (most computers come with built-in Ethernet adapters) and a length of Ethernet Category 5 cable long enough to reach the hub, switch, or router you're using to connect the network.

If you run out of LAN ports (RJ45 connectors for Ethernet cable) on your hub or switch, you can either buy a new, larger device (one with more ports), or add a second hub or switch and daisy-chain it to the existing hub or switch. Connect Ethernet cable between the Uplink port on the existing hub/switch to an empty port on the new device.

> **Note. . .**
>
> Refer to the distance maximums between hubs and switches documented earlier in this appendix.

> **t i p**
>
> Unlike older hubs and switches, today's devices accept regular Ethernet cable to connect the Uplink port to another hub/switch. Older equipment required a special cable for this connection.

If you're using a router as your connection point and you run out of ports, buy a hub or switch and connect it to one of the router's ports. Use the new hub/switch for the connection you're removing from the router, and for the new computers you're adding to the network.

## WIRELESS MINIMUM REQUIREMENTS

To add a wireless computer to your wireless network, you need only a wireless network adapter. If you plan to use the new wireless computer in a location too far from the router to get a reliable signal, buy an access point and place it between the computer and the router.

If you're adding a wireless computer to an existing wired network, you must purchase an access point to bridge the wireless connection to the wired network.

## POWERLINE AND PHONELINE MINIMUM REQUIREMENTS

To add a powerline or phoneline computer to your existing powerline or phoneline network, you need a network adapter for the computer. If the phoneline network adapter doesn't come with a telephone cord, you must buy the cord.

If you have a phoneline network and you want to put the new computer in a room that lacks a telephone jack, buy a longer telephone cord and plug it into a jack in another room, or daisy-chain the new computer to an existing computer by connecting the telephone cord between the two network adapters.

# COMPATIBILITY ISSUES

The only network equipment compatibility issues you're likely to run into are for wireless networks and wireless devices. The first compatibility issue is the operating system. If you're really interested in wireless networking, every computer in your house should be running Windows XP. The earlier versions of Windows just don't offer the support for wireless communications and wireless security that Windows XP offers.

Windows XP also has better (and easier-to-use) features for networking, regardless of the topology you're using to connect your network. Consider upgrading to Windows XP even if wireless networking isn't the motivation.

## UPGRADE TO WINDOWS XP

If you're running Windows 98, 98SE, or Me, you can update your computer to Windows XP Professional Edition or Windows XP Home Edition if it meets the hardware requirements. If you're running Windows 2000, you can only update to Windows XP Professional Edition. Here are the minimum hardware requirements for your computer if you want to update to Windows XP:

- PC with 300MHz or higher processor clock speed
- 128MB or more of RAM
- 1.5GB of available hard-disk space
- Super VGA (800 x 600 or higher resolution) video adapter and monitor

Microsoft has a tool called the Upgrade Advisor that checks your system hardware and software to see if you can upgrade your computer to Windows XP. You can download the software, or run it while connected to the web site. The advantage to running the Upgrade Advisor while connected to the Internet is that if your system needs updates that are available on the Windows Update web site, the software finds and installs what you need right away. Go to Microsoft's web site (*http://www.microsoft.com/*) and search for the Upgrade Advisor.

## UPGRADE WINDOWS XP COMPUTERS TO SERVICE PACK 2

Microsoft's release of SP2 for Windows XP introduced a host of new features, many of which are aimed at networking and wireless security. Because you're running a network, and because you might be using wireless components in that network (or might introduce them in the future), considering upgrading your Windows XP computers to SP2 (*http://www.microsoft.com/windowsxp/sp2/default.mspx*).

## WIRELESS ALPHABET SOUP COMPATIBILITY

Most of the wireless equipment you'll find today is 802.11g. If your existing equipment is 802.11b, the 802.11g network devices interoperate with wireless-b devices (this is called *backward compatibility*, or *downward compatibility*). Some 802.11g equipment is marked "wireless g-b" to indicate the compatibility, but even if you don't see that designation on the box or on the web site specifications, you can buy 802.11g devices with full confidence that they will work with your existing 802.11b equipment.

## WIRELESS SECURITY COMPATIBILITY

When you buy new wireless adapters, routers, or access points to expand your network, you're going to find devices that support Wi-Fi Protected Access (WPA) security

technologies. WPA is a higher-level security standard than Wired Equivalent Privacy (WEP), the previous security standard. WPA substantially raises the level of data protection and access control for wireless networks. WPA provides several benefits to enhance security, not the least of which is its support of user permissions and passwords for allowing network access. The data encryption level provided by WPA is more robust than that of WEP.

To use WPA security you must have an access point or a wireless router. (All wireless routers have built-in access points.) All of the wireless devices on your network must support WPA. Your existing wireless devices are probably not WPA-enabled, but you don't have to toss them out and buy new ones. Instead, you can download a firmware upgrade from the manufacturer's web site. After you install your WPA access point or router, you can upgrade the network adapters gradually. WPA and WEP can coexist on the same network (the WEP devices just ignore the features available in WPA).

Don't even try to use WPA on any version of Windows other than Windows XP. Although you can probably configure a WPA network on Windows XP without updating to SP2, it isn't easy. The built-in support for WPA in SP2 makes upgrading imperative.

**One of the big differences between WEP and WPA is the method by which the systems encrypt data. WEP uses 64-bit or 128-bit encryption keys, but WPA offers 256-bit encryption keys, which are exponentially harder to decode.**

**WEP encryption keys are static. WPA keys are dynamic and automatically change as often as you specify when you configure the wireless device (most manufacturers default to 50 or 60 minutes, which is quite acceptable). Hackers who try to learn your encryption key by eavesdropping on your network would have a hard time breaking in. Even with powerful encryption-breaking software, by the time they gain the information they need to decode the current key, your network has switched to a new key.**

# SIGNAL INTERFERENCE ISSUES

All network topologies face a risk of interference with the signal, causing a cessation of communication or an agonizingly slow rate of communication. As you expand your network and try to fit more stuff into your rooms and walls and along your cable runs, you might inadvertently cause yourself some problems.

## WIRELESS INTERFERENCE

Wireless networks have the greatest risk of interference because RF technology swirls around the room, potentially bumping into other RF devices. Cordless telephones and microwave ovens are the two most common causes of interference problems because they use the same 2.4GHz frequency band as your wireless network.

However, beyond frequency interference, wireless communications experience interference from metallic objects in your home. Metal furniture, metal studs, nails, foil-backed insulation, and even lead paint can reduce the speed and distance of a wireless signal. In addition, high-density materials such as concrete and plaster are more difficult to penetrate and absorb some of the signal's energy, shortening the distance the signal travels. Porous materials such as wood or drywall are more "wireless friendly."

You can overcome most interference problems by moving your devices around the room, or the house, until you reach acceptable levels of speed and distance. Also, try testing the signal by manipulating the antennas on access points, including your wireless router (are you old enough to remember television rabbit ears, which we spent hours bending and twisting until the reception was acceptable?). In addition, depending on the placement of your devices, you might want to experiment with directional antennas to replace the multidirectional antennas that came with your wireless devices.

## ETHERNET INTERFERENCE

Ethernet cable runs into interference if it's too close to fluorescent fixtures, and many computer experts insist that running Ethernet cable too close to electric lines within the wall can also interfere with the data signals. There are also reports that ham radio transmissions can interfere with Ethernet communications because they use the same frequencies.

## POWERLINE INTERFERENCE

Any equipment that filters or monitors electrical signals can cause interference with powerline data transmissions and therefore slower performance. These devices include uninterruptible power supplies (UPS) or surge protectors. In addition, some older wiring (e.g., knob and tube) degrades performance.

## PHONELINE INTERFERENCE

Some performance degradation can occur if the connection from the network adapter is in a splitter rather than a jack (use the empty RJ11 connector in the adapter to plug in telephone instruments). If you're using a DSL modem and the line is split back at the telephone company's central office instead of at your house, you probably have filters for telephone jacks that have telephone instruments attached. Do not connect a phoneline network adapter to one of those splitters; the data signal won't get past it.

# NIFTY NETWORK DEVICES

You can equip your network with some rather cool devices and features, some of which I consider to be almost as important as the basic necessities. In this section, I'll discuss some of these devices.

## ROUTERS WITH FIREWALLS

If you're using a router, you can protect your network from Internet intruders at the router, instead of installing a software firewall on each computer. However, router firewalls prevent only incoming intrusions and do not prevent computers from sending data out to the Internet.

Outgoing data is a problem if a computer sends data to some computer on the Internet as a result of a virus designed to collect files. When an unauthorized software application tries to send a file to a computer on the Internet, software firewalls ask users whether they want to allow the transmission. Router firewalls never ask because they permit all outgoing transmissions (the same is true of the Windows XP built-in firewall). Don't use a router firewall unless your computers run antivirus software that you update regularly.

## PRINT SERVERS

Instead of connecting a printer directly to a computer, you can use a print server (a standalone hardware device) to connect the printer to your network. The print server becomes a network node, the same way a computer is a network node. After you connect your printer(s) to the print server, you connect the print server to your hub or switch to make it available to all the computers on the network. It has a name and IP address just like the computers, so you can easily access it.

Using a hardware print server to share printers on a network, instead of using the standard printer-sharing features offered by Windows, provides the following benefits:

Location
> You can put your printers in a convenient place for all users on the network.

Speed
> Print servers move data faster (they're not victimized by the overhead of other processes that a computer might be experiencing).

Availability
> The print server is available all the time, while a printer attached to a computer is available only when the computer is running.

If you're using a wired print server, use the RJ45 port (the LAN port) on the back of the print server to attach it to your network hub, switch, or router. Use a standard Ethernet Category 5 patch cable to make the connection.

If you're using a wireless print server, connect the print server to an Ethernet device (a hub, switch, router, or computer) to install the drivers and configure the print server. After you complete the setup and configuration, the print server uses its antenna to communicate with your wireless network.

> Note. . .
> **Print servers are available for both parallel and USB port printers.**

Print servers come with software installation CDs, which walk you through the process of setting up the device. You have to install printer drivers for the print server to use, and then you must install the printers (as network printers located on the print server) on the network computers.

## STANDALONE HARD DRIVES

You can buy a standalone hard drive that connects to your hub, switch, or router and becomes a network node that all the computers on the network can access. It's always available, providing file storage space independent of a computer (which might not be turned on).

> **Note. . .**
> Hard drives that connect to the network as independent nodes are known as Network Attached Storage (NAS) devices.

You can use the NAS device as a backup drive for all the computers on your network (see Chapter 8 for information about backing up). NAS is also a handy place to store large music and video files.

# MULTILINK PHONE MODEMS TO INCREASE SPEED

Are you unable to get DSL service at your house? Does your cable company not offer Internet access in your neighborhood? Are you jealous of your friends who have high-speed Internet connections? Is the speed (rather, the lack of speed) of your modem driving you nuts?

If the answer to these questions is Yes, you might have a way to lower your frustration level when you access the Internet. The solution is multilinking—a hardware solution for faster Internet communication. Wait, before you say "This is great," you should ask "What do I need for multilinking?" because the necessary components might not be available. Here's what you need:

- An ISP that supports multilinking
- Two modems
- Two phone lines

> Don't confuse multilinking with software applications that are supposed to speed up your modem communications. Multilinking is a hardware solution, and it works!

Multilinking means both modems dial out to your ISP and work in a coordinated manner to exchange data over the Internet. You should be able to double your speed. The modems don't even have to be the same model.

To get started, set up a multilinking account with your ISP. Then install both modems using the standard procedures required by your version of Windows. You don't have to create a new Internet connection for your double-power access; you just configure the existing Internet connection to use both modems.

## CONFIGURE WINDOWS 98SE/ME FOR MULTILINKING

In Windows 98SE and Me, open My Computer and open Dial-Up Networking. Right-click the icon for your dial-up connection and choose Properties. The General tab of the connection's Properties dialog box displays the name of the modem you selected for this connection (see Figure A-2). Note which modem this is because you'll have to select the other modem in the next step.

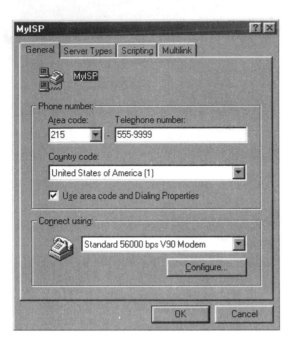

Figure A-2. Take note of the modem that's already linked to your dial-up connection.

Click the Multilink tab and select the "Use additional devices" option. Then click the Add button to open the Edit Extra Device dialog box. In the Device Name field, select the other modem from the drop-down list, and enter the telephone number this modem dials if your ISP provides a second telephone number (see Figure A-3). Click OK, and your second modem is listed in the Multilink tab. Click OK again to close the Properties dialog box.

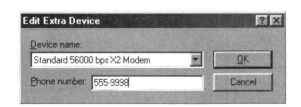

Figure A-3. Add the second modem to your dial-up connection.

# CONFIGURE WINDOWS XP FOR MULTILINKING

Configuring Windows XP for multilinking is easier because the dial-up connection automatically adds the second modem to the modem list on your dial-up connection as soon as you've installed the modem. However, the second modem isn't selected for use, so you must open the Properties dialog box for your dial-up connection and select the new modem (see Figure A-4).

Figure A-4. Check the box next to the second modem to enable multilinking.

If your ISP has provided separate phone numbers for each modem, *uncheck* the "All devices call the same numbers" box. Next, select each modem and fill in the telephone number. Click OK to close the Properties dialog box.

## USING THE MULTILINK CONNECTION

To connect to your ISP using your new handy-dandy-twice-as-fast multilink connection, just do the same thing you did before—double-click the connection and follow your normal procedure. You'll hear the first modem squawk as it makes a connection, then you'll hear the second modem squawk as it makes its connection. Proceed as usual. Well, not as usual—proceed at double-speed!

While you're connected, Windows puts a connection icon on the task bar. You can open the icon and click the Details button to see the details of this connection. The bottom of the dialog box has a Suspend button. Click it to hang up the second modem if you need the telephone line. The connection speed drops to single-modem rates, and the button changes its name to Resume. When you click the Resume button, the second modem reestablishes its connection.

## HOME ENTERTAINMENT DEVICES

Manufacturers offer all sorts of devices that play the digital music and video files stored on your computers on your television and stereo units. Most of the devices offer wireless connections, which make everything convenient to use (and don't clutter up the house with additional cabling).

Connect an entertainment device to your stereo system or television using standard video/audio connectors. Then connect the device to a computer with either a wireless or an Ethernet connection. Pick a file from your hard drive, and send it to your family's media center. The music you're storing on your network computers is available for the whole family's enjoyment using better audio and video than your computer offers.

### *How Multilinking Works*

With multilinking, your computer makes two separate connections to your ISP, one for each modem. The multilink software at the ISP tracks the two connections assigned to your account, intercepts the data packets, and splits them in half. It sends one partial packet to each of the two modems. When they arrive, Windows reassembles them. When you send data, Windows and your ISP reverse the process.

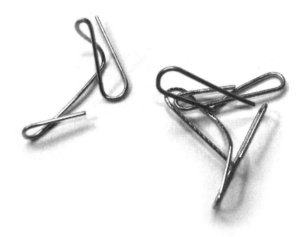

# Index

Notepad, multiple users and, 91
NovaStor Corporation web site, 176

## O

online backup services, 176

## P

password-reset disks, 43
passwords
    eliminating, 42
    hints, 45
PC MACLAN web site, 104
persistent connections, overview, 118
phoneline maximum distances, 191
Phoneline Networking Alliance (PNA),
    3
Ping utility, 65
    failures, 66
    firewalls and, 66
    pinging specific IP addresses, 66
PNA (see Phoneline Networking
    Alliance)
ports and port scanning, 149
powerline maximum distances, 191
power settings, denied to limited users,
    46
printer redirection, 114
printer sharing services, installing, 62
printing annoyances (see network
    printing annoyances)
PrintScreen button, 174
Print command trick, 173
print files, overview, 116
print jobs, 98
print servers, 198

## Q

Quick Launch toolbar, adding network
    window to, 58

## R

Readme file, 185
rebooting after installing updates, 155
Recycle Bin annoyance, 88
registry, making changes in, 47, 71
remote computer, running software
    on, 95
remote computers, 56
remote files, saving, 89

remote files in applications, 89
remote users, disconnecting, 170
removable media for backups, 175
routers, 148
    firewalls and, 198
    locating physically on the network,
        192
    settings, documenting, 172
    stateful inspection, 149
routers, configuring, 28–35
    Automatic Private IP Addressing
        (APIPA), 32
    DHCP and, 30
    laptop with multiple local network
        connections, 35
    logging on to different net-
        works with Alternate
        Configuration, 34
    login data
        changing, 30
        lost, 29
    MAC addresses, 31
    network switching programs, 34
    switching laptop IP address set-
        tings, 32
    User Profiles, 36
Run command, opening without a
    mouse, 104

## S

screen capture network settings, 173
security annoyances
    firewalls for broadband-based ICS,
        148
    firewalls for older computers, 148
    routers, 148
Segment, 2
Send To folder missing, 88
Send To menu item, cannot locate, 178
Service Set Identifier (SSID), 159
share, defined, 56
shared broadband annoyances
    cable access upload and download
        speed differences, 131
    cable company support, 138
    cable data transmission versus cable
        television signal, 138
    cable modem, protecting from low
        voltage, 139
    cable modems, buying, 133

cable modem replacements, 138
cable modem speed test web site,
    131
cable modem speed variations, 131
debunking cable speed cap myth,
    132
DSL
    buying from third-party vendors,
        135
    filters, 134
    home security and, 135
    increasing speed of, 133
    line filters, 135
    telephone line problems and,
        139
    upload and download speeds,
        134
email
    Eudora, installing on multiple
        computers, 141
    Outlook Express on multiple
        computers, 140
    settings remain the same, 139
outgrowing router, 130
recycling modem, to reduce support
    calls, 137
routers
    connecting phoneline and pow-
        erline devices, 137
    firewalls and, 136
    lack of ISP support, 137
    not specific to modem types,
        136
    wireless access to wired routers,
        136
    upload speed versus download
        speed, 132
    wireless routers in wired networks,
        130
shared internet annoyances, 121–144
shared network annoyances, 55–82
shares, disabling search for new, 72
sharing documents on a file-by-file
    basis, 166
signal interference issues, 197–198
    Ethernet, 197
    phoneline, 198
    powerline, 197
    wireless, 197
Simple File Sharing, 165
simultaneous use of a single file, 91

## Z

## Colophon

Our look is the result of reader comments, our own experimentation, and feedback from distribution channels. Distinctive covers complement our distinctive approach to technical topics, breathing personality and life into potentially dry subjects.

Emily Quill was the production editor and proofreader for *Home Networking Annoyances*. Audrey Doyle was the copyeditor. Emily Quill did the typesetting and page makeup. Matt Hutchinson and Claire Cloutier provided quality control. Reg Aubry wrote the index.

Ellie Volckhausen designed the cover of this book using Adobe Illustrator, and produced the cover layout with Adobe InDesign CS using Gravur Condensed and Adobe Sabon fonts. The cover was based on a series design by Volume Design, Inc.

Patti Capaldi designed the interior layout using Adobe InDesign CS. The text and heading fonts are Rotis Sans Serif, Lineto Gravur, and Myriad Pro; the code font is TheSans Mono Condensed. Julie Hawks converted the text to Adobe InDesign CS. The screenshots and technical illustrations that appear in the book were produced by Robert Romano and Jessamyn Read using Macromedia FreeHand MX and Adobe Photoshop 7. The cartoon illustrations used on the cover and in the interior of this book are copyright © 2004 Hal Mayforth.

LP506    108